Big Bluestem

JOURNEY INTO
THE TALL
GRASS

6-

Big Bluestem

JOURNEY INTO
THE TALL
GRASS

BY ANNICK SMITH

WITH PHOTOGRAPHY BY HARVEY PAYNE

COUNCIL OAK BOOKS

TULSA, OKLAHOMA

In memory of
Elizabeth Kirkpatrick Doenges

Council Oak Books, Tulsa, Oklahoma 74120
©1996 by The Nature Conservancy
All rights reserved. Printed in Hong Kong
Photographs by Harvey Payne ©1996
All photographs not otherwise credited are by Harvey Payne.

Library of Congress cataloging-in-publication data
Smith, Annick, 1936 –
Big Bluestem : journey into the tall grass / by Annick Smith ;
with photography by Harvey Payne.   c.   p.
"The Nature Conservancy."
1. Tallgrass Prairie National Preserve (Okla.) 2. Smith, Annick,
1936—Journeys—Oklahoma—Tallgrass Prairie National Preserve.
I. Nature Conservancy (U. S.)   II. Title
QH76.5.04S65   1996
333.74'16'09766—dc20   96–28419 CIP

Designed by Carol Haralson

00 99 98 97 96   5 4 3 2 1
ISBN 1-57178-031-9

This book is dedicated to
Joseph H. Williams,
without whom The Nature
Conservancy's Tallgrass Prairie
Preserve would still be just
a dream.

Big Bluestem

urely we must have made a mistake, I thought while walking across a freshly burned prairie for the first time. It simply cannot look *this* bad, this desolate, this lifeless.

It was springtime in Osage County, Oklahoma, and the burned prairie was part of the historic Chapman-Barnard Ranch, now home to The Nature Conservancy's Tallgrass Prairie Preserve. The ground, normally bursting with hues of bronze, crimson, and yellow, was a blackened moonscape of soot and ash. The head-high grasses were gone, burnt to nubs. With each step, a small puff of dust rose at my feet.

Continuing to walk the prairie, I began to appreciate the life-giving magic of the controlled burn — fires deliberately set and orchestrated for purposes of conservation. Making my way across a meadow, I was suddenly surprised by the bright flashing movement of a Swainson's hawk up ahead. On the horizon, a coyote appeared and vanished.

And looking closely at the ground, I realized that all around me, tiny green shoots were pushing their way up through the desolation. Among the clumps of burnt grasses and shrubs, new and vigorous plant life — the biological heart of the prairie ecosystem — was asserting the power of life.

Under my feet, the prairie was renewing itself.

Such moments of renewal are emblematic of the Conservancy's work on this 37,500-acre swatch of tallgrass. Here, on one of the finest remaining landscapes of its kind in the nation, the Conservancy has joined with local partners to bring back a very special part of America's natural and cultural history.

Bigflower coreopsis in the morning dew on The Nature Conservancy Tallgrass Prairie Preserve

Photo by Harvey Payne

Walt Whitman once called it "our characteristic landscape." The prairie remains firmly embedded in our collective consciousness as the image of our nation's heartland. For centuries, it gave sustenance. It was home for generations of Native Americans, and then for early European settlers whose wagon wheels cut their way into the landscape and the American story.

When you consider that the tallgrass prairie once extended over some 140 million acres, from Indiana to Kansas, and from Canada to Texas, you appreciate the importance of the Conservancy's Tallgrass Prairie Preserve. The tallgrass prairie — once the largest contiguous ecosystem in North America — is a vast chunk of nearly vanished Americana; by the most recent estimates, perhaps as little as two percent remains.

To bring it back to its pristine glory is to help reclaim our past. In preserving a functioning, healthy prairie for generations to come, we preserve an important cultural current that runs deep in our shared memory.

Surely that thought was on the minds of many of the hundreds of people who gathered on October 18, 1993, for the historic reintroduction of bison to our preserve. But fewer of those in attendance realized that something equally extraordinary was happening *ecologically*.

In returning bison and fire to a large, intact expanse of tallgrass prairie, the Conservancy is attempting to restore an ecosystem that has been essentially extinct for a century. Drawing on the latest findings of conservation science, we are replicating the intricate play of the natural processes that shaped this landscape — native grazers and wildfires. Our hypothesis was that reintroducing these long-altered processes would also return to balance the populations of hundreds of plant and animal species.

Standing there at the bison release along with our neighbors from Osage County — the civic, business, and other community leaders — and other supporters and conservationists from all over, listening to the pounding hoof beats of 300 returning bison, I felt privileged to be part of an historic moment.

Here in text and photographs, *Big Bluestem* captures at once the fascinating and multifaceted history of the American tallgrass prairie and the Conservancy's work in restoring a wonderful stretch of it. This book celebrates both the American spirit and the American conservation ethic.

"O prairie mother, I am one of your boys," Carl Sandburg once wrote. "I have loved the prairie as a man with a heart shot full of pain over love." Whether or not you have walked the tallgrass, this book will open your eyes to this treasured landscape of awe and wonder.

And as you turn its pages, I know you will join The Nature Conservancy and me in thanking the generous benefactors without whose assistance the story of the Tallgrass Prairie Preserve could not have been told in this form. Our deep gratitude goes to CITGO Petroleum Corporation, The Robert S. & Grayce B. Kerr Foundation, Mary Lawrence and Ruth Hardman, MidFirst Bank, Sooner Pipe & Supply Corporation and Dr. Rainey and Martha Williams for making this publication possible.

JOHN C. SAWHILL
President and Chief Executive Officer
The Nature Conservancy

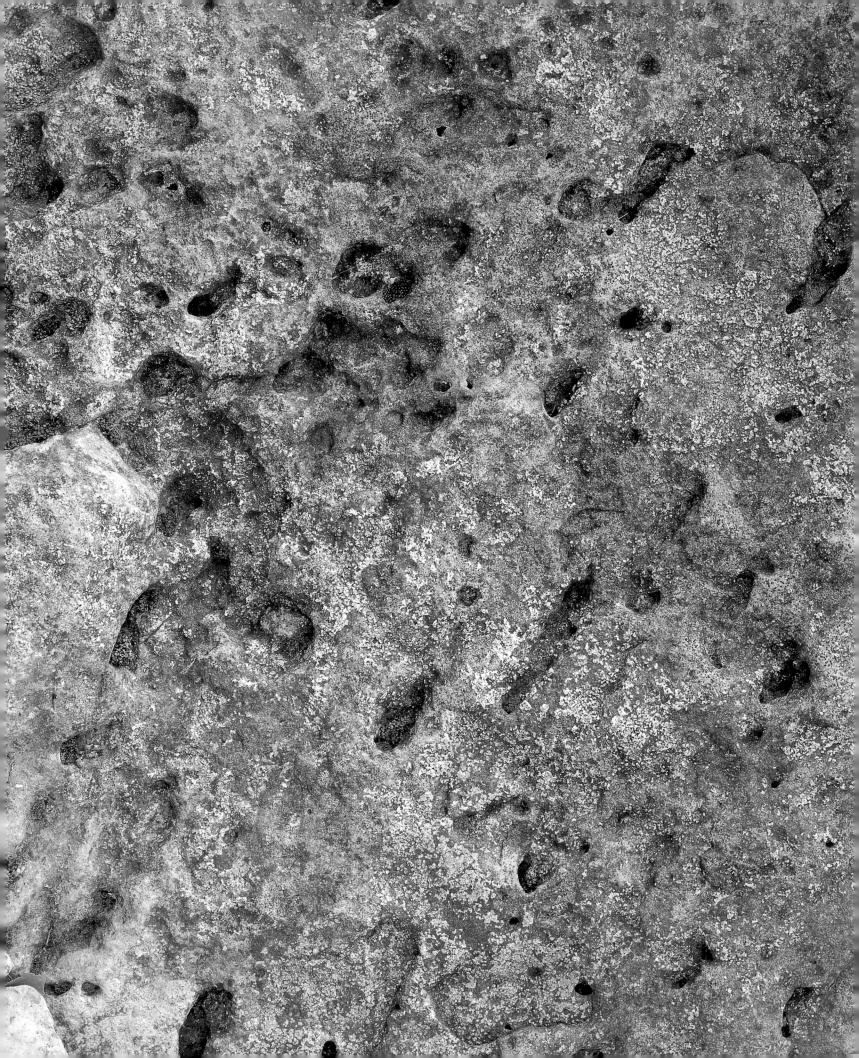

When I decided to write a book about the bluestem prairies of Osage County, Oklahoma, and The Nature Conservancy's Tallgrass Prairie Preserve, I had no idea how high the grass grew or what stories lay under it. I walked into the grass and it has taken me three years to find my way out. This book tracks my journey. There are no direct roads through the great meadows and blackjack groves of the Osage, and my wanderings through that country have followed dim paths, switchbacks, and multiple crossings — like game trails leading to water. The intellectual map that emerges is as complex and convoluted as the landscape. It is rife with impressions, conjectures, and byways of the mind that turn travelers like me toward new understandings of the world and their relation to it. This, I believe, is the purpose behind any voyage seriously taken.

The vast webs of interconnecting life in a prairie ecosystem are beyond human comprehension — especially as seen through geologic millennia and historical time. Still, we seek to know as much as we can know, and our knowledge of prairies is increasing while the last wild grasslands themselves disappear. Oscar Wilde said we kill what we love best; but it seems more true that we often love best what we have killed.

Nostalgia for America's historic heartland prairies has become a turn-of-the-century preoccupation. Native-seed companies are flourishing. Towns across the country are spawning nurseries that specialize in regional trees and plants. In bookstores in suburban shopping malls, people who never set foot in a wild prairie are buying gardening books that teach them to cultivate indigenous wildflowers. Trendy tastes run to rare, native exotics such as the double blossomed trillium, which sell for thirty dollars a plant in New

Subtle colors of the Prairie Preserve: Lichens on sandstone, left, and four eggs in a dickcissel nest.

Photos by Harvey Payne

York City. Other gardeners — often Midwesterners — want to recreate a sample of the original prairie in their backyards: big bluestem, Indiangrass, black-eyed Susans, purple prairieclover, plains beebalm.

A plot of prairie grass in the backyard, in an old cemetery, or along an abandoned railway right-of-way is no substitute for the genuine. Thus, for years many Americans have wanted to establish a tallgrass prairie national park that would bring them closer to the realities of what was once the dominant natural system west of the Mississippi. Yet the prairies have been so denuded, used for agriculture, grazing, and cities, and so tied up in political feuds over private property that only a few sites remain. Still, one can find small preserves throughout the original tallgrass region where folks can roam through head-high big bluestem, knee-high little bluestem, or bunchgrass. People can walk out and sing praise to the morning with meadowlarks, watch raptors, lie down on unbroken sod and study the work of grasshoppers and ants.

Intimate and lovely as such pleasuring grounds can be, they are tiny islands, not large enough to harbor the charismatic beasts — bison, elk, bear, wolves, wildcats — whose patterns of predation, grazing, and foraging were vital to prairie ecosystems. Such animals need whole mountain ranges, forests, grasslands, and riversheds to survive in their wild state. Which is why people who treasure America's historic wildernesses want to be assured that enough land is set aside to preserve entire habitats. They know that offering sanctuary to popularly loved animals such as bison or elk ensures protection for less popular but equally important flora and fauna, and can mean survival for many species that are equally necessary to the natural life of a place.

You don't have to come face to face with a grizzly bear to be glad she exists. She will amble through huckleberry thickets with her cubs, alive in your imagination, if you are sure she is walking in nature somewhere. Without wild grasses, old-growth forests, pure waters, birds, insects, and mammals, human beings will become a lonely species, turned in on themselves, hunting each other, perhaps doomed to a short life on old earth.

Connection to nature lies deep in our genes. Humans became human in a world of biological and botanical diversity. We are still a young species, genetically as close to Paleolithic as to contemporary man, but far more sophisticated in our tools of creation and destruction. What distinguishes you and me from our hunting and gathering ancestors is an accumulation of knowledge — the cultivation of abstract reasoning and language, mostly through the use of metaphors. Metaphoric thinking, however, like the virtual realities of electronics, will not satisfy our inborn hunger for actual relationships with wild animals and lands.

Conservationists are aware of this basic human need. So when the long campaign to create a National Park Service tallgrass preserve in Kansas or Oklahoma came to defeat, in stepped The Nature Conservancy. In 1989 the Conservancy purchased nearly 30,000 acres of the historic Chapman-Barnard Ranch near Pawhuska, Oklahoma, and since then has added some 6,000 acres of Osage prairie lands in what has become their largest project, ever. The Conservancy's intention on the Osage prairie is to protect, indeed to reclaim, a complex mosaic of grasslands and oak forests, as well as the watershed that nurtures them. The Tallgrass Prairie Preserve embodies a dynamic and holistic land management approach, which is significant because it offers a new model for land restoration.

The ranchlands of the preserve are far from pristine. Although the sod there has never been plowed, the rich grasses have been grazed by cattle for generations, altering growth patterns of grasses, forbs, and woodlands. Oil pumps, roads, and the remnants of ranching mark the wide meadows, the creek bottoms and timbered ridges. The Nature Conservancy's goal is not to erase all signs of industrial and agricultural use, but to increase biodiversity within this landscape as it exists. By introducing periodic fires and grazing bison — forces that shaped historic grasslands — the preserve's managers hope to rekindle a unique biome. The restoration they seek is not duplication of what existed long ago, for that is impossible. What they are after is a revitalization unpredictable and surprising as life.

This book will look at the natural ecosystem of the Osage tallgrass prairie: plants, animals, geology, and evolutionary forces such as climate and fire. It will describe the region as it exists today, and find evidence to indicate what it was like in pre-European eras. And it will chronicle the work of land managers and scientists as they take the first steps toward influencing the preserve's evolution in years to come.

The book will also investigate historic human uses of the prairie that helped shape its physical attributes, largely determined its present animal and plant populations and its patterns of settlement. There will be stories of Indians, cowboys and ranch women, of oilmen and settlers, explorers old and new. Some of the stories are mythic, others are common and individual as blades of grass.

All stories that emerge from the prairie illuminate a human response to a place in nature — a trail through the grass, or a home. Like paintings in ancient caves, like tribal hands painted in desert canyons, like shards of pottery buried in mounds, such stories help us to understand our own places in the world and to have empathy with others.

You might think of this as a case study centered around the connections and sacred stories that inspire any effort at preservation. The interdependent influences of a landscape on the people who live within it, and of people changing the nature of land, is what this book will be about. To an uncomfortable degree, we are what we touch and are touched by. We must think carefully about what we destroy, what we preserve, and what we choose to reclaim. To survive with some grace and sanity, I believe we must learn how to live more lovingly on the land, encouraging the natural diversity that sustains us.

ANNICK SMITH

❧

The writing of this book has been a communal effort. My first thanks go to the Oklahoma women who, in honor of The Nature Conservancy's Last Great Places, call themselves "The Last Great Broads" — women whose enthusiasm made this project possible. I am grateful to Mary Barnard Lawrence for the inspiration and contributions she offered, and to other Barnard family members who helped along the way. The Tallgrass Prairie Preserve staff and crew — especially Harvey Payne and Bob Hamilton — gave generously of their time in educating an outsider about the natural history of the grasslands. I am also indebted to the Oklahoma Nature Conservancy and the national office of The Nature Conservancy for their support. Special thanks to Marty Marina for her efforts during the initial stages, and to Scott Anderson for his editorial assistance.

Dan Flores led me to valuable primary source material, and historians Jim and Jeanne Ronda offered crucial research and editorial aid. The annotated bibliography at the end of the book is a compilation of the Rondas' recommendations and my own for readers wishing to learn more.

I am grateful to Geoffrey and Sean Standing Bear and other members of the Osage Tribe for their insights and assistance, and I owe many thanks to Pawhuska area citizens and ranchers such as the Drummond family, Betty and J.B. Smith, Holton Payne, and Helen Christenson.

My editors and publishers Paulette Millichap and Sally Dennison gave invaluable help and support during three years of hard work, and designer Carol Haralson helped to create a beautiful book. Finally, I must thank my companion, Bill Kittredge, and my four sons, Eric, Stephen, Alex, and Andrew for standing by me and encouraging me on my long and rocky road through the tallgrass.

—AS

Begin with Grass

"I believe a leaf of grass is no less
than the journeywork of the stars."

WALT WHITMAN

MY FIRST SIGHT OF THE OSAGE GRASSLANDS is in late August when seedheads droop heavy and the lush green of summer has begun its fade to colors more earthen. The hot, humid air reminds me of the Midwest, where I was raised in Chicago, the "prairie city" with no prairie in sight. Chicago, where "the fog creeps in on little cat's feet," was celebrated by the poet Carl Sandburg, who also celebrated the much older songs of grass. "The prairie sings to me in the forenoon," wrote Sandburg, "and I know in the night I rest easy in the prairie arms, on the prairie heart."

Sandburg's Illinois, and mine, was tallgrass once, a broad open stretch of big bluestem like the Oklahoma prairies of Osage County. But the Osage does not have the rich, deep, tillable soil of Illinois. It grows cattle, not corn, and beneath its skin of limestone and sandstone lie reservoirs of oil and gas. Driving the 16 miles of gravel road from Pawhuska to the Chapman-Barnard Ranch headquarters of the Tallgrass Preserve, I feel spooked. I am a stranger in a land I have never seen, know nothing about, and am as bewitched and bewildered as the pioneer women who arrived on the Kansas and Oklahoma frontiers to claim Indian lands more than a century before.

"Lost! Out here on this lonely prairie," wailed Martha Lick Wooden on a June night

Comets of sturdy purple coneflower (*Echinacea pallida*) shoot upwards in spring.

Photo by Harvey Payne

Where the land is so intractable people can only travel through it, dig holes into it, or trail their herds over it, the landscape remains more or less intact. This is the prairie where soil is so thin and rocky it could not be plowed and farmed, so this is the prairie that survives.

⚭

in 1878. Martha's husband had missed the wagon trail to their Kansas homestead, and the howls of coyotes seemed to her like hyenas — wild dogs laughing at the imbeciles who could not find their way in a wilderness of grass.

"It was such a new world, reaching to the far horizon without break of tree or chimney stack; just sky and grass and grass and sky . . ." Lydia Murphy Toothaker said, recalling her first night on the prairie in 1859. "The hush was so loud."

Lillie Marcks was seven when she rode into the grasslands. "As we drove on the prairie, Mother and I could hardly stay in the wagon. The wild flowers covered the prairies in a riot of colours like a beautiful rug. How we longed to gather some."

The Oklahoma prairies that run on all sides of my rented Mazda partake of the West, where I have lived in Montana for more than thirty years. Broad horizons where grass meets sky are western. I feel at home in windy blue spaces, but this is not the dry, light high plains or the mountain meadow of my homestead ranch, swept by cool breezes even in the dog days of August. This is borderland, a place where West begins.

Always the hunting ground of nomads — a grazer's paradise — the Osage prairies once thronged with bison and elk, antelope and prairie chickens. Now, many native animals have been hunted out, replaced with cattle and horses. I know there are trails in the deep grass made by Indians, explorers, ranchers, and oilmen. And if I looked closely, I would notice that the land is littered with decaying signs of their industry and settlement. But I am overwhelmed with undulating prairies that sweep to every horizon. To my newcomer's eye, the immense landscape shows few signs of habitation. I see only grass, oaks, and sky. The grass swallows every artifact.

Urban civilizations from their origins along the Euphrates have taken hold around places where agriculture and irrigation offered stable sources of food, or at the crossing of major trade routes. Where the land is so intractable people can only travel through it, dig holes into it, or trail their herds over it, the landscape remains more or less intact. This is the prairie where soil is so thin and rocky it could not be plowed and farmed, so this is the prairie that survives.

When I stop my car along the gravel road, I catch scents of musk and dust and rotting stems, an electric charge of ozone. The Oklahoma air is warm, moist, and oppressive. Southern. All I see is grass and more grass, nothing but grass which, when I step into it, envelops me. Claustrophobia panics me, and I push the coarse, enclosing leaves away from my face. I cannot anchor myself to the soil at my feet or the wind at my back through connections of memory or experience. I feel the sky descending.

In the fall of 1832, just back from a long sojourn in Europe, Washington Irving set out on an expedition to see the wild prairies of Indian Territory. He was anxious to reroot himself in the American experience, and what could be more American than the western frontier? In *A Tour on the Prairies,* Irving describes what he saw. He was standing on land not far from where I stood watching the grasses shake their heads in the rustle before a storm.

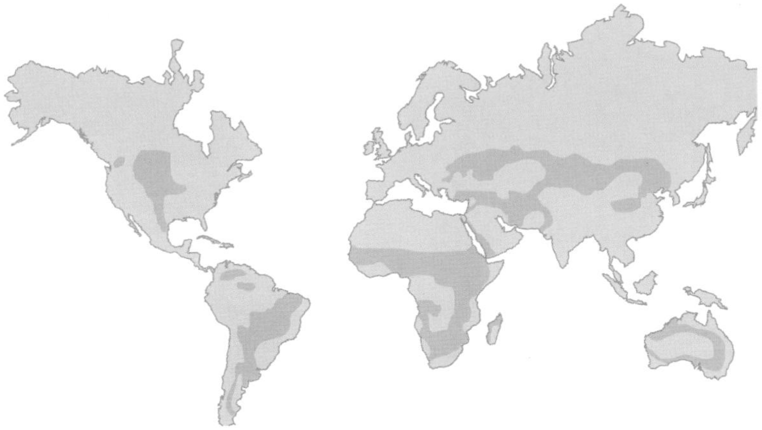

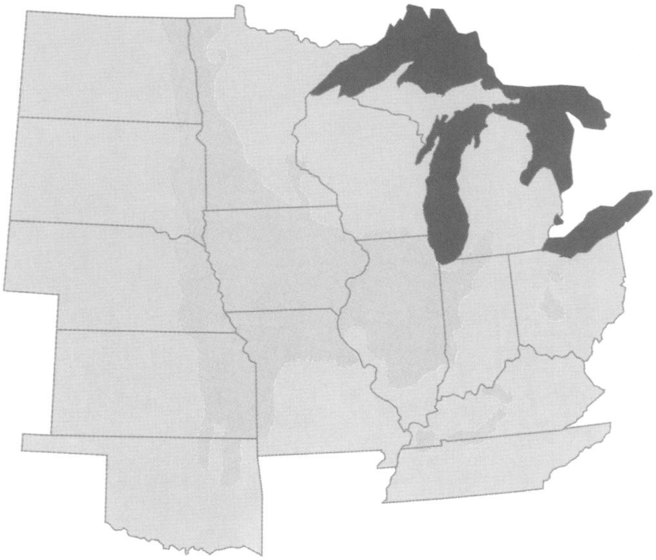

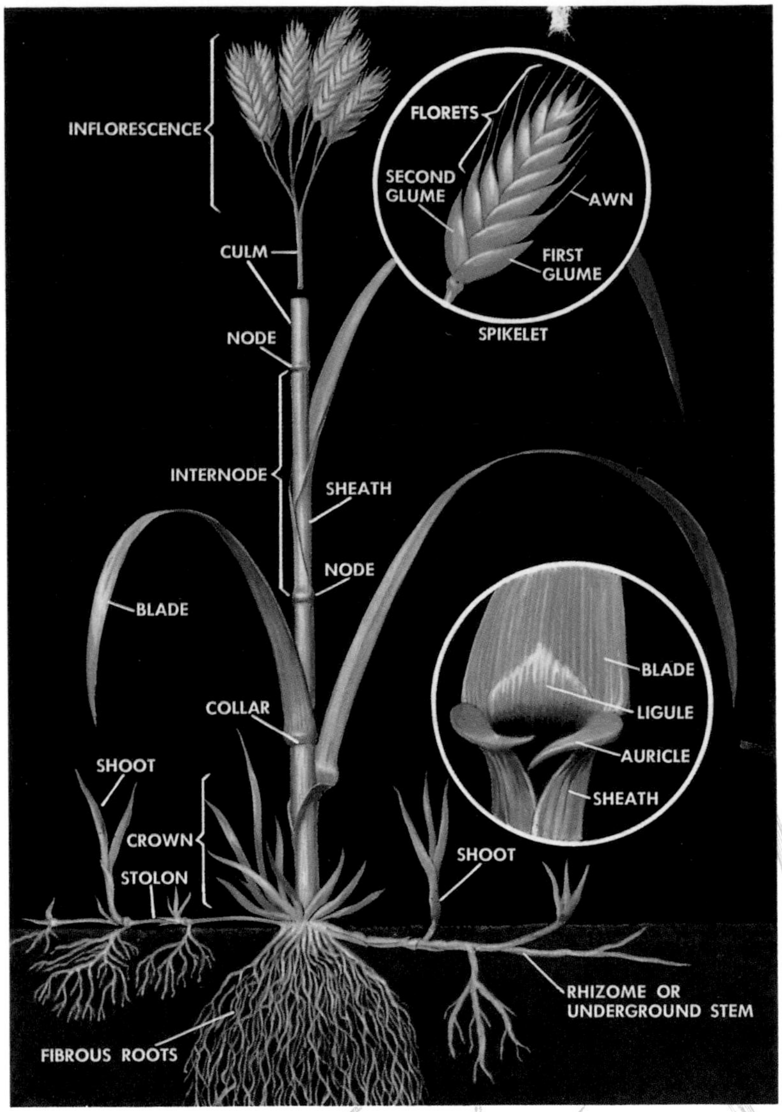

INFLORESCENCE

FLORETS

SECOND
GLUME

AWN

FIRST
GLUME

CULM

SPIKELET

NODE

INTERNODE

SHEATH

NODE

BLADE

BLADE

LIGULE

COLLAR

AURICLE

SHOOT

SHEATH

CROWN

STOLON

SHOOT

RHIZOME OR
UNDERGROUND STEM

FIBROUS ROOTS

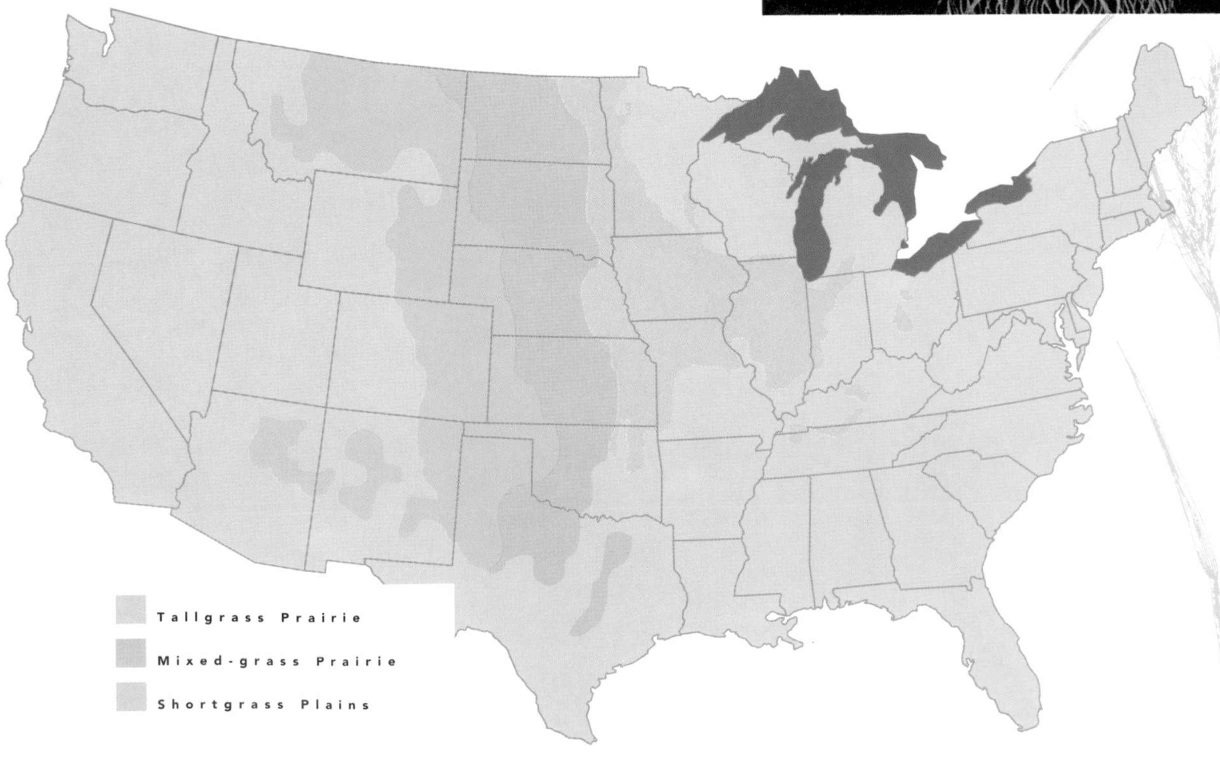

Tallgrass Prairie

Mixed-grass Prairie

Shortgrass Plains

To one unaccustomed to it, there is something inexpressibly lonely in the solitude of a prairie. The loneliness of a forest seems nothing to it. There the view is shut in by trees, and the imagination is left free to picture some livelier scene beyond. But here we have an immense extent of landscape without a sign of human existence. We have the consciousness of being far, far beyond the bounds of human habitation; we feel as if moving in the midst of a desert world.

The green prairies all around me spoke of a fecundity no desert ever has, yet in an emotional sense, Irving was right. A land seems desolate if you know nothing about its geology, botany, and biology, know no histories or stories. Even in my ignorance, I knew this place, like every place, holds a long history of habitation by birds, insects, small and large mammals — including humans — that this prairie's story is underpinned by the tall grasses and flowering plants, the roots beneath my feet.

If I could become familiar with the prairie I stood upon, the meadows and gullies, dark peninsulas of post oaks and blackjack oaks, the trickle of streams over outcropped limestone, I would not be lonely. The red-tail hawk riding air currents is not lonely, nor the spider spinning its gossamer. To know the stories of this place, I must begin with grass. To understand grass, I will have to descend to its roots, and beneath roots to soil and bedrock. But first, as always, was the sky.

"I believe a leaf of grass is no less than the journeywork of the stars," wrote Walt Whitman, America's great poet of grass. The evolution of the tallgrass prairie may be thought of as beginning in stars, in the forces that created the landforms of our continent.

ONCE UPON A TIME, say 65 million years ago during the Cretaceous Period, there were no Rocky Mountains and no great American grasslands either. North America was a level, forested country from sea to shining sea. Its climate was more even, also warmer and wetter than today's, with no deep-freeze winters or steaming summers. Then the bedrock began to heave and lift under pressures of clashing tectonic plates. During the Laramide Revolution, the continent's western edges rose up in great bulging faults and folds which eventually became the Rocky Mountains, the Sierra Nevada, and the Sierra Madre of Mexico.

Prevailing winds, which have always come from the west bearing Pacific moisture, ran up against the new mountains. Instead of dropping their rain burdens evenly across an even landscape, the air masses were forced upward over peaks and ridges. Clouds rapidly cooled as they rose, condensed, then let go of their moisture in great falls of snow and rain. By the time the Pacific westerlies reached the Continental Divide they were exhausted of vapors, having crossed the coast ranges, the Sierras, and the Rockies, and having released most of their wet freight on the westerly slopes and peaks of each range.

Facing page: Grass diagram from the series *Pasture and Range Plants,* published by Phillips Petroleum Company in 1956, used by permission of Hayes State Alumni Association; maps of prairie areas by Chris Mitchell; drawing of big bluestem grass by permission of the University of Nebraska Press.

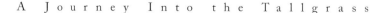

A J o u r n e y I n t o t h e T a l l g r a s s

The result was what we call a rain shadow. In the dry shadow on the eastern side of the Rockies, about 25 million years ago, the great North American grasslands began. For eons they seeded their slow way eastward, aridity and wind helping grass devour forests in a continual movement across the continent.

In addition to the drying effect of the rain shadow, a climate shift to warmer, drier air opened holes in the overstory of weakened forests. The sun shone where it had never shone before. Pines gave way to more drought-tolerant hardwoods, which in turn gave way to grass. Trees could not survive as well as the deep-rooted grasses in increasingly extreme temperatures and under the pressure of high winds. Winds blew grass seed and spread lightning-caused fires. Fires opened new areas.

Giant herbivores such as mastodons, mammoths, and ground sloths kept the forests open. Smaller mammals, including horses, camels, bison, and swift antelope, evolved hypsodont teeth, digestive systems, and hooved feet designed to take advantage of the grassland environment. Carnivores preyed upon the grass-eaters in a cyclic chain of eat-and-be-eaten, but there were enough grazing animals to keep fuel sources low, diminishing the destructive force of fires and increasing diversity.

The grass kept growing eastward beyond the edges of the rain shadow to a region where westerlies collided with the warm, wet currents of air blown inland from the cupped Gulf of Mexico and southern seas. This created the turbulent climate where tornados flourish and the tallgrass thrives near borders of forest lands.

As centuries passed, the Atlantic's cool, moist atmosphere would become dominant for a spell, and the tallgrasses would give way to trees edging in from the east, returning to hegemony when the air warmed once more. Climate remains the crucial force in creating prairies, but nothing stays static on this earth for long, especially climate. Long dry millennia alternated with ice ages. Glaciers slipped down from the north in powerful rivers of ice. They scooped and leveled the northern plains, creating glacial soils that later, blown into drifts by constant winds, became the rich deep Midwestern soil called loess. Although dry spells stopped the glaciers before they reached southern Kansas and Oklahoma, the influence of ice traveled south with seeds carried by wind and birds, and on the hides of migrating animals.

The Osage tallgrass prairie is only about eight thousand years old. It lies in the southern portion of what was, until only a couple of hundred years ago, a huge contiguous grasslands ecosystem of about 142 milion acres. Think of a picture of North America taken from outer space in 1803, when Jefferson made his fateful Louisiana Purchase. Focusing in on the continent's center, you would see the Osage as the southwestern fingertip of an immense deep-green stripe of tallgrass prairie country that began in Manitoba and ran south more than one thousand miles to the Gulf of Mexico. At the eastern edges of the tallgrass stood massive forests of pines and maples, beech and oak. On its east-west axis, the widest and most central tallgrass region extended from western Indiana well into Nebraska.

Aerial view of farmland.
©Richard H. Smith 1944/FPG
International

As I flew over the plains from Missoula to Tulsa on my tallgrass journey, I saw a land where once huge stripes of grass had been replaced with checkerboards and circles of corn, wheat, and other domesticated grains. Lights of hundreds of towns lit the night like stars roosting. I realized that the mechanically transformed landscape below the airplane's wings was not much older than I.

Continuing to trace a west-moving line across the continent, you would see the grass-lands gradually becoming shorter — from head high to knee high — melding in my imaginary map into a paler stripe called the mid-grass plains, which hooked south from Saskatchewan through the Dakotas to Texas. Then, at the 100th Meridian, where the high, dry climate cannot support grasses dependent on abundant moisture, the green turns even paler. The westernmost stripe would be shortgrass plains — predominantly bunch grass — which ran south from Alberta to New Mexico, and kept running toward the sunset until they hit the Rockies.

As I flew over the plains from Missoula to Tulsa on my tallgrass journey, I saw a land where once huge stripes of grass had been replaced with checkerboards and circles of corn, wheat, and other domesticated grains. Lights of hundreds of towns lit the night like stars roosting. I realized that the mechanically transformed landscape below the airplane's wings was not much older than I.

That first day on the Osage, coming sixty, my children grown, my hair turned white, I looked east. Dark stands of oak and blackjack seemed to be pushing their way into the prairie. The muted landscape was feather-soft and cushioned. A wind at my tail stirred plumes of big bluestem and switchgrass in the dipping and rising folds of great meadows. Clouds flew over the wind-tossed grass casting deep purple shadows on silvery greens and grays. Below the roof of advancing storm, turkey vultures circled with outspread wings.

The Ranch Headquarters, or Bunkhouse (at right, 1940s) was restored for use by the Nature Conservancy in 1991 after the Barnard portion of the ranch became a nature preserve. Fencing pliers, below, were part of a cowboy's toolkit.

Photos courtesy of Mary Lawrence; fencing pliers photo by Harvey Payne

The main building of the Tallgrass Prairie Preserve is a one-story red brick, U-shaped structure called the Bunkhouse or Headquarters. Before The Nature Conservancy bought the Barnard portion of the Chapman-Barnard Ranch from the Barnard trusts and refitted the old ranch house for organizational uses, it was an actual bunkhouse as well as the ranch's headquarters. Built in Texas ranch style in 1920 for the oil-rich owners, James A. Chapman and Horace G. (for Greeley) Barnard, the building is gracefully proportioned, sitting solid but not obtrusive on a wide lawn above Sand Creek.

In its prime, the Chapman-Barnard Ranch encompassed 125,000 acres, one of the great cattle empires of the region. When Chapman died, the ranch was divided. The Conservancy's preserve includes nearly 30,000 acres from the Barnard portion, as well as about 6,000 acres of additional property. It centers around the Bunkhouse, barns, sheds, and a few nearby houses and cabins for crew, cowboys, and researchers.

The Bunkhouse had bedrooms for the owners in its far wing and a long central section reserved for visiting and eating. There was a kitchen large enough to provide grub for forty hands, and behind it the cook's quarters, and then another wing where cowboys

bunked. The original, arcaded porch faces the lawns and looks down on the wood-fringed bottoms of the creek.

I arrive at the Bunkhouse near dusk to meet and dine with some of the key figures behind the slow transformation of a working cattle ranch into an experimental grasslands preserve. First to greet me is Harvey Payne, the tall, wry, taciturn director of the Preserve. Harvey is a local citizen, raised on a ranch in Osage County. He is a lawyer, a conservationist, and a talented photographer whose greatest joy seems to be roaming the far reaches of the preserve at dawn or sunset, catching on film the deer, prairie chickens, grasses, wildflowers, and bison in their most secret and beautiful hideouts.

Next I meet Bob Hamilton, the preserve's scientific director and ranch manager. Bob is a wildlife biologist, a Kansas prairie boy — literally boyish in his checked shirt, jeans and brown tousled hair. I am struck by Bob's enthusiasm and energy in tackling what many would call an impossible task. I will soon come to appreciate his easy-going leadership and his knowledge of the tallgrass plains.

Sitting with me at the long, scarred hardwood table that has endured countless cowboy suppers of beef and spuds, are two eminent authorities on prairie grasses and forbs. On my right is Dr. Jerry Crockett, a retired professor of botany from Oklahoma State University. Crockett has published numerous scholarly treatises, but amateur that I am, I prefer to listen and take notes as he talks about bluestem grasses and wildflowers on the Osage.

William C. (Dick) Whetsell, on my left, is a rancher as well as a scholar, with lean and weathered looks, boots and western jacket. Whetsell was for many years president of the Oklahoma Land and Cattle Company and manager of the K. S. Adams Ranch. Although semi-retired, he oversees the Adams' cattle operation on the preserve. But Whetsell is here to inform me about the region's plant life rather than its cattle, for he is an expert who helped develop the manuscript and botanical illustrations for *Pasture and Range Plants,* published by Fort Hays State University. Originally commissioned by Phillips Petroleum as a series of pamphlets to encourage better range management, the black-bound volume would become my prairie bible — the drawings so lovely I am tempted to tear them out and frame them.

"The best way to see the prairie," he says, "is horseback."

"Will you be my guide?" I ask, delighted at the prospect of riding the plains like the Indians, explorers, and cowhands of yesteryear.

A horseback expedition is tempting, but I have homework to do before I allow myself such a treat. My brain whirls with bits of information about the prairie, its cattle ranching history, the Conservancy's plans. As I read myself to sleep on the cool yellow sheets of a bunk in one of the guest rooms, I wonder if I will ever come to understand even the broadest outlines of the interwoven natural and human histories of the ranch.

Harvey Payne, director of the Tallgrass Prairie Preserve, has photographed the 37,500 acres of the Tallgrass Prairie Preserve in all seasons and at all times of day for over twenty years.

Photo by Harvey Payne

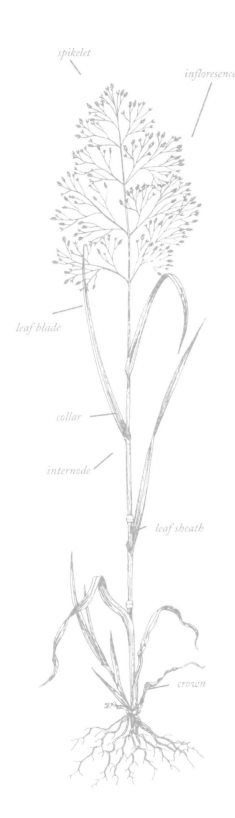

spikelet

infloresence

leaf blade

collar

internode

leaf sheath

crown

By next evening, my task seems more comprehensible. Perhaps because I am in the company of women. The Oklahoma women who surround me have a familiar western sense of humor, a self-irony that enables them to name the group they represent the "Last Great Broads" in honor of The Nature Conservancy's Last Great Places. The Last Great Broads had raised funds to help establish the Tallgrass Prairie Preserve, and some of them were gathered now to turn their energies toward the telling of its many instructive stories.

Sated with pasta and wine, we recline on benches along the narrow Bunkhouse porch. The storm that has been gathering for two days blows toward us with cooling gusts of wind, splatters of rain. There's Jenny Hendrick, retired associate dean of Oklahoma University's Medical School; and tall Judy Kishner, from a family of pipeline entrepreneurs and philanthropists; and Liddy Doenges, the delicate blond fundraising wizard, who would shortly be struck down with cancer. Paulette Millichap, with her soft southern drawl, is the link that brings us together. A friend from long-ago faculty-wife days in Montana, she is the Tulsa editor and publisher who had called me one morning in May and asked if I would like to write a book about the prairie. Marty Marina, at that time the Oklahoma Conservancy's development director for the preserve, bustles in and out, making sure every detail runs right and everyone is satisfied.

The woman who impresses me most, however, is Mary Barnard Lawrence. Mary is in her early seventies, a tall, elegant ranchwoman. She is the Barnard daughter and heir whose desire to turn the old ranch into a symbol of the living prairie made the effort possible. Mary, in her long, divided skirt and crisp white blouse, was, it seemed to me, the generous heart behind the preserve. She leads me to a rise where we experience the force of the engulfing storm.

"There are so many great stories about the ranch, this country," says Mary, lifting her arms to encompass the yellow lighted windows, the dark outlines of barns and sheds, the roaring night sky. "I want to be sure someone tells them right."

As if to punctuate Mary's words, a clap of thunder rolls toward us like timpani, and lightning streaks the sky irridescent blue. A great rain begins to fall. Mary has given me a tall order, but I am more grateful than worried. I feel like taking off my shoes and leaping into puddles like my sisters and I used to do during the warm, summer storms of a Midwest girlhood. I believe I am complicit again with sisters.

After the storm, in the misty light of a blue moon, cicadas begin a strident chorus in a hundred-year-old hackberry tree that dominates the courtyard outside the Bunkhouse porch. I am not used to the voice of this insect, its shrill buzz of life. That hackberry has seen some things. I want to know its secrets, to be the bluebird in its branches or the insect who sings a song of the prairies. Then, under the croak and buzz of cicada wings, I hear a muffled, thumping sound.

The ghost drum of Osage Indians, I think, as the hairs on my arms rise. Spirits dispossessed. "We are here, where we belong: boom, boom," the drum seems to say. "Who the hell are you?" This is an ominous sign and I am frightened. Better get out of here. Pack my bags and slink away.

NEXT MORNING, Bob Hamilton informs me that the rhythmic pulse is only an oil pump on the prairie, giving voice to an oil producing presence that is still here, still viable. There is so much to learn. I am glad to have Bob as teacher.

We walk into the tallgrass under a sky of pure blue with powderpuff clouds skittering like sheep across the pastures of heaven. In the wake of the storm, the temperature dropped during the night, taking summer away with the heat. In a space of 12 hours, the prairie has turned toward autumn. Amid the green meadows, I notice dark splotches where bunches of big bluestem have darkened from the rain and the cold. By October, the whole landscape will turn russet and brown. In winter it will be drained of color, white with snow. Not until the young shoots spring up next April will green return.

Bob leads me into a stand of grasses that rise from ankle height to stems almost ten feet tall. As I pick a bouquet, he names the grasses.

"Big bluestem. That's the tallest. You can tell it by the three-part seed head. Looks something like a turkey's foot. That's why some people call it turkey-foot bluestem."

Big bluestem is the king of tallgrass. It loves moisture and good soil and thrives in valley bottomlands throughout the Great Plains. A native, warm-season perennial, this grass has short, scaly underground stems. The sod underneath is a massed web of big bluestem roots, which can reach down almost 12 feet in search of moisture and nourishment.

Bob Hamilton speaks of grass with the pride and authority of a father praising his prodigal children. The underground vitality of species such as big bluestem, he explains — their deep and pervasive root systems — enables the grasses to survive drought, fire, sub-zero temperatures, even intensive grazing.

In early April, the young shoots begin to sprout, their lower leaves covered with silky hair. Growing in large leafy clumps, big bluestem is the richest and favorite forage of livestock, relished by bison and cattle. If the grass is not grazed down below four inches during the growing season, it regenerates fast. Like other grasses, big bluestem sows its seed on the wind and also spreads by rhyzomes. Its discarded, curled leaves provide a protec-

Big bluestem (top) and little bluestem (bottom) are chief among prairie grasses.

Drawings this page and facing page by permission of the University of Nebraska Press

tive mulch that creates new topsoil as well as fuel for wildfires that are crucial to prairie evolution.

Bob reaches down and picks a delicately fringed stalk from a knee-high bunch of grass. "This is little bluestem," he says. "It's one of our dominant warm season grasses, along with switchgrass and Indiangrass."

I learn that little bluestem was the most abundant grass of the American prairies, native in every plains and western state except California, Nevada, Oregon, and Washington. There's a smattering of little bluestem on the wildgrass borders of my Montana meadow, and in small forgotten patches throughout the Midwest. One of the most nutritious and abundant of all prairie grasses, little bluestem was the wild hay that pioneers cut and stacked as they settled the West. You can identify this hardy perennial by its flat, bluish basal shoots and folded leaf blades. Spread by seed, tillers, and short underground root-stocks, little bluestem shoots from the earth in April, and when it drops its seeds in the fall, the stalks may reach to a person's thighs.

High as the bison logo on my baseball cap, the prettiest tallgrass within reach of my gathering hands has a perfect plume of yellow seedheads at its top and foot-long leaves spreading at 45 degree angles from its stalk. I would love to pick a great armload of this grass and stand it in a vase beside my fireplace.

"That's Indiangrass," says Bob. He points to the claw-like ligule that emerges from the stem wherever a long leaf grows. "It's one of the most nutritious grasses on the prairie."

Indiangrass is a sod-making warm season perennial that reproduces from seed and from short, scaly, underground stems. Its seedlings can withstand extremes of temperature and drought, and so the grass invades disturbed lowland pastures where other less resilient grasses have died out.

Before I am finished, there will be a host of other grasses in my wild bouquet, with common names so descriptive you can imagine what they look like: switchgrass, foxtail, blue grama, hairy grama, windmill grass, sand dropseed, purpletop. The names are poetry. Knowing the names, I am no longer claustrophobic. I believe I could feel at home in the tallgrass, like the bobwhite quail, or the blue dragonflies that hover amid the spiky leaves, or the common garter snake who wisps away from my invading boots, a creature almost indistinguishable from the mottled earth.

All flesh is grass, says the prophet Isaiah in the Bible. My nostrils are filled with the sweet scent of grass. The tingle of grass brushes my hands. The itch of grass is in my eyes. I am tempted to shout "Yes" to the grass. All flesh is one.

THERE IS MORE IN THE TALL-GRASS THAN GRASS. There is a vivid splendor of color. I point to the understory, where August's dark greens and browns are made bright with yellow petals and blue rosettes.

The sod underneath is a massed web of big bluestem roots, which can reach down almost 12 feet in search of moisture and nourishment.

THE BIG FOUR

....

BIG BLUESTEM (top left, *Andropogon gerardi, A. furcatus,*) is a native warm-season perennial of the prairie.

LITTLE BLUESTEM (top right, *Andropogon scoparius*), also a prairie perennial, is slightly shorter than Big Blue.

INDIANGRASS (bottom left, *Sorghastrum nutans*), is a tall native perennial with beautiful golden plume-like seed heads.

SWITCHGRASS (bottom right, *Panicum virgatum*) is a sod-forming tallgrass with vigorous roots. It can be identified by a small nest of hair where the blade attaches to the sheath and its large sprangled seed head.

Drawings from the series *Pasture and Range Plants*, published by Phillips Petroleum Company in 1956, used by permission of Hayes State Alumni Association.

PRAIRIE GRASSES AND FORBS
....

HAIRY GRAMA (top left, *Bouteloua hirsuta*,), a short grass, grows from 10 to 18 inches. It is found throughout the Great Plains on sandy, rocky soil too thin for taller grasses.

COMPASSPLANT (top right, *Silphium laciniatum*), is a deep-rooted native forb growing 3 to 7 feet in height where the rainfall exceeds 30 inches or more annually. Because it decreases where native rangelands are overgrazed, it is an important indicator of range condition.

WITCHGRASS (bottom left, *Panicum capillare*), sometimes called ticklegrass, is abundant on sandy soils. The stems are somewhat sweet-tasting while young but become hard and woody when mature.

YELLOW BRISTLEGRASS (bottom right, *Setaria lutescens*), an annual sometimes called yellow foxtail, was introduced to the prairie from Europe and now is found throughout the United States.

Drawings from the series *Pasture and Range Plants*, published by Phillips Petroleum Company in 1956, used by permission of Hayes State Alumni Association.

"Wildflowers!"

"Forbs," says Bob, using the more specific name for broad-leaf plants. "And that one you're picking, it's a legume."

Any gardener should know a pea legume when she sees one — the dark green opposing leaves like feathers on a stem. The cupped blooms that will fruit into pods. The legume that I add to my bouquet is called showy partridge pea because of its hot yellow flowers. Many legume species, including clovers, are native to the prairies and provide food for animals, insects, and birds. Legumes are a natural fertilizer, returning nitrogen to soils.

Here are a few that have caught my attention: tickclover, with hairy seed pods that cling to clothing or hair like a tick; wild alfalfa, a nutritious June-flowering plant with tiny purple blossoms; purple prairieclover, which rises with spring grass and is high in protein; roundhead lespedeza, covered with fine silvery hair and topped by soft golden flower heads; and the accurately named blue wildindigo, which is slightly toxic, but whose sap turns purple when crushed and exposed to air.

Also yellow, but taller than the legumes, is goldenrod, which I thought made me sneeze. But I am wrong, for goldenrod is pollinated by insects, not by pollen-spreading winds that infect some of us with hayfever. A tasty prairie tea made of goldenrod warmed explorers who came to witness the tallgrass. Henry Ellsworth, U.S. Indian Commissioner for the West, introduced Washington Irving to prairie tea during their expedition to Oklahoma in 1832. "It is *sudorific, gently stimulating* and an active diuretic — in large quantities it is laxative," wrote Ellsworth. "Mr. Irving is so much pleased with it, that he has ordered a quantity for New York."

Goldenrod has gleaned its bad reputation by consorting with the extremely sneezeable ragweeds. Bob leads me to another place on the prairie, a spot of scorched earth dominated by forbs rather than grass. Western ragweed grows in rough, bushy clumps on all sides of me. I notice more goldenrod and prairie dropseed, and lots of tall, aptly-named broomweed, whose open-fingered seedheads look like upended umbrellas.

The Conservancy burned this piece of ground during the summer to mimic the seasonality of historic prairie fires — an unheard-of practice for ranchers who prize high grass. Then bison devoured the young bluestem shoots that sprang up in fire's wake. Now local ranch folk drive their pickups along the preserve's gravel road. On one side they see thick grass; on the burned side, a weedpatch. "Look at the weeds!" they say, confirmed in their suspicion that the preserve's managers are out of their minds.

The notion of weeds as demonic forces to be destroyed is a value judgment outside of nature's order. Agriculturists despise the rugged invading armies of "pioneer" plants such as ragweed that rise up where grasslands have been heavily disturbed by fire or grazing. Such forbs have a role in a healthy ecosystem, but hold no nutrition for people or domesticated animals, and are therefore deemed useless. Ragweed spreads rapidly by means of its long underground stems. Cattle don't like it much, and if a dairy cow eats ragweed, her milk will have a bitter taste.

Prairie goldenrod (*Solidago missouriensis*) flowers from June to October. Some Native American tribes chewed the leaves and flowers to relieve sore throats; chewing the roots was said to relieve toothache. The pollen is highly desirable to many species of bees.

By permission of the University of Nebraska Press

Ordinarily we fight such weeds with herbicides. But on this preserve, any native growth is permitted. Bob Hamilton is a patient manager. He knows that in time the grasses will return with no need for human interference. The bison have already moved on to better patches, and next year the "Big Four" late successional grasses — big bluestem, little bluestem, Indiangrass, and switchgrass — will begin their comeback. By the second year, if there is no fire, this stand will hold more grass than weeds; and by year three, says Bob with a hopeful grin, "the late successional grasses will triumph."

My attention is diverted by a scattering of delicate blue-flowered pitcher sage, and a few red-purple bunched heads of tall, stalky ironweed. I scan the meadow for rosy blooms of blazing star or button snakeroot, but find none.

"I thought there'd be compassplant," I say, looking in vain for the giant stalks with yellow sunflowery blooms.

A clan of Osage Indians who called themselves Walkers-in-the-Mist used seven-foot tall compassplants to plot their routes across fog-bound prairies. Wagon-train scouts marked trails for their followers by tying flags to the flower's stalks. I would love to see the foot-long oak-shaped leaves that give this characteristic tallgrass prairie forb its name — leaves whose long sides point north and south, and whose flat horizontal edges face the rising or setting sun.

Bob shakes his head a bit sadly, for compassplant is rarely seen on some of these meadows. Because cattle have grazed here for so many years, devouring broad-leaf plants along

PRAIRIE FORBS

··························

COBAEA PENSTEMON (left, *Penstemon cobaea*) is a native, warm-season, long-lived perennial forb which reproduces by seed and underground stems.

HEATH ASTER (right, *Aster ericoides, A. multiflorus*) is a native deep-rooted perennial whose rapid new growth stands well above the grasses in May.

Drawings from the series *Pasture and Range Plants*, published by Phillips Petroleum Company in 1956, used by permission of Hayes State Alumni Association.

~ ~ ~ BIG BLUESTEM ~ ~ ~

with grass, many typical prairie wildflowers have grown scarce or disappeared. Herbicide use by previous managers has also contributed to this decline. Although much of the land has never been plowed, its plant life has been diminished on fenced pastures managed to fatten cattle.

"About 75 to 80 percent of a cow's diet is grass, the rest forbs," Bob explains. The Conservancy hopes to bring a more natural distribution back to the grasslands by returning bison to the prairies, for bison do not like to eat forbs.

"At least 90 percent of a bison's feed is grass alone," Bob continues. "In our bison pasture, we expect to see a resurgence of more broadleaf plants."

Fire is the second element necessary for restoring the prairie. Except for controlled spring burning, which encourages the growth of favored grasses, the Osage ranchers have suppressed wildfires over the years, and so changed the life of the prairie.

Some native plant species that were grazed heavily or killed with herbicides spread by previous ranchers may be scarce now, but there are clusters of surviving forbs in remote byways where cattle have not grazed. Their seeds will return on prairie winds, or be carried by birds. Other seeds are storing their energies under the sod. Fire will open the land to sunlight. Bison will not devour them. Given the right conditions, the wild garden is returning.

Clockwise, pale purple coneflower, tall thistle (*Cirsium altissimum*), and golden coreopsis (*Coreopsis tinctoria*) are three common prairie forbs, or wildflowers. On the facing page, woolly yarrow (*Achillea lanulosa*) keeps company with the shorter bigflower coreopsis (*Coreopsis lanceolata*).

Photos by Harvey Payne

"During the summer of '95," says Bob, "a previously burned patch within the bison area produced pitchers sage, blackeyed susan, showy evening primrose, and lemon monarda.

"When we completed our plant count on the preserve," he continues, "we found 650 species. They were all here to begin with. We don't expect any new species to turn up. But the abundance and distribution will change." I imagine a host of many-colored wildflowers harboring roots and seeds in underground beds, like bears in hibernation.

"We are trying to get comfortable with change," says Bob. Not an easy trick.

AS WE WALK BACK TOWARD THE BUNKHOUSE, Bob points out the soils that underlie the preserve's landscape. To the west are limestone-based soils, the most productive for tallgrass. I see bluestem meadows edged by a fringe of brush and oaks. To the east, a cross-timber forest of blackjack oaks and post oaks juts into the grasslands. The tree-growing soil is sandstone-based, often exposed, thin and rocky. In loamy creek bottoms, the only land that can be farmed, grasses grow ten feet tall.

This particular stretch of ground, Bob figures, has been prairie for only eight thousand to ten thousand years. It was shaped by natural forces such as drought, intensive grazing by nomadic herds of bison, and fires ignited in lightning storms like the one that raged last night. Native Americans, who hunted and camped in the region as long as the grass has grown here, also changed the landscape through fire. They set fires for defense and to produce more and better feed for the elk and bison they depended on for food and shelter. They were the first human land managers.

"The Conservancy's policy," Bob says, as we enter his book-lined office, "is to reintroduce randomness in order to encourage the biodiversity of the prairie ecosystem. The best way to do this is to create a similar dynamic of disturbance through carefully controlled use of bison and fire.

"We are not trying to recreate a snapshot in time," says Bob. "We are trying to restart the engine, mimic what we think is a functional landscape."

I pause on my way to my room to study the old hackberry tree in the courtyard. Here, the grass is clipped short, a green undifferentiated lawn made for the limited uses of modern people — a place where you could picnic in comfort, play croquet, spread a blanket in the shade and read a book. This is what most folks think is a functional landscape.

My arms are still grasping the huge bouquet of grasses and flowers I have brought back from the prairie. What will I do with this sloppy bunch of stems and leaves already shedding seeds and petals? It is too fragile to pack in a bag, wrap in plastic, stow in the narrow compartment above an airline seat. I cannot hold on to this bunch of grass except in my mind and memory. And that is where the landscape I have just traversed becomes most functional for me. The new landscape in my mind has opened my imagination to a world of grass dizzy with motion, form, and color. I am ecstatic, addicted, and I am not alone in this.

Rolla Clymer was a newspaperman in El Dorado, Kansas, who traveled through the Flint Hills for 39 years on his way to and from Topeka. He always loved the prairies, but did not write his regionally famous editorials about the land of tallgrass until he was an old man, retired and reflecting. At the age of 85, voiceless from surgery, he continued to put pen to paper in rhapsodic paeans to his great obsession and joy. "Now, as midsummer nears," he wrote, while his own life waned:

A COMPLEX DANCE

A goldenrod spider embraces its prey, a common sulphur butterfly, on a light poppy mallow.

Photo by Harvey Payne

FLOWERS AND FRUITS IN MANY FORMS

A few of the forms taken by the fruits of wildflowers and shrubs of the prairie: from the left, a follicle, a schizocarp, a capsule, utricles, capsules, drupes, a pome, a berry, a nutlet, and achens.

By permission of the University of Nebraska Press

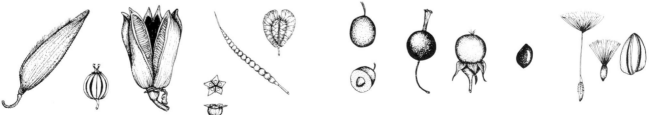

A J o u r n e y I n t o t h e T a l l g r a s s

PRAIRIE BIRDS

Clockwise from top left: a male wood duck on the water; killdeer in a snowy wetland; common nighthawk resting on a fencepost; mature bald eagle; male cardinal on an ice-covered limb; and scissor-tailed flycatcher on a barbed-wire fence.

Photos by Harvey Payne

The same sweet grasses bend their heads before the South Wind's vagrant whim; the same riot of wildflowers runs glitteringly through the expanse; the same anthems of birdsong rise from feathered throats; and the same smoky haze dances afar off where the sky bends downward to earth. Over all this comely region the same great solitude prevails — a silence that is its distinctive symbol — a reflective calm with healing in its wings.

I promise myself to return to the prairie in June, when the great wildflower show takes place with sulphur butterflies and Monarch butterflies, hummingbirds, daisies, larkspur, purple coneflowers, and fragrant wild roses. The new grass will be emerald, thick as the carpet of a Persian queen, and I will lie down in it. I recall two favorite lines from Andrew Marvell's poem, "The Garden" — *ensnared with flowers/I fall on grass.*

"I would be converted to a religion of grass," writes Louise Erdrich in an essay about the prairies of her Ojibwa ancestors near Wahpeton, North Dakota.

There's a sensible religion. One I could embrace. We should be baptized in grass. Grass, our nest. Grass, our spiritual home. And we should adhere to the tenets of the faith Louise has proposed: Sleep the winter away and rise headlong each spring. Sink deep roots. Conserve water. Respect and nourish your neighbors and never let the trees gain the upper hand.

Then, like the tallgrass prairies of Oklahoma, we might become humble in our strengths: "Bow beneath the arm of fire. Connect underground. Provide. Provide. Be lovely and do no harm."

Spider's web in the morning dew. Below, a grasshopper on a stalk of big bluestem.
Photos by Harvey Payne

"The Conservancy's policy . . . is to reintroduce randomness in order to encourage the biodiversity of the prairie ecosystem."

Beasts of the Field

"I know the joy of fishes
In the river
Through my own joy, as I
go walking
Along the same river."
CHUANG TZU,
TRANSLATED BY
THOMAS MERTON

O UT OF A FAWN-COLORED SWALE LEAP FAWNS. And does. A clutch of young stags. They hold their long, furry, white tails high, and the tails wave over their haunches flagging danger. Four, five, six deer bound across the open meadows below our viewpoint on a promontory of rocks. Then, from the next dip in the pale green prairie hills, another bunch takes flight, joining with the first. I lose count at fifteen deer.

White-tailed deer do not usually congregate in herds. But here is a herd running full tilt for shelter. As they cover ground in the almost comical, bouncing stride of deer, their airborne front hooves nearly meet their rear hooves above the tallest stalks of last year's grass. The deer move swiftly, spanning up to fifteen feet in one bound. They tilt back their large, tawny ears. They uplift their long necks and pointed black snouts, alert to any new threat of predators.

I feel my heartbeats quicken. My breath comes fast. Adrenalin surges in my bloodstream. I look over at Harvey Payne, director of the preserve, who has led me to this viewpoint. Standing tall and still in his red cap and canvas jacket, Harvey peers through his binoculars, tracking the deer.

"I've never seen so many deer out here in a bunch," says Harvey. When, at last, he lets go of his field glasses, his eyes gleam. Harvey is as excited as I am.

The thrill that comes with the sight of big game is an old experience. I feel it every April, when sometimes thirty elk materialize out of the pine woods at dusk to graze the

WINTER AND SPRING

A white-tail doe pauses with her fawn beneath snow-laden branches. Inset above, the exuberant mating dance of the male greater prairie chicken.

Photos by Harvey Payne

A Journey Into the Tallgrass

My adrenalin rush is a wake-up call. Here is your beautiful prey, it says. A hunter does not hate her prey, she loves it, often worships it. Here is the animal you love, says my blood, the animal that will nourish you, the animal you must capture and kill.

white-petaled flowers called spring beauty that grow on the edges of my Montana meadow. The elk are dominant, huge as my horses. The bull will arch his dark brown, fur-fringed neck, antlers raised high, and sniff the air. He advances toward the seep-spring by my stone pile, his harem following in a scattered line. In the dim evening light, the herd's butter-cream rump patches glow like small moons. Some nights the yearlings are frisky as kids, and they chase each other in a game of elk tag. Once I saw the young elk playing with a few white-tail deer who had come to drink at the seep. An unseemly adolescent mule who thinks he owns the meadow bucks and charges the invading elk. When the elk take flight, running with high-stepping grace, they remind me of camels. The coming of elk signals spring, as much as the bluebirds and robins, the yellow buttercups in my pasture.

There is a hole in my life if the elk do not come. I feel their absence in the wide April meadows of the Oklahoma prairie. Once the elk, also called wapiti, roamed here in abundance. At home in forests and prairies, elk were major herbivores on the American grasslands, but were hunted mercilessly until none were left there. Only a remnant population found safe harbor in the remote mountains and valleys of the Rockies and the Northwest, where they are carefully preserved for today's hunters.

In back-country Montana where I live, some of the last charismatic beasts survive. I wish they were on the prairies where they also belong. If I could hear wolf songs, or see elk herds or a bull moose knee-deep in a swampy lowland or pronghorn antelope running or a pale prairie grizzly stripping berries in the brush, I would feel the surge of excitement that deer bring. When I go hiking in the high wilds of the Rockies and the bear I spot is a grizzly, my breath nearly stops. My emotions rise to heights of love and fear.

Navajo Deer Hunt,
Narciso Abeyta,
(Navajo, b. 1921),
watercolor.

Philbrook Museum of
Art, Tulsa, acc. no.
1946.29.5

Why, I wonder, do Harvey and I share the same feelings at the discovery of deer in the wild? We have seen countless deer in our lives—deer, these days, common as coyotes or cowbirds.

The answer, I believe, lies partly in our genetic heritage. Human beings evolved as hunters. On African savannas of grass and trees, a land thick with grazing, hooved beasts, our ancestors learned to eat meat as well as the nuts and fruits their primate progenitors had thrived on. The best hunters were the best survivors. And, if you accept any part of Darwin's theory of natural selection, it makes sense that traits promoting successful hunting would eventually become genetically coded.

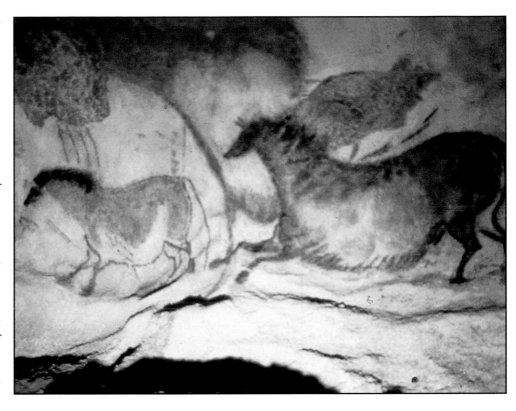

Horses in the caves of Lascaux, France.

Photo by Dordogne Tourist Board

Homo sapiens are a predator species. In their patterns of predation, humans are not vastly different from the cat family or the dog family. Anyone who owns a cat or a dog has seen the transformation such an animal goes through when it spots some favorite prey. Nostrils twitch. Ears rise. Tails switch or wag. Soon your sweet kitty will be creeping, silent and totally focused, toward the mouse in the corner, the bird pecking seeds on the feeder in your backyard. Your obedient dog will run away from you, nose to the ground, oblivious to your calls, on the track of a rabbit or a squirrel.

"Man is naturally an animal of prey," wrote Washington Irving, infected by the bloodlust so many white hunters felt when they encountered the animal feast of the prairies, "and however changed by civilization, will readily relapse into his instinct for destruction. I found my ravenous and sanguinary propensities daily growing stronger on the prairies."

My adrenalin rush is a wake-up call. Here is your beautiful prey, it says. A hunter does not hate her prey, she loves it, often worships it. Here is the animal you love, says my blood, the animal that will nourish you, the animal you must capture and kill. Harvey Payne hunts with his camera; I hunt with my notebook and pen; and many hunt dollars rather than meat. Our genes don't care. They just instruct us in ways of being alive, the old ways of being the animal we are.

The two bison, Lascaux, France.

Photo by Dordogne Tourist Board

RECENTLY I HAD THE LUCK to visit the limestone grottos of Lascaux along the Vezere River in France. We entered the enormous cavern overhung with crystallized white ledges. From every gleaming surface — walls, ceilings, passageways — the forms of huge animals surrounded us in a layered, multi-dimensional frieze. Painted in earth reds, ochre, browns, and outlined in black, the vivid beasts seemed to emerge alive out of the dripping, stony darkness.

I was stunned by the brilliance, the immediacy, the spiritual force of a gigantic, black and red prehistoric cow. Painted into the curved and recessed heights of the cave, the cow's curled horns, her drooping belly — heavy as with child — her great haunches and flowing tail slanted upwards, above the other animals. Her front legs were spread as if flying or falling, and they hung over a white ledge, creating a sense of motion and perspective. But it was the great cow's hind leg, raised and bent forward, as if running, that surprised me. Some experts call her the Falling Cow, assuming she has been wounded by a shaft near her throat. I prefer to see her as the Flying Cow, forever lifting her pregnant body toward light and fresh air.

~ ~ ~ BIG BLUESTEM ~ ~ ~

The cows in the cave were of a kind we have never seen. Like the great black bulls with arcing horns who tower over the main gallery, they are aurochs — an extinct bovine species that evolved to become the domesticated oxen of Europe, and Spain's wild fighting bulls. The painted bestiary with ibex, lions, cave bear, red deer, swimming stags, and black curly-haired rhinos tells us that the valleys of Perigord teemed with life. The first etchings go back 30,000 years, but the great artistic tradition began in the Magdalenian Period about 18,000 years ago and lasted about 4,000 more years. This sweep of centuries saw the waning of one great ice age, the sudden warming of earth, and then another cold spell.

Buffaloes in the Salt Meadow, left, and *Buffaloes,* top, by George Catlin (1796-1872), capture the great beasts in oil on canvas. Immediately above, a bison bull in winter, one of the herd reintroduced to the Tallgrass Prairie Preserve by the Nature Conservancy.

Catlin paintings, collection of the Gilcrease Museum, Tulsa, acc. nos. 0176.2172, 0176.2123; bison photo by Harvey Payne

Stalking the Buffalo by George Campbell Keahbone (Kiowa, b. 1916), watercolor.

Philbrook Museum of Art, Tulsa, acc. no. 1948.13

Horses roamed everywhere on the walls of Lascaux, painted and etched throughout the age — stallions racing, fecund large-bellied mares, horses with manes, horses perfect in their proportions, almost Grecian. And then I saw the famous opposing bison. Some experts say they are fighting, but how can they fight when they face in opposite directions? To me the molting bison are dancing.

The bison on Lascaux's walls were images of *Bison priscus,* now extinct, an animal much larger than the rare European *Bison bonasus,* or its Eurasian cousin, *bison antiquus,* who traversed the Bering land bridge from Siberia to Alaska more than 50,000 years ago. Those bison were killed off, but some of their kin evolved into *Bison bison* — the prolific American breed we call "buffalo" — our symbol of the Great Plains.

The dancing beasts in that French cave reminded me of the vital, humped, and shaggy bison I had seen roaming the tallgrass a few months before. I stood in one of the world's sacred places and offered thanks to turn-of-the-century conservationists who had preserved a few remnant herds so that the primordial, life-giving bison would not go extinct in North America.

I thought of paintings by George Catlin, John Mix Stanley, and Karl Bodmer —

inspired artists of the nineteenth century whose precisely observed images portray a more recent prairie paradise. George Catlin traveled among Plains Indians from 1832 to 1839, and sketched their visages, dress and customs. When he reached the southern prairies, two hundred miles southwest of Fort Gibson, Catlin wrote, "I am already again in the land of the buffaloes and the fleet-bounding antelopes; and I anticipate, with many other beating hearts, rare sport and amusement amongst the wild herds ere long."

Catlin's Oklahoma images include a playful herd of wild cayuse horses with flying tails and manes. And white-tail deer plunging into a river to escape a grassfire that sweeps

The Osage Indians living along the Arkansas and Neosho Rivers as Catlin would have seen them in the 1830s.

Courtesy of the Museum of the American Indian, Heye Foundation

A J o u r n e y I n t o t h e T a l l g r a s s

down from the bluffs. And buffalo thick as ants, trailing in furry lines across lime-green prairie hills. Catlin portrays his vision of the West. The art in Paleolithic caves is also visionary.

No one knows what the ancient peoples who painted realistic animals on the walls of European grottos were up to. The paintings could be a way of prayer and thanksgiving, a form of healing or initiation, a celebration of fertility and the hunt, or art for art's sake. Most probably all of the above. It doesn't matter. The power and the beauty matter, and the fact that we can stand where our ancestors stood 20,000 years ago and gape in awe at the great beasts, as they must have gaped.

An Osage family living in the Pawhuska area at the turn of the century.

Osage Tribal Museum Archive and Library, Pawhuska

JOHN JOSEPH MATHEWS was a child of the Osage, its historian, story-teller, and scholar. He was a man of mixed blood, descended from a white missionary who married an Osage woman. Although educated at Oxford in England and serving as a pilot in World War I, Mathews prized his Osage identity. The Native American side of himself — his formative years on the Osage Reservation — led him to write several novels and a memoir. But his great tome was *The Osages, Children of the Middle Waters,* an utterly original telling of the story of his tribe, based on the oral histories he heard from its elders.

"I thought of myself as a paleontologist," Mathews writes in his introduction. Recording the ancient stories was his way of trying to preserve life on the borders of extinction. The stories of Osage elders, who had lived the traditional life of Plains Indians, were dying with the old story-tellers, dying with their language during the 1940s and 1950s, when Mathews conducted his research.

"I became almost at once aware of the importance of oral history," he continues, ". . . each word had a certain sanctity. The history was a part of them, of the informants and the tribe, and they could not be detached from their narrative as were literate Europeans detached from their written narratives."

This portrait of Julia Lookout, wife of chief Fred Lookout, was made by Todros Geller, a German-American painter commissioned by the Works Progress Administration to work among the Osage Indians in Oklahoma during the years of the Great Depression. During his two-month stay he made a remarkable number of sensitive and enduring portraits. Visible on the hands of this woman is the spider tattoo that signifies her membership in the No-Ho-Zshinga or "Little Old Men Society." The tattoos worn traditionally by Osage women were a visible record of tribal history and clan associations. Only women wore spider tattoos.

Courtesy of the Osage Tribal Museum, Archive and Library. Photos by Harvey Payne

The intricate and lengthy Osage creation story that Mathews retells is notable for its "harmony with the natural flow." Its many-layered structure covers many aspects of tribal organization and ritual, but its core story is based on an immutable relationship among the forces of sky and earth.

The "Little Ones," as the Osage called themselves, originated among stars. By seeing themselves as "little," the Osage recognized their humble stature on the broad reach of earth. They were a creature among many; not better, not worse. Their myth of creation details the connections of human beings to a specific natural ecosystem inhabited by a plentitude of diverse and thought-provoking life.

The stately great blue heron. Over 300 bird species make their home on the Tallgrass Prairie Preserve.

Photos by Harvey Payne

When the Children of the Middle Waters . . . came down from the stars, they floated into a red oak tree, and when they alighted they loosened acorns which clattered down among the leaves. . . . They floated down from the sky with their legs outstretched to the tree tops, and their arms up like the wings of an alighting eagle, since it is this great bird's landing which they later imitated in their creation dances.

The Osage ancestors came to live along the banks of the Missouri River, just west of its juncture with the Mississippi. Although this land is north of the Oklahoma prairies that have been the tribe's home since the 1870s, the mammals, reptiles, insects, and birds that inhabited those Missouri meadows, rivers, and forests in pre-Columbian times were the same creatures that inhabited the more southerly hunting grounds where the Osage would ultimately settle.

In the Osage creation myth, as in most creation stories, naming plays an important role. "We received our names from nature and nature revealed its names to us," explains Geoffrey Standing Bear, a contemporary Osage. "It was . . . through communication with the creatures, beings and elements of this world that people conceived of the physical attributes of what is now called the world and of themselves."

To learn at least one version of the whole story, you will have to read Mathews' book. Here, I will list some of the animal-teachers or clan symbols of the Osage, leaving out the crucial flora, such as willows, rushes, herbs, flowers, and trees. It is a bestiary of great mammals, birds, fish, and small insects, each especially adapted to survive in its niche on the hungry earth. Lucky for us, although some are threatened or endangered, and some fled from the prairies, all of these creatures remain somewhere in America to teach their lessons to any who take the time to listen and observe.

First among the instructing animals was buffalo — generous buffalo who gave the people the four colors of maize as well as squash, told them how to use his hide, fat, sinew, and horns.

The crayfish dug from the mud the four sacred colors, red, blue, yellow, and a color called merely "dark." Wily, swift, strong-swimming panther showed the Osage delectible lotus fruit and the wisdom of growing old through stealth.

One clan claimed as its symbol the sandhill crane, because the bird was almost as tall as a man and saw everything that moved on the prairie. Another claimed black bear, for she is black like the night and carries a small white spot on her chest, like the moon; and still another clan claimed black bear again, but painted the animal red and revered it as a life symbol because, to quote Mathews, "the wrinkles on his neck and feet and the under parts of his body were symbolical of old age," survival into old age being one of the most desired goals of any individual, for elders keep the old ways and stories alive.

Snakes were not forgotten when the clans named themselves, especially rattlesnake, who was a symbol of merciless killing, but also, because rattlesnakes shed their skins, a symbol of rebirth. The most sacred symbol, however, was a bird of prey.

The Osage worshipped the peregrine falcon with shrines and used its skin as the sacred central object in medicine bundles. They revered falcons for their swift courage, clean killing, alertness, and freedom. Golden eagles were more problematic because they were eaters of dead things, but they became one clan's symbol because they had valor, ruthlessness, and the ability to "remain in the eye of the sun."

Trumpeter swan became an important military tribal symbol because the swan not only embodied beauty, endurance, and strength, but held its dignity and grace in three elements: water, land, and air. The swan would let no enemy approach its home. White pelican, on the other hand, was a symbol of peace. Known as He-Who-Becomes-Aged-While-Still-Traveling, pelican was the philosopher of old age, a huge, heavy bird that, "even when old, travels on the strong wings of youth."

Strange as it seems, the fresh water mussel became the symbol for a major clan division — the Children of the Waters. The mussel could jet water like a fountain; its wrinkled shell denoted prized old age; and the mussel proposed to teach the people how to move through water and make no trails. Artisans carved mussel shells into round gorgets, which clansfolk tied around their necks with strips of deer hide. The mussel ornaments signified the sun.

The list continues with white-tail deer, adopted for fleetness, its cleverness in finding refuge and foiling enemies. The water strengths of beaver, otter, turtle, and eel brought these river rovers into the cosmology. Even red perch and black perch were taken as symbols.

The common spider became a symbol for the Earth People. "I am a little black thing," said the spider, "but remember this: wherever I go I build my house, and where I build my house, all things come to it. . . . And whoever enters my house will break their necks therein." The people were convinced. Sometimes women affirmed their identities by tattooing a spider symbol on the backs of their hands.

"We received our names from nature and nature revealed its names to us," explains Geoffrey Standing Bear, a contemporary Osage. "It was ...through communication with the creatures, beings and elements of this world that people conceived of the physical attributes of what is now called the world and of themselves."

A white-tail buck in late summer.

Photo by Harvey Payne

I will end the Osage litany of sacred beasts with Mathews' telling of the elk's story:

The Children of the Land say that when they first came near the great wapiti, the o'po'n tonkah, he stood and gazed at them, his antlers like the branches of a winter hickory. Then he turned and trotted off with knees high, and as he splashed through the edge of the water, his great bull hooves slashed the mud exposing the sacred colors of clay.

On seeing this, they followed him through trees, then he stood and waited for them and offered himself as their symbol. They might see, he suggested to them, that when he threw himself upon the earth, he left hairs, and these hairs became the grasses of the land. He turned and asked them to note his rounded buttocks. Those humps, he said, were the rounded prairie hills; and the right side of his body was the level land, the plains; the ridge on his back, the land ridges; and the gaps in the ridges were represented by the downward curve of his neck between his head and the hump of his shoulders. The tip of his nose would be the peaks of the earth, and the knobby base of his antlers, the humble rocks strewn over the land. The large tines of his antlers were the river systems, and the smaller tines the creeks.

AFTER JEFFERSON'S LOUISIANA PURCHASE in 1803, the first government-sponsored scientific explorations of the frontier lands west of the Mississippi began. Everyone knows about Lewis and Clark's 1804-1806 expedition across the Great American Desert and over the shining mountains to the Pacific. Explorations of the more southeastern and southwestern plains and woods of Oklahoma, Arkansas, and Texas are less familiar to us. Now, however, we can read the accounts of explorer Thomas Freeman and naturalist Peter Custis in Dan Flores' book, *Jefferson & Southwestern Exploration*. The impressions of early visitors to this region are important to our story because they give us a glimpse of life on southern prairies before the great waves of settlement changed everything.

In 1804, Jefferson appointed Thomas Freeman, a surveyor and civil engineer, to lead a twin expedition to Lewis and Clark's up the Red River from Louisiana through Texas, and westward across the plains to the mountains of Santa Fe, where, rumor had it, the river began. Freeman was to map the region, describe its geology, flora and fauna, and to discover the Red River's headwaters. Then, Jefferson instructed Freeman, he was to locate the origins of the Arkansas River and descend it through the cross-timbered central region and grassland plains of what is now Oklahoma. Osage Indians foiled Jefferson's plans and limited the range of the Freeman Expedition. The Osages dominated the region, and they threatened to attack any intruders on their prairie hunting grounds. To avoid trouble Jefferson amended his instructions in 1805, so that only the Red River, well south of Osage domination, would be explored.

Camanchee Indians Throwing the Lasso by George Catlin (1796-1872), oil on canvas.

Collection of the Gilcrease Museum, Tulsa, acc. no. 0176.2163

Jefferson appointed a young naturalist to accompany Freeman. Peter Custis was twenty-five years old, a medical and natural history student at the University of Pennsylvania, and the first naturalist ever sent on a United States expedition to the West. Custis noted several "new" species as his party penetrated the post oak savannas of Texas nearly to the Oklahoma border — an ecoregion that marked the transition from eastern forests onto the southern great plains. Among the birds Custis identified were many that would also be found further north on the tallgrass prairies. These include the migrant lesser yellowlegs; the peregrine falcon; the ruby-throated hummingbird and rufous hummingbird; cardinals; northern bobwhites; the merlin, or pigeon hawk; barred owls; and countless wild turkeys — probably the eastern wild turkey, which biologist Victor E. Shelford estimated in his study, *The Ecology of North America,* numbered from 50 to 200 birds per 10 square miles in pre-settlement eastern forests. By the end of the nineteenth century, according to environmental historian Dan Flores, the species along the Red River was "totally extirpated."

Custis's notes on rarer birds included the now extinct western Carolina parakeet, a bright green and yellow parrot which was last spotted along the Arkansas River in 1849, and the ivory-billed woodpecker, largest of all American woodpeckers, also extinct.

Although Custis does not mention them, perhaps because they were so common, he must have also seen huge flocks of passenger pigeons, today long gone from any skies.

But Custis's most scientifically notable discovery was the Mississippi kite. If Custis had not neglected to give this striking bird a Latin name, its addition to the *Birds of America* would be attributed to him, rather than to the more eminent birdman, Alexander Wilson, who named it *Ictinia mississippiensis* in 1810. Here is Custis's description:

> Cere, ores and bill black; legs yellow; head and neck blueish white; body and wing coverts lead color; quill and tail feathers black-brown, each tail feather with white stripes extending halfway across; claws black; belly blueish; wings below with white & ferruginous spots; inside fulvous. 14 inches long.

Fish that Custis spotted in the Red River are also found in other rivers within the Mississippi drainage. They included black and white buffalo fish; spoonbills or paddlefish, herring and gar. He mistakenly listed freshwater crayfish as "shrimp," and noted many catfish — some that weighed in at 59 pounds.

A page from the *Codex Canadiensis* by Louis Nicolas (early 17th century) shows marvelous beasts thought to inhabit the New World. Left, passenger pigeons, like this one from an engraving in *Harper's Weekly* ca. 1870, once filled the prairie skies, but now are extinct.

Codex, Gilcrease Museum, Tulsa; engraving, Ridgway Gallery, Ridgway CO

Title page from the 1819 report of Thomas Nuttall on his travels in Arkansas Territory; below, Nuttall's itinerary.

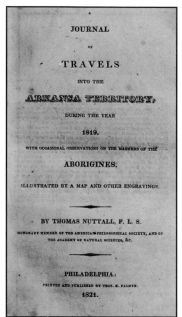

The list of quadrupeds Custis observed includes numerous black bears, white-tail deer, striped skunks, eastern moles, gray lobo wolves [now extinct, along with prairie wolves], cougar, beaver, otter, and a large rabbit, the black-tailed jackrabbit, not catalogued as a new species until 1837.

Although he saw some bison along the river, Custis never witnessed the great herds of the plains. But, he reports: "I am told by Hunters that in the large plains about the Panis Villages many thousands may be seen at a view. Some say they have seen Ten thousand at a sight; this is most probably an exaggeration."

There were also herds of small, easily-tamed, many-colored mustangs, which ran wild on the southern plains in the early years of the nineteenth century, but Custis does not mention them. These were offspring of Spanish horses brought to the Americas by explorers and soldiers beginning with Hernando Cortes's invasion of Mexico in 1519. But the wild horses of the Texas, New Mexico, and Oklahoma plains more likely had

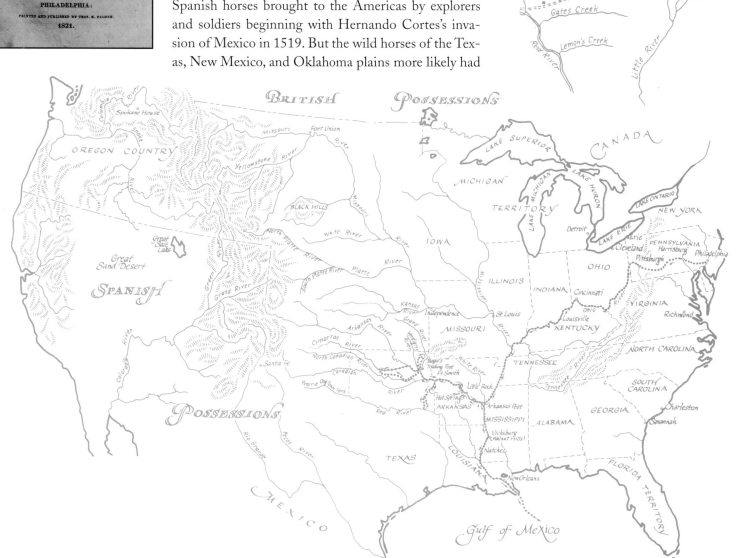

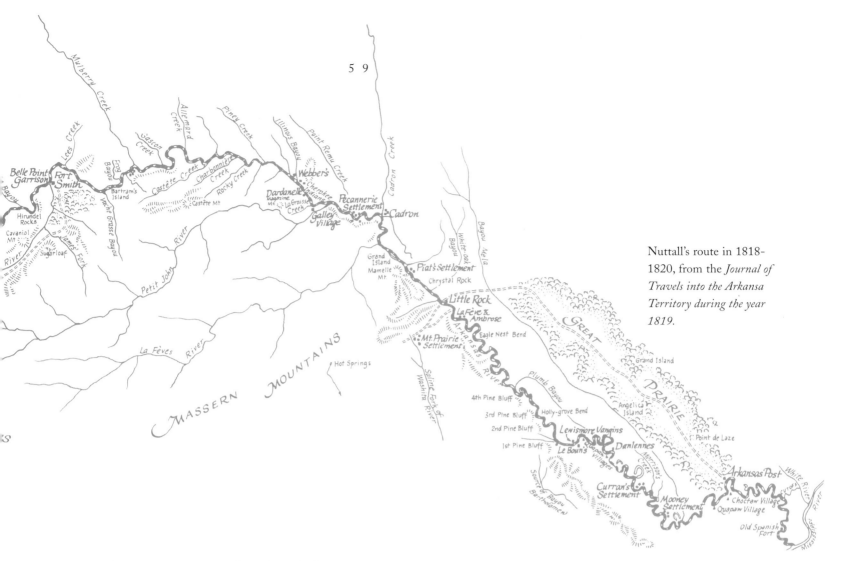

Nuttall's route in 1818-1820, from the *Journal of Travels into the Arkansa Territory during the year 1819.*

their origins in escaped or discarded animals from DeSoto's Mississippi exploration in 1541, which touched the eastern edges of the bison prairies; and even more likely, from Coronado's large mounted expedition into the southwest during 1540-41.

Although the bloodlines of wild horses on the southern plains may be obscure, their presence changed the course of history. By the late 1600s, the Apaches were mounted, and then the Comanches, and by the 1730s, horses had exploded into the cultures of plains buffalo-hunting tribes, from south to north.

Horses, of course, were present in America before any humans stepped into the bestiary. If Custis had visited the plains, say 20,000 years ago, he could have hunted native American horses. Ironic, isn't it? Horses evolved in North America and became extinct through Paleoindian hunting. Some, however, escaped to Eurasia over the Bering land bridge and eventually were interbred and domesticated to create the animals that Spanish conquerors carried back to transform the Indian cultures of the New World.

Explorers such as Custis stepped into new territory with wide-eyed wonder. It was like a modern astronaut stepping onto the moon. Custis's notes become curious, sometimes incredulous, when he dutifully reports information taken from other people's sightings of

Thomas Nuttall in 1824

The barred owl (*Strix varia*).
Photo by Harvey Payne

"Nothing could at this season exceed the beauty of these plains," wrote Thomas Nuttall, on his 1819 journey through present-day Oklahoma, *"enamelled with such an uncommon variety of flowers of vivid tints, possessing all the brilliancy of tropical productions."*

such real, but strange, creatures as flying squirrels, and pronghorns, "a species of Antilope near the head waters of R. River." Given the fantastic beasts newly come to his eyes, we should hold our laughter when Custis reports the amazing "unicorn" rabbit a Lieutenant Osborn told him about. Osborn said:

> There is a rabbit on the upper parts of Arkansas about the size of a common Buck; but shaped like the common hare or rabbit, is of a light red color, sometimes mixed with white, or spotted; its hair is uncommonly coarse and so thick as to render it almost impossible to discover the skin through it & is about 3 inches in length particularly about the hind quarters; the flesh is equal to Venison and a little like it in flavor, but rather more juicy. — It is described by John Frazier a Chicasaw Indian who has killed of them as having one horn in the middle of its forehead bending downwardly & inwardly. This animal is most generally found in the neighborhood of the Osages. — I have seen the skin of one of these animals which weighed 5 lbs. english weight. — The skin is now to bee seen at Arkansas [Post] in possession of a Mr. Hendry of that place.

In 1819, the famous English botanist Thomas Nuttall arrived in Oklahoma's rich Three Forks region, where the Grand River joins up with the Verdigris and the Arkansas. He traveled up the Arkansas through what is now Tulsa and westward onto the plains, taking notes that would be published in his book, *A Journey of Travels into Arkansa Territory during the Year 1819.* "Nothing could at this season exceed the beauty of these plains," wrote Nuttall, "enamelled with such an uncommon variety of flowers of vivid tints, possessing all the brilliancy of tropical productions."

Among the new creatures that flashed before his eyes was the mockingbird.

> In my solitary, but amusing rambles over these delightful prairies, I now, for the first time in my life . . . hearkened to the inimitable notes of the mockingbird (*Turdus polyglottus*). After amusing itself in ludicrous imitations of other birds, perched on the topmost bough of a spreading elm, it at length broke forth into a strain of melody the most wild and varied, and pathetic, that ever I had heard from any thing less than human. In the midst of these enchanting strains, which gradually increased to loudness, it oftentimes flew upwards from the topmost twig, continuing its note as if overpowered by the sublimest ecstasy.

A spur-throated grasshopper dines on a compassplant (*Silphium laciniatum*); and a cicada emerges from its outgrown "skin" — prairie sights that offer themselves to the careful watcher.
Photos by Harvey Payne

Nuttall's ears were keen as his eyes. On camping on the Cedar prairie in southeastern Oklahoma in early May, he was kept awake all night by swarms of mosquitoes. In the darkness he noted "how greatly the sound of objects, becomes absorbed in these extensive woodless plains." There were no echoes on the plains but strange music, such as a species of frog "which almost exactly imitated the lowing of a calf." Also "the cheerless howling of a distant wolf," and an all-night serenade "with the vociferations of the two species of whip-poor-will."

Further north that summer, on the "Great Osage plain, toward the mouth of the Verdigris," Nuttall walked twenty miles in pathless grass "three feet deep, often entangled with brambles, and particularly with the tenacious 'saw brier.'"

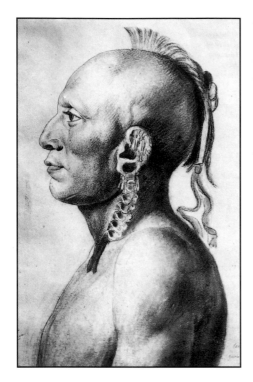

The Osage Cachasunghia
[Cashesegra], by Charles B.J.F.
de Saint Mémin, portrait made
in the early 19th century.

Collection of The New-York Historical
Society, New York City

The grass was soaked in honeydew, a whitish, oily film made of water, amino acids, and sugars secreted by sapsucking insects such as aphids, whiteflies, plant lice, and plant hoppers. "The honey upon the grass," wrote Nuttall, "was so universally abundant, that my mockasins and pantaloons were soaked as with oil."

He slept on the prairie that night with no fire, food, or water, tuned to a cacophony of crickets, grasshoppers, catidids, and stocking-weavers. Around his bed, "every tender leaved plant, whether bitter or sweet, by thousands of acres, were now entirely devoured by the locust grashoppers [sic], which arose before me almost in clouds."

In August, heading west beyond what would someday be Tulsa and in hopes of reaching the Rockies, Nuttall was struck with yellow fever. His observations mirrored his discomforts: the plains were "monotonous"; the "dazzling light . . . proved oppressive and injurious"; there was no shade in forest "pervious to the sun"; green blow-flies "filled even our clothes with maggots, and penetrated into the wounds of our horses, so as to render them almost incurable." To save his life, Nuttall turned back.

Another accomplished naturalist, S. W. Woodhouse, accompanied the Creek Boundary Expedition of 1849-50 to Indian Territory in what is now central and northern Oklahoma. This expedition was charged with drawing boundary lines to separate Creek Indian lands from Cherokee lands — which included a good portion of the Osage's traditional prairie hunting grounds.

Neither the Creek nor the Cherokee were familiar with Oklahoma. Under President Andrew Jackson's Indian Removal Act of 1830, the Five Civilized Tribes (Choctaws, Chickasaws, Cherokees, Creeks and Seminoles) had been forced to leave their ancestral lands in Georgia, Florida, the Carolinas, and the Mississippi Valley for new lands west of the Mississippi in Indian Territory. These southeastern tribes were "educated" Indians, who had attempted to adapt to white civilization. Unlike the intransigent "wild" tribes of the Great Plains, they were farmers, sometimes slave owners, literate, and mostly Christian converts. And they were new as any settler to the Oklahoma prairies—the land that was being staked out for them—its oak thickets, swamps, and savannas.

The story of these people's "Trail of Tears" is one of the ugliest in American history, but we will talk about that in a later chapter. Here the subject is animals. And that was Woodhouse's job: to catalog the natural life he encountered along the expedition's route. Without repeating the actual lists of flora and fauna that Woodhouse collected, I will quote some excerpts from a recent book, *A Naturalist in Indian Territory,* that reprints Woodhouse's journals. These entries were jotted down as Woodhouse journeyed northwest with the boundary party from Fort Gibson, up the Verdigris River, then west to the Arkansas River.

Friday [June] 22d Clear & hot shower in the afternoon . . . after hunting all morning I returned without having discovered anything new . . . ticks very troublesome I picked 6 off me this morning.

Tuesday [July] 10th packed my things saddled my horse and at started it was fine and moonlight. The sun rose and the scene was realy charming you could see for miles a beautiful roling prarie . . . We found Mr S and his men here they having been here all night his face was tremendously swolen which he attributed to the musquetoes which he said made such a noise that he could not hear a wolf howl . . . .

Wednesday [July] 11th . . . On Monday morning as Mr Smith was getting up he spied a small Animal in the tent and he called Mr Burgess to know what it was and he answered a young Bear at the same time got out of bed and went off at a distance this surprised Smith and he demanded again what it was when Mr B cried out Skunk shoot it . . .

By September, Woodhouse's party was encamped in a small Creek town called Tallassee. "Our Camp is situated on top of a high hill on a Cattle stamp next to a corn field," wrote Woodhouse. These days you can find this spot at the intersection of Brady Street and Union Avenue in the city of Tulsa. But you are not likely to find similar company.

"Some Indians passed with their horses loaded with buckeye root which they said was to poison fish in the Verdigris," Woodhouse reported. Traditional Osages did not eat fish, fowl, or small mammals because large mammals offered more plentiful sources of protein. Besides, according to the French explorer Victor Tixier, the Indians said, it was "annoying to have these small bones in your mouth." However, they were not averse to using fish or birds as trade items.

Next day, having flushed an opossum from a log with his dog, and then finding nothing more worth shooting, Woodhouse met an Osage Indian in his camp. ". . . he was not troubled much with cloathing having nothing on but a breech clout his hair was cut close to his scull exepting a scalp lock and was painted with Vermilion his ears were slit and filled with beads." The Osage, hoping to trade for more vermilion dye, was on his way west and south with a large party of men, women, and children on their annual buffalo hunt.

On his own trips westward, Woodhouse would see many bison and deer, and what he calls a "wild Cat." This is an excerpt from his final report:

On the 11th of Sept. [1850] Mr. Isaac Smith shot a wild Turkey (M. gallopavo) in a thicket but before he could get at it, it was carried off by a leopard cat (Felis pardalis, Linn.). In passing down this stream a short distance farther he saw another of these beautiful and daring little animals. He dismounted from his horse and was in the act of shooting when another jumped from out a tree and came near alighting on him.

Amusing as it is, the wildcat anecdote interests naturalists because in it Woodhouse identifies the cats as "leopards," which would mean they were ocelots rather than the much more common bobcats or lynx. Ocelots range from Mexico north to the Red River, but no one has spotted an ocelot in Oklahoma since, perhaps, Woodhouse himself.

I, too, have seen an Oklahoma wildcat. One fall evening on the Tallgrass Prairie Preserve, while walking the road toward my quarters, a feline animal with sun-tinged mottled fur streaked across my path. He raced out of the tall grass on one side of the road and into the brush along Sand Creek. I knew immediately this was no domestic cat, but a bobcat. The bobcat is larger and heavier — a compact package of muscle and hide whose wild energy seems to radiate from its sleek head to its naturally bobbed tail.

And, I am told, there are a few mountain lions who come through the region. A young researcher named Chris Wilson spotted one while counting birds. "I saw this cat coming out of the woods," he said. "It just moseyed around the edge of the trees. With that big, long tail, it couldn't have been a bobcat."

My personal list of animal sightings on the prairie during only a couple dozen walks in spring, summer, and fall attests to the vital animal life that anyone might see there. I have spotted white-tail deer all over the place; and a raccoon along the Sand Creek bot-

toms; also several howling coyotes in the evening hills; and a flash of red fur that could have been a red fox. Once I saw a fox squirrel in an oak tree; and often, gray squirrels among acorns. My headlights on the preserve's gravel road have drawn jackrabbits into a dangerous path and spotlighted small owls. I have stepped over snakeskins in burned grass and noticed the burrows of voles, also mice and other rodents I could not identify. I wish I could see a black bear in a thicket, but bears are long gone from these prairies.

One dew-filled August morning I walked through grass hung with hundreds of glistening spider webs. I have seen sulphur butterflies warming yellow wings in the sun, grasshoppers and blue dragonflies, and water skippers in shallow pools among the stones of Dry Creek. Evenings, the sawing buzz of cicadas has teased me to sleep. Awakening, I

The prairie in autumn; immature red-shouldered hawks (*Buteo lineatus*) in their nest; and a widow dragonfly on a stalk of big bluestem.
Photos by Harvey Payne

Deer Nibbling at Bushes, Acee Blue Eagle (Creek/Pawnee, 1907-1959), watercolor. Many paintings by Indian artists of Oklahoma capture the spirit and gesture of wildlife in the prairie landscape.

Philbrook Museum of Art, Tulsa, acc. no. 1973.18.1

have heard croaking frogs, the trill of field sparrows in the grass, and the songs of meadowlarks.

My bird list includes eastern bluebirds in a hackberry tree, lesser and greater yellowlegs, and American avocets near a pond. Also, the huge, prehistoric white pelican, wimbrels, willets, killdeer, sparrows and a cardinal — my bright red favorite. The autumn skies are filled with raptors hunting the tallgrass for rodents and small birds: red-tail hawks, red-shouldered hawks, American kestrels, many marsh hawks (low-flying northern harriers with a white stripe at the base of their tails); also American bald eagles, an occasional migrating golden eagle, and turkey vultures. I must have seen scissor-tailed flycatchers — Oklahoma's state bird — but did not know what I saw.

Driving toward Kansas, I stopped on a bridge over the Verdigris River to spy on a great blue heron. Near the fishing bird I saw mallards and what I thought might be wood ducks; and further upstream, a couple of cranes took wing — sandhill cranes, if I could have my wish. Although I have not tried to fish the rivers and streams that cut through the prairie, I know they hold at least 23 species of fish including largemouth and spotted bass, catfish, gar, darters, and five kinds of sunfish.

One memorable October evening, as I walked through a prairie swale, I scared up about twenty bobwhite quail. On the ridge above me, a huge old oak spread gnarled arms. It stood black against the peachy sunset sky, and as I stepped through untracked grasses, I felt as if I might be in Africa. Overhead, a hunting great horned owl

Below, a whitetail fawn nibbles pale purple coneflower in the tallgrass. Left, Canada geese (*Branta canadensis*) float in the morning fog.

Photos by Harvey Payne

caught my full attention. The owl's body was heavy, its underside tawny, flashing like copper in the low light. Suddenly, the owl rose in the air, turned sideways, dipped toward earth, exposing open, dangling legs. Striking prey, it disappeared into a thigh-high mass of sere bluestem.

And, most memorable, I have seen the booming dance of prairie chickens. When Woodhouse's party embarked on its homeward-bound journey to Fort Smith from Fort Gibson along the Arkansas River in 1894, he saw thousands of passenger pigeons and flocks of what he called grouse — meaning greater prairie chickens. Woodhouse's journal entry for November 6 says, "we saw great numbers of wild pigeons all day in some places the trees were almost breaking down with them. Grouse also in great flocks in one of which I counted 72 and some flocks there were greater numbers." In a later report, he notes that the prairie chickens were "feeding among the oaks upon the acorns; hundreds were to be seen at the same time."

Poor prairie chickens. Once so abundant they were standard dinner fare for settlers, they are gone now from most of their range, even getting scarce in the tallgrass plains of Kansas and Oklahoma, where people are allowed to hunt them in season. But they are not extinct as the passenger pigeons or endangered as peregrine falcons. There are still prairie chickens on the preserve, and they are prized and protected from human predation.

IT IS EASTER SUNDAY in the Osage Hills, a misty morning heady with the rebirth of spring, colored pink with the blossoms of redbud. I have never before seen redbud bushes, the salmon-pink blossoms like paintings on a Japanese vase. There is redbud along the banks of Sand Creek, and in brushy gullies the diffused rose-tinted petals blush among pale green budding leaves of buckbrush, wild plum, and Osage orange. The scene is resplendent as Monet's garden.

Redbud blooms outside the researcher's quarters called the Stucco House or the Barnard House, where I bunk next to a floor-to-ceiling picture window. But when I raise myself from my bed this Easter dawn, the hour is 4:15 a.m., and the world is dark.

In the kitchen, I put water to boil for the pot of coffee I prepared the night before. I fill a cup and grab a chocolate-chip cookie from the sack lunch that stands ready on the hall table, along with my pocket binoculars and automatic camera. At five o'clock sharp, as I pull wool socks over my longjohns, I hear a knock at the door. There stands Harvey Payne, wide awake and smiling at my morning dim-wittedness.

I do my best to smile, too. He has come a quarter hour early, I believe, to test me. To see if I will be game as a true country woman, game enough to rise before the birds.

We climb into his 4 x 4 rig and head off for the hills. There is a knoll Harvey spotted a few days before where the rocky earth is just beginning to green up with this year's grass. At its edges rise stalky remnants of last summer's big bluestem. This is a prime spot for a lek, or booming ground. Lek is a strange word. When I look it up in my American

Poor prairie chickens. Once so abundant they were standard dinner fare for settlers, they are gone now from most of their range, even getting scarce in the tallgrass plains of Kansas and Oklahoma, where people are allowed to hunt them in season. But they are not extinct as the passenger pigeons or endangered as peregrine falcons. There are still prairie chickens on the preserve, and they are prized and protected from human predation.

Heritage dictionary, I find it means an Albanian coin or, capitalized, names a tributary of the Rhine flowing 40 miles through the Netherlands. No mention of spawning beds or booming grounds, which are also called leks.

In the halcyon days of the Osage, an April traveler might have heard chickens booming on mounds all over the prairie. These days leks are becoming rare as Albanian coins from overhunting, overgrazing, the intrusions of industry and commerce. Prairie chickens like to perform their mating dances in solitude on bare heights with nearby grass cover and a view to surrounding territories. They may return to the same lek generation after chicken generation.

Harvey scans both sides of the road as we drive slowly through hillocks that look identical to me. He finds the exact location he seeks and we park at road's edge. With the headlights off, the outlines of the horizon are edged in the east with a silvery luminescence that precedes the sun. I hear a few sharp bird calls. Not the cackle or cluck of prairie chickens. But Harvey taps my shoulder. "Look!"

On the round flat top of the hill, I make out one heavy-bodied winged silhouette. Then another, and another. "Males," says Harvey. "Staking out their territory."

The cocks rise and fall in the hopping motion of the mating dance, but they seem lackadaisical, just warming up. Now the sky holds a tinge of lemon light and I see more prairie chickens appearing as if out of nowhere, wings spread low, heads and tails curving downward as they circle and land.

"Here come the hens."

I roll down my window. Frost creeps in. I listen intently and hear the unmistakable booming call of the male dancers. Whoom, whoo-a-woo-woo, whoom. A dozen leaping, strutting cocks. The hens stroll around seeming oblivious, pecking at seeds. They are dull brown, plump and sedate. Although morning has arrived, I can see little detail or color in the washed rays of dawn.

Suddenly, the booming stops. First hens, then cocks take flight. "What happened?" I ask Harvey.

He points to another, much larger-winged bird that circles above us. "Hawk scare. They'll be back in a while."

We take advantage of the intermission to drive off the road and up the sloping ridge to a spot much nearer to the booming ground. I'm afraid we will scare off the birds, but Harvey knows what he is doing. Within ten minutes, the first cocks return. Then the more-cautious hens.

Delighted that we are close enough to see line and color, I return to observing the birds' ritual, looking for details through my binoculars. Some cocks are dancing, jumping straight up and down in full mating display. They have raised the stiff brown feathers that lie athwart their mottled brown and white necks. The erect neck feathers look like long pointed ears, and under them, fully exposed, are bright orange air sacks. Puffed and pulsing, the air sacks glow like small rising suns.

The cocks hold their tails up in a rigid fan. Their spread wings are cupped backwards, parallel to the ground. The orange of their neck sacs is mirrored in bright oval rings around their eyes, and as they frantically jump or explode into cockfights, one or another will suddenly stop in his tracks to sing his booming song. The hens, meanwhile, prefer to ignore the dancing and fighting cocks.

ON THE BOOMING GROUND

On the booming ground, or lek, male greater prairie chickens (*Tympanuchus cupido*) display their plumage and fight with each other to establish dominance prior to mating.
Photos by Harvey Payne

They walk a circle, taking their slow time, deciding which one of these courtiers will be their chosen mate.

I have seen this ritual dance before, not on the booming grounds of prairie chickens

or those of sage grouse, who perform similar dances on the short-grass western plains, but in the tented pavillions of Indian powwows. In traditional dances, painted men will jump straight into the air. They imitate wings in the low-spread motions of arms. On their hair are upright feathers. Bright bustles adorn their backsides. The booming in Indian dances comes from drums, the wailing from singers. And, like elegant prairie hens, the women circle in rhythmic deliberate steps. Their graceful shawls move with each beat. Their hands hold brightly-plumed fans.

Here on the primeval grasslands, as the sun rises full in the sky, the dance of the prairie chickens wanes. The mated pairs disperse as swiftly as they appeared, out of the air, and then back into it.

I feel honored to have seen this Easter rite. And I know it is only one of many rebirths. Bedded in thickets, does will soon give birth to fawns. Coyotes, bobcats, and rabbits are denning with their young. Birds feather their nests. Snakes shed their skins. Life begets life on the prairie, and we are here, too, walking the streams among insects, rodents, birds, and mammals, rejoicing with the fishes.

Seeding With Fire

> "And the flames folded, roaring fierce within the pitchy night. . .
>   In black smoke, thunders, and loud winds, rejoicing in its terror,
>   Breaking in smoky wreathes from the wild deep, & gath'ring thick
> In flames as of a furnace on the land from North to South."
>
> WILLIAM BLAKE, AMERICA

A PALL OF SMOKE HOVERS OVER PAWHUSKA TOWN. As I pass through blackjack thickets on the skirting hills, I smell the grasslands before I see them. Then I am driving amid clouds of brown vapors edged scarlet with tines of flame. It is late March and the flames are burning winter's tallgrass. The high green of summer is reduced to blackened soil, ash and scorched rocks.

After snow and ice melt, the old grasses lie in a tinder-dry mat upon the earth. New grass is fingernail high. With no wet green growth to hinder its spread, a spring wildfire lit by lightning sweeps across the prairies until the flame front is doused by rain or hits a moist riverbank, a swamp, a lake, or rocky ground with no fuel. A grassfire in March is like Blake's fiery furnace, running far and fast with the wind.

The fires I see on the prairie today are not wild, but man-caused and man-controlled. Every rancher in the county seems to be firing his pastures. That's because early spring fires enable the big four grasses to be reborn in profusion. Big bluestem, especially,

A controlled burn on the Tallgrass Prairie Preserve.

Photos by Harvey Payne

Prairie Fire, by Blackbear
Bosin (Kiowa/Comanche,
1921-1980), watercolor.

Philbrook Museum of Art, Tulsa, acc.
no. 1953.7

responds well to fire. Burning will create more feed for cattle, more profit for the cow business. But why, I wonder, are the preserve's pastures also black and smoking? Its mission is to nurture a prairie ecosystem, not to raise cattle.

My question is answered as I drive back roads with Bob Hamilton. The Conservancy does, indeed, lease some of its land for cattle grazing, but only for a limited time. "The tallgrass prairie has always been a disturbance-dependent ecosystem," Bob explains again. This is his litany. This, the justification for the preserve's management philosophy. "Fire is the most dramatic recurrent natural disturbance. Intensive grazing is the other."

In the old days, bison provided the grazing disturbance. Looking for new grass, herds followed fires; where bison did not forage, grasses dried in deep layers, creating fuel for future fires; then bison grazed the newly-fired patches. The chain went on and on and the prairies stayed healthy and diverse.

"WE WANT TO MIMIC the foraging patterns of bison," says Bob, "for the health of the ecosystem." According to his plan, by the year 2003, about 32,000 open-range acres on the preserve will be grazed by 2,000 bison. Cattle will continue to graze 1,000 acres each summer in a pasture set aside to com-

pare the habits and effects of the two bovine species. As the original 300 head of bison increase, so will their grazing acreage. In the meantime, intensive summer grazing will continue. If you don't have enough bison, the next best grass eaters are cattle.

Soon, when the grass is hand high, outside ranchers will truck large numbers of cattle — mostly yearling steers — onto the preserve. For about twelve weeks, steers will convert grass into beef, and then they'll be shipped off to markets. Although the Conservancy will receive money from early summer grazing leases — funds to help pay their operating expenses — their purposes in placing cattle on the land are more ecological than pecuniary.

Spring burning is part of the cattle deal. Among other effects, it will improve forage, control encroaching woodlands, restore a historically appropriate ecological balance, increase the vitality of the grassland plant community, and keep down the accumulation of fuels, averting dangerous wildfires. Not all cattle pastures are charted for burning, however, and twenty percent of areas grazed only by bison will also be burned each year. But the preserve will keep one-half of its land fire-free annually to ensure adequate habitat for prairie nesting birds and to provide refuge for insects and mammals.

In talking to old-time cowboys who worked the Chapman-Barnard Ranch in its heydays, I discovered that cattlemen have been burning this land each spring for more than half a century.

MAN-MADE AND NATURAL BLAZES

A blaze on the Tallgrass Prairie Preserve, above, is set to mimic nature's own fiery housekeeping. Left, in *Prairie Meadows Burning*, George Catlin (1796-1872) caught the crackling grasses with brushstrokes.

In the photograph of a prescribed burn on the next two pages, the head fire is racing across the prairie. The Indians called such racing fire "red buffalo."

Collection of the Gilcrease Museum of Art, Tulsa; photos of tallgrass burns by Harvey Payne

Bob Hamilton, director of science and stewardship and assistant preserve director, carefully sets a prescribed burn with a drip torch.

Photos by Harvey Payne

"I've set a lot along this ranch," said Dink Talley. "Old Man Chapman used to burn it off every year. He'd make fire balls out of gunny sacks. He'd fold 'em up so they wouldn't be much bigger than your hand. And soak 'em in kerosene and motor oil, crude oil and everything else. [And I'd] fasten one up on a rope, and start out with it. I drove one up five miles before it burnt out, one time down the creek."

In a cattle operation, control means everything. No one wants an uncontrolled burn — especially in summer, when grazing is prime. Wildfires can wipe out homes, barns, kill horses and cattle, and endanger families living out on the prairies. Nature, however, having no care for ranchers and cattle, sets its own fires. One of the most dangerous cowboy tasks was putting out wildfires with crude equipment.

Marvin Griffin, another veteran cowhand, described one that went clear to Kansas.

> . . . the wind was blowing a lot higher than it is right now. And that grass was about that high [pointing to his belt]. You didn't have a snowball's chance in a hot place of putting it out. They tried to put it out when it got to that highway going toward Cedar Vale. They backfired it on both sides, but it still jumped it. It burned up oilfield houses, burned up cattle and everything else. It was rough.

Sometimes even controlled fires got out of hand. "We had pretty good equipment," Marvin continued.

> We had a pressure pump. You had to pump it, you know, pump air into the tank . . . And on the bottom of our pickups (now you never seen this before), come off on the front bumper with a quarter-inch steel plate, and go plumb back past the transmission. And when you was fighting the fire, why you went down the fire line as close as you could follow it. Well we had about 150 to 200-footer hose on it, with a spray nozzle, but you slid the pickup off over them big rocks. If you couldn't get off, why, you'd get up enough speed to just [slide]. That panel would just hold everything off. It slid, you slid on off, and kept a-goin'.

Fighting fire is a tedious and tough business — not the work a horseback cowboy felt was his birthright, especially at night. The most famous foreman on the Chapman-

THE DEEPER STORY

Beneath the surface of the prairie lies a three-dimensional embroidery of life-sustaining roots — some 6,000 to 7,000 pounds of them per acre in the first six inches of soil. Roots hold the plants aloft in prairie winds, while nourishing the leafy grasstops with water and minerals. The roots of perennial grasses also serve as storage centers for plant food.

Diagram from the series *Pasture and Range Plants*, published by the Phillips Petroleum Company in 1956, used by permission of Hayes State Alumni Association

Barnard spread was Ben Johnson, Sr., a world-champion rodeo roper, the hero of the Osage. Ben Jr., his son, known as "Son" Johnson, would also become a world-champion roper, and a movie star to boot. But when Ben Jr. got his start, he was just a green hand.

Marvin Griffin's memories include one fire-fighting anecdote that stars a rebellious teenaged "Son" Johnson:

> I remember one time . . . the John Lee was on fire. And we'd fought one fire that day, and that was at night. Went over there to fight it out, and Son got mad. And he got a box of matches out of the pickup, and as we come back, he burnt the whole country off. . . . Old Man Johnson, I think Johnson knew he was doing it. And when we got in, Old Man looked back, and he said, "My God that whole country's on fire. I thought we got it out." Ben said, "I don't think there's any use to go back."

At this point in the story, Marvin let out a big guffaw. "Yeah, ol' Son was sittin' there in the back of that pickup, just strikin' those matches, throwing 'em down. He set a fire from over at the Western Wall plumb on through."

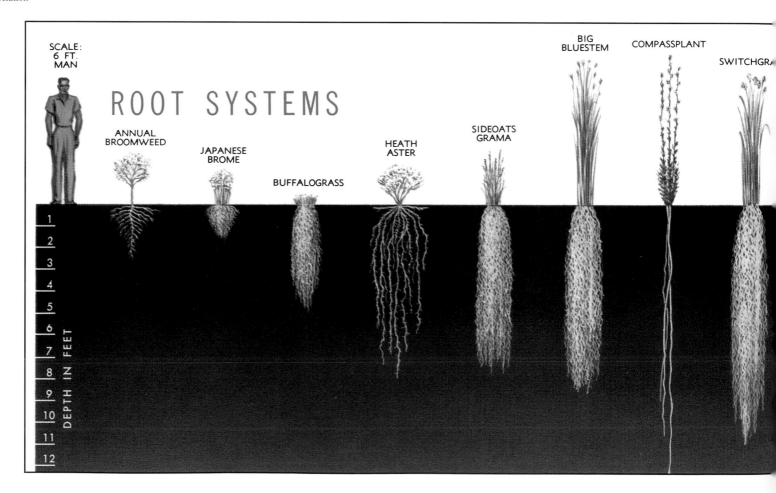

ROOT SYSTEMS

SCALE: 6 FT. MAN

ANNUAL BROOMWEED

JAPANESE BROME

BUFFALOGRASS

HEATH ASTER

SIDEOATS GRAMA

BIG BLUESTEM

COMPASSPLANT

SWITCHGRA[SS]

DEPTH IN FEET

1 2 3 4 5 6 7 8 9 10 11 12

FIRES WORLDWIDE, whether caused by lightning or volcanos or set accidentally or deliberately by humans, are most destructive when the biomass holds great stores of fuel. When fire intensity in a forest is high, the effects may be catastrophic. We who watched Yellowstone burn in 1988 know the terrors of an inferno. Heat may become so fierce it sterilizes soils. Crown fires running in treetops devour not only weak, but mature trees. Heat and smoke choke animals, insects, and plants. After high-intensity forest fires, nature takes a long time reconstructing an ecosystem of great diversity.

When forest fires are frequent, fuels do not accumulate and intensity is lower. Sporadic, low-intensity burns enrich soils with ash; they clear brush, promote grass, toughen healthy trees, and do not permanently diminish animal or insect life. Biological diversity is enhanced by spatial and temporal diversity of fires, which create mini-environments: new growth among climax old growth; redistribution of insects, rodents, birds, mammals; patches of pioneer plants; savanna openings in deep woods.

If frequent small forest fires promote diversity, so do frequent fires in prairies. But fires in grasslands run with different rules. Even if fuels are heavy and heat is intense during a

Fires worldwide, whether caused by lightning or volcanos or set accidentally or deliberately by humans, are most destructive when the biomass holds great stores of fuel.

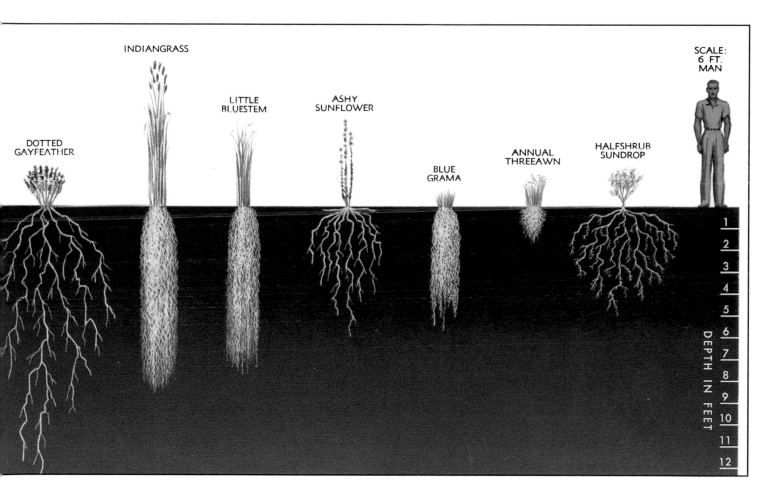

A   J o u r n e y   I n t o   t h e   T a l l g r a s s

The Tallgrass Prairie burn crew controls a prescribed burn; below, "Daisy" with Kevin Chouteau and Perry Collins.

Photos by Harvey Payne

prairie fire, the sod acts as an insulator, protecting seeds and root systems. Heat does not get high enough for a long enough time to sterilize soils. The scorched earth of spring prairies does not remain black for long. When I walked into a meadow a couple of weeks after it was fired, I saw pale leaves of grass sprouting through the ash, like lettuce leaves in my garden. "Hair," the ranchers call this grass, as in "the south pasture's haired-up enough to move the cattle in."

I like the notion of grass as hair. Cut it, and it grows back. Burn it, and it grows back. That's because the heart of grass lies in its roots — with tallgrass, really deep roots. And the skin that protects grass is the insulating sod that a root system builds. Depending on air temperatures, humidity, wind, and fuel loads, grass fires create surface temperatures ranging from less than 200° F to more than 1,000° F. But even the hottest fires move rapidly across grasslands, and the heat does not usually penetrate more than an inch or two below ground. The same adaptations that make grass resist drought and extreme cold will allow regeneration after grazing and fire.

The growing points of grass lie under the sod. Trees are different. Even hardy, deep-rooted bur oaks expose their growing points and buds. Drought and fire will kill trees from the top down. Although fire is necessary for the germination of species such as lodgepole pine, it will kill an oak tree's seedlings. Fires bring down forests and open grasslands to sun and rain, promoting more grass. Which is why, if you come to the preserve on a hot day in summer or on a cool October's noon, you might witness a wall of flames.

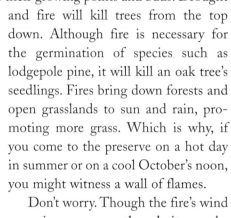

Don't worry. Though the fire's wind roars in your ears; though its smoke sets you to choking; though its color is scarlet and clouds of sulphurous fumes burn to beat the sun, this fire has been mapped, planned, choreographed as elegantly as a ballet. It is a controlled burn, and Bob Hamilton has set it.

In an era of fire suppression, August and September blazes are rare, for ranchers cannot bear to see good grass destroyed. Nature has no such qualms. There was never a consistent pattern of disturbance on the prairies, says Hamilton, and random fires raged in most seasons, with October being the most fire-prone month. So, in the bison-fire unit where Hamilton is trying to mimic in miniature the forces that created and maintained a prairie landscape, he sets 20 percent of his fires in late summer, and 40 percent each in early spring and late fall.

The grass where I stand is so tall I cannot see over it. I could be engulfed by flames with no sense of where to run for safe ground. But my fears are unfounded. Bob has planned this burn to resemble a natural summer fire, and I am safely outside its perimeters. The fuel mat will incinerate, but the fire's intensity will be checked by damp green growth.

Summer fires in a normally wet year are patchy — smaller than conflagrations in the dry tallgrasses of spring or fall. Yet a summer burn can mean death for trees. Summer and fall blazes are tree-killers because they hit trees in full, mature, and drying leaf. Late season fires can turn trees into torches, while spring fires merely skim the surfaces of bare-armed green trunks wet with sap.

Bob has set this fire on a piece of ground bordered by exposed sandstone hills where cross-timbered blackjack and post oaks grow in thickets. Beyond the tree line, brush has been creeping into the tallgrass. If nothing is done to disturb the land, the sumac, wild plums, and Osage orange will advance ahead of oak trees onto the sun-dried prairie earth. Brush prepares the soils under its leaves for trees by creating shade where grass has a hard time growing, but where seedlings can take root. Bob wants to know if summer fires will tip the balance of regeneration toward grass rather than trees. He wants to know how many fires it will take to make a difference.

Bob has a whole list of things he wants to find out, but first comes the fire for which he is responsible. He started the day by checking air temperatures. For a good burn, you need air no cooler than 40° F, no hotter than 80° F. There must be moderate humidity — nothing below 40 percent. And a steady wind from 5 to 15 miles per hour.

"You want a good, consistent wind," says Bob. "Light and variable winds are the worst. One second you're lighting a backfire, and the next thing you know that sucker starts to act like a headfire."

Bob set a test fire this morning. Then he and his six-man crew sat around it, waiting and watching the wind to see if the conditions for safe burning would pan out. When Bob was sure the weather was perfect, he gave the go-ahead and his multi-purpose, fence building, bison-herding, cowhand crew stepped into their sunflower-yellow flame resistant jumpsuits and stuck their heads into hard hats, breathing through respirators.

First would be the job of "blacklining," which means igniting a slow-burning backfire on the downwind side of the area to be burned. A backfire will set the borders — seal in the main burn. Then Bob, riding an all-terrain vehicle, uses a drip torch jetting flame to set the fire line.

His crew guards the margins, backed up by three spray rigs, including a huge, bright yellow fire-fighting behemoth called "Daisy." Daisy has four-wheel drive and a John

Deere chassis and engine. Its tractor tires stand four feet high and are two feet wide. The front, driving section is hinged to a truck bed carrying a 960-gallon water tank and long hoses pumped by an 18 hp engine. There are also hoses attached to Daisy's front end. Some of the crew rides shotgun on Daisy. Others tote five-gallon backpack pumps that weigh about 50 pounds. Some carry rubber mats attached to wooden poles, tools called "flappers," because that's what they are for — to slap out any roving flaming leaf or clump of sparking grass that floats over the fire line.

Bob and his men keep in moment-to-moment contact using hand-held radios. Having burned a safety zone of 150 to 200 feet on the windward side, Bob gets the head fire going.

Flames fly twenty feet high. The blazing wave moves fast, devouring what it touches. When the front hits a canyon, the inferno literally roars with the wind it has created. Canyon fires are especially dangerous, but Bob and his crew have this one well in hand. White smoke billows hundreds of feet into the air, melding with black smoke, darkening the sun-bright day. Grass, forbs, saplings, brush turn to ash. A few small oak trees flare. Birds rise in alarm. Mice and small rodents skitter for shelter. Grasshoppers fry. Snakes are burned into black coils.

Fire has no mercy. But it is not immortal. When its fuel is consumed, it, too, will die. This fire will smolder all night. Crew members will watch for hot spots. They will patrol the fire lines to make sure some errant tongue of flame will not blow havoc into a neighboring pasture. Someone will be on the lookout, night and day, until the earth cools and is safe.

Fire has no mercy. But it is not immortal. When its fuel is consumed, it, too, will die.

WHEN I RETURN TO THE PRESERVE in October, I walk through a mixed brush, tree, and grass area that was burned in the spring. This day my guide is not Bob Hamilton or Harvey Payne, but Chris Wilson, an intern who is helping to conduct research on the preserve. Chris is lean, blond, and knowing for a young man in his twenties. He has a master's degree in wildlife biology from Oklahoma State University. He calls himself a biotechnician.

We are studying some ground above Sand Creek, where I had seen my first redbud blooms in April. Five months ago, the soil was black and barren from a recent fire. Burned sapling stems streaked my tan pants with charcoal. But pale green shoots and buds tempered the devastation, and along the creek, where fire had done no harm, redbud petals glowed with pink burning light.

Today, a cold wind blows stalks of russet grass. The oak leaves are a deeper brown and clatter as wind moves through them.

"This area," says Chris, "has more trees than the open prairie. It shows the dynamic of a savanna — always changing. That's what I love," Chris continues. "Always changing."

I notice many oak saplings are gone. Dry black sticks, they have disintegrated into smashed coals, enriching the earth. Chris digs under the charcoal layer and brings up a handful of reddish dirt.

"Here we've got sandstone-based soil, which is good for tree growth," says Chris, letting the fine grains sift through his fingers. "Trees have a hard time on the limestone soils of the western meadows, where the best grass grows. Fire does play an important role, but the soil itself tends to keep those meadows clear of forests."

But in this no-man's-land of sandstone savanna, fire makes a difference. "What you have here was a hot burn — a top-burn," says Chris. "We killed a lot of trees, but as you can see, some of the oaks are coming back."

Oaks are among the most fire and drought resistant hardwoods. Bur oak, with deeply lobed leaves and tough, heavy-hatted acorns, is especially suited for invading prairies. But on the Osage, the most prevalent invaders are post oaks and blackjack oaks. Such oaks put down tap roots before their tender shoots bud out, and by July the roots may reach several feet into the earth while the stems are less than a foot above ground. Fires can check tree growth, but fire alone cannot turn a forest environment into a prairie. For such transformations you need winds, occasional drought, extreme temperature variations that favor grass.

The pattern of trees on the prairie maps the presence of moisture and reveals the nature of various soils. Fire alone cannot sculpt the wooded areas.

Photo by Harvey Payne

A Journey Into the Tallgrass

A PRAIRIE MOSAIC

From the upper lefthand corner, a bumblebee on a handsome blazing star; a bobcat in the tallgrass; a spider on a compassplant; a coyote in a patch of lemon monardas; a rough green snake; and a monarch butterfly caterpillar — prairie life takes numberless forms and colors all fitted in splendid arrangement.

Photos by Harvey Payne

The ground we stand upon is a borderland. Its climate is moist enough to harbor oaks, but windier and drier than the forest climate of Arkansas to the east. This savanna, after years of suppression, has weathered fire again — fire intense enough to begin the process of natural thinning. If there had been no fire and not enough grazing to keep saplings in check, the blackjacks and post oaks would be taking over in the storm-ridden, relatively moist tallgrass environment of the Osage Hills.

"Within the last one hundred years," Chris explains, "there has been an expansion of cross-timber areas. When trees reach a certain size, annual fires won't make an impact because there is not enough fuel under the trees. You have to cut them down, then burn, or apply herbicides and bulldoze, which is in itself harmful to diversity."

Several large oaks are black — charred from top to bottom. Their sparse leaves are dark, their gnarled branches are nearly bare, and dying. Others, also touched by fire, have risen from the ashes with new stems, new branches. I notice fresh-sprouted saplings that have pushed up from old roots. Everything wants to endure, to replicate. The struggle for dominance is not only a trait of men and women, but the habit of trees, of grass.

Once more I am struck by the complex checks and balances of a natural ecosystem: soils, rain, drought, wind, and fire made this place what it is. Bison and cattle made it, and people have added their influences. Also small rodents. Large mammals and birds can usually escape fire, but what about the tiny creatures who are vital to a prairie's life?

There have been some studies about the effects of prairie fires on mouse, gopher, and vole populations, but they are not controlled or extensive enough to reach reliable conclusions. Mostly, the studies confirm common-sense observations. Species that depend for food and nesting sites on the debris of prairie floors will suffer immediately after a fire. These are the fire-negative mammals such as northern short-tailed shrews and other diminutive creatures who forage on invertebrates in the litter layer. Prairie voles, meadow voles, hispid cotton rats — all animals who live in dense foliage and eat plant leaves — are also fire-negative. Rodents who nest above ground rather than deep within it, such as white-throated wood rats, western harvest mice, and some vole species, are doubly vulnerable. Quick-moving rodents who prefer more open grassy habitats and feed on seeds and/or insects are called fire-positive. They seem to thrive after fires. These include the hispid pocket mouse, southern grasshopper mouse, deer mouse, white-footed mouse, and thirteen-lined ground squirrel. Quick-footed jumpers such as the meadow jumping mouse also have positive responses to fire.

Of course fire will burn or asphyxiate many small creatures. And, on bare grounds newly opened by fire, raptors and coyotes have a field day feasting on the injured and exposed little critters. For those who escape, fire causes shifts in population densities and changes of location. After their forced march out of a burn, some mammals, birds, and insects will choose to stay in new territory, some will come home, and others will find the burn site more appealing than the place they already inhabit.

If there had been no fire and not enough grazing to keep saplings in check, the blackjacks and post oaks would be taking over in the storm-ridden, relatively moist tallgrass environment of the Osage Hills.

The Antelope, Ben
Quintana.(Cochiti,
1923-1944),
watercolor.

Philbrook Museum of
Art, Tulsa, acc. no.
1995.7.91

The indirect effects of a fire will cause certain species to
change the levels and timing of reproduction, and may alter
patterns of mortality. But in the long run, say three to ten
years, if there is no more fire on the land that was burned, the
conditions of both plant and animal life that existed before the grass
fire will resume. In the meantime, the mosaic patterns of prairie diversity will
have been enhanced.

CHRIS DRIVES OFF in his pickup,
and I wander out onto the undulating meadows that roll eastward toward a rim of trees.
Here, a few widely separated ancient post oaks — maybe 300 years old — stand huge in
the grass. Heavy-limbed, they are twisted by sun and wind and wrinkled with age. Their

trunks have been blackened and hardened by recurrent fires in their youth. Crows gather in the high, open-armed branches above my head. I listen. I think they are crowing "savanna."

The word savanna is one of those magical, connotative words that sing like music and bring pictures to the mind's eye. For me, the word conjures images of faraway lands and prehistoric times. I imagine wide-crowned baobab trees under a red sky. Between the scattered shade-givers, I envision great sweeps of tall grasses, yellow and bent by a gentle wind. And honey-maned lions in the grass, with their mewling, playful kittens. I see elephants, gazelles, giraffes. And then I imagine the strange, upright ancestors of human beings emerging from dark, smoky forests. They squint into bright sunlight, carrying spears in one hand, fire in the other.

The picture in my mind is Africa, first Eden. It is not so different from the red-fringed Oklahoma autumn prairies all around me. In savannas, at the edges of forest, looking out to hills alive with gilded grasses, humans may recognize the original, ancient home of our species.

The Osage myth of creation says the Little Ones came down from the stars. In the Judaeo-Christian birth story, God created Man fully formed, and then created Woman from Adam's rib. But in the tale of origins Science tells — at least in the one I am about to relate — the great force behind human evolution was Fire.

The evolution of landscapes and life is a complex, theoretical, and speculative field where a student will find many, often conflicting answers to the questions of human beginnings that have obsessed us since the invention of language. In an intriguing essay called "Landscapes and Climate in Prehistory: Interactions of Wildlife, Man, and Fire," W. Schule of the Institute of Prehistory at the University of Freiburg offers one theory that I find compelling. Schule says:

> Landscapes are more than a simple function of geological, geomorphological, climatic, and botanical parameters. Animals play an important role. Their behavior, especially their trophic habits, is a major force in the forming of landscapes. Herbivores consume the product of the primary biomass production. Fire and man have been doing the same since they appeared on Earth. Moreover, both are not only herbivorous, but carnivorous, devouring whatever animal wherever they can.

PRAIRIE POINTS

Flint tools like these points were made by the Wichita Indians, members of the Caddoan culture who occupied the Tallgrass Prairie Preserve area before they were driven out by the Osage. From left to right, an axe head, spear point, and knife were made of flint mined in the area.

Photos by Harvey Payne

The two-leggeds could not outrace swift animals, but they could trap them in encircling flames. They kept wolves, lions, cave bears at bay by building the bonfires we still love to sit around. It is no accident that the symbol of family and home is the hearth.

Well before our hominoid ancestors emerged into the grass and tree-dotted savannas of Africa, interactions of fire, flora, and fauna had created a landscape of diversity. Mega-herbivores such as mammoths and sloths evolved to browse brush and the lower branches of trees. Their tree-trimming habits opened the forests and strong, tall trees flourished. Then grass invaded the open regions, and ungulates such as horses and bovids evolved teeth and digestive systems to eat the grass. Grazing animals controlled the accumulation of fuels by where and when they grazed. The result was a strong herbivore-fire interaction. It seems likely that during frequent, low-intensity wildfires, the swiftest hooved mammals survived. They could smell smoke from a distance and run before they were devoured. They could also run from predators.

All creatures except our kind are so afraid of fire they will flee if they can. We are afraid, too, but also enticed. Early upright walkers learned to eat the fresh-singed remains of huge animals unable to run from fires. Our ancestors were not scavengers of putrid meat, but they alone among primates discovered the pleasures of roasted prey. The two-leggeds could not outrace swift animals, but they could trap them in encircling flames. They kept wolves, lions, cave bears at bay by building the bonfires we still love to sit around. It is no accident that the symbol of family and home is the hearth. In all these trials by fire, and by solving the mind-expanding puzzles of how to use wood, stone and metals as tools, hominoid species evolved the intricate cerebral cortex connections that keep us populous and predominant because our wits override our weaknesses.

According to Dr. Schule and most scholars who study such things, the American continents came to be populated by Upper Paleolithic hunters from Eurasia. About 25,000

A storm on the prairie. Weather, fire, and bison are the three main forces shaping the prairie.

Photo by Harvey Payne

Council Call of the Crows, Joseph Henry Sharp (1859–1953), oil on canvas.

Collection of the Gilcrease Museum of Art, Tulsa, acc. no. 0137.345

years ago, the first Americans occupied Beringia — an ice-free arid grassland country that stretched from Siberia to Alaska — and some crossed over the Bering land bridge, following prey.

Those first Paleoindians, known as Clovis Man, can be identified in archeological remains by a genetically distinct attribute: they had a shovel-shaped hollow tooth. At first their colonies were confined to the Arctic steppes and North Pacific coasts by the great American ice sheet. Then, probably about 12,000 years ago, the ice melted enough to open a passage west of the Rocky Mountains, and the hunters wandered south into the unknown.

Wind Spirit, Blackbear
Bosin (Kiowa/Comanche,
1921-1980), watercolor.
Drought, lightning, fire,
and wind all help shape
the prairie.

Philbrook Museum of Art, Tulsa,
acc. no. 1955.9

Recent discoveries in South America indicate there may have been more than one type
of early human settler on the American continent. There may have been semi-agricultur-
al peoples as well as the aviel Clovis hunters. Whoever they were, they found temperate
lands, with open forests and grassland savannas, like Africa. But unlike Africa, Europe,
and Asia, where Neanderthal and other varieties of human hunters and gatherers had
existed alongside their prey for eons, this was virgin territory. Here were great numbers of
gigantic herbivores and smaller ungulates who had never seen thin-skinned two-legged
creatures and had no inherent fear of them.

What a paradise for America's Adams and Eves! Walk up to a mammoth, drill it with
spears, and gorge your whole clan for a week. I am oversimplifying. It was no easy task to
puncture mammoth hide with hand-held spears. Courage, strength, and perseverance
were needed to bring down huge beasts fighting for their lives. Still, the Clovis hunters
were successful. Digs in Nevada and throughout the continent show mammoth bones
chipped by the obsidian Clovis points that a person can gather by the handful in some lake
beds and river bottoms of the Great Basin.

Fossils indicate that during three million years, right up to the end of the Pleistocene,
about twenty genera of large mammals became extinct in North America. Then came
Clovis hunters skilled in the use of spears and fire. In a few thousand years they helped to

exterminate all the giant mammals in the Americas, several species of huge flying and flightless birds, and many of its largest reptiles. No more horses, camels, *Bison antiquus*, mammoths, rhinos, dire wolves, sabretooth tigers. Thirty-three genera died out, including about 100 species. The only large native grazing mammal to survive was the antelope, who could outrun hunters and fires.

Some experts believe climate may have played a strong role in the animal holocaust of the Americas, but paleontologists such as W. Schule, Paul Martin, and E.O. Wilson lay

A controlled burn in the tallgrass.

Photos by Harvey Payne

A J o u r n e y I n t o t h e T a l l g r a s s

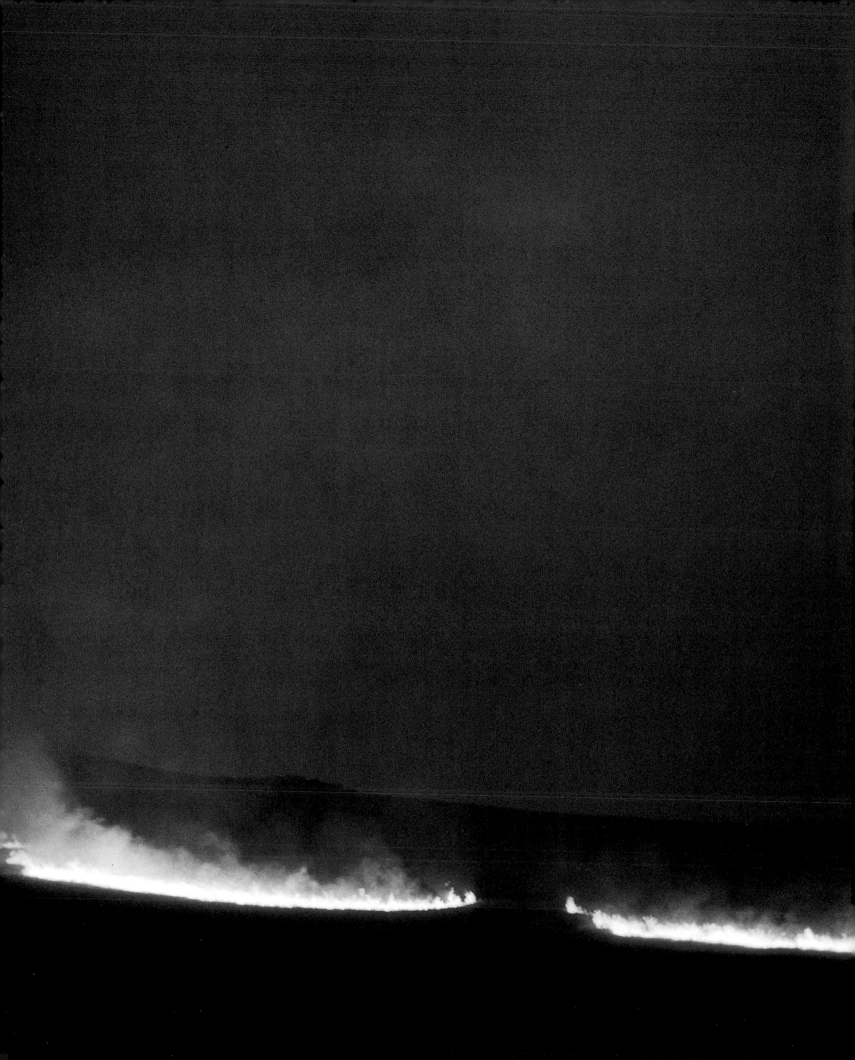

Purple skies above a manmade fire at night, facing page. At left, a single bloom of tall wine cup (*Callirhoe digitata*).
Photos by Harvey Payne

the blame mostly on humans. Heedlessness seems to be the oldest human sin. Perhaps we were always voracious, never innocent.

Then times got tough. With few animals to control the biomass, fuels built up. When changing climate brought drought, fire intensity in forests and grasslands was devastating. Vegetation became depleted along with animal life. Starvation ruled for hunters and beasts. But not for long.

With less pressure from herbivores and human predations, the North American forests

Crucified Land, Alexandre Hogue (1899-1995), oil on canvas. Hogue immortalized images of the ruined landscape of the 1930s Dust Bowl areas where prairie sod had been broken by the plough.

Collection of the Gilcrease Museum of Art, Tulsa, acc. 0127.2000

and grasslands recovered. Now, however, the woods were dense, the prairies invaded by brush and small trees. Again, Eurasian immigrant species such as bison, elk, bear, and beaver came down from the north. Again came northern hunters tracking their prey, and the landscape changed.

The hunter-educated bison, deer, bear, and elk populated prairies and roamed the woodlands. They were smaller-boned than the original American herbivores, swifter, wary of humans, and fire-wise. Intensive grazing by herds of bison in their millions jump-started grass production; grazing lowered accumulation of fuels and diminished the intensity of fires, if not their frequency. The prairie ecosystem as we know it was born.

THE AMERICAN PRAIRIES may be imagined as vast grass and flower gardens sown by fire — a paradise for animals, including humans. Gardens need cultivation, and the hunters, who were also gatherers, soon became domesticators and agriculturalists as well. One of their primary instruments was the burning-tool.

The extent of the American prairies and the shaping of their ecosystems were determined in crucial ways by Indian fires. Like earlier Clovis hunters, indigenous plains tribes and the more recent immigrant tribes who came from the east used fire for hunting, war, self-defense, and to increase grass. But necessity teaches. During their primacy on the prairies, American Indians learned to control the flaming force they called Red Buffalo more wisely than their Clovis precursors. Preservation of resources meant preservation of human lives.

Indian fires helped clear the grasslands of trees and shrubs, and thereby helped feed bison and elk — the tribes' best sources of protein. Even when the climate became cooler and wetter a couple of thousand years ago, promoting a return of trees, Indian fires were instrumental in holding the prairie system to its old drought-induced limits.

Joliet mentions wildfire, but does not comprehend its importance. Later, in their journals for March 6, 1805, Lewis and Clark noted: "a cloudy morning & smoky all Day from the burning of the plains, which was set on fire by the Minetarries for an early crop of grass, as an inducement for the Buffalow to feed on. . . " In a letter to his mother, Lewis elaborated the theory that western prairies were formed by Indian fires.

Thomas Freeman, leader of the expedition Thomas Jefferson sent to the Red River country in 1806, propounded this theory in greater detail. In his report, Freeman wrote:

> The extensive prairies which are found in this rich and level country, appear to be owing to the custom which these nations of hunters have, of burning the grass at certain seasons. It destroys the bushes and underwood, and in some instances the timber, preventing the future growth where once timber is destroyed. The small spots of wood with which these prairies are interspersed, are found in the poorest spots, and on the margin of the water courses, where the under growth is less luxuriant, or the water stops the progress of flames. It is observed, that where these prairies are enclosed, or otherwise protected from fire, they soon become covered with bushes and timber trees, a circumstance which proves, that neither the nature of the soil, nor any other natural cause, gives rise to these extensive and rich pastures, with which Western America abounds.

Freeman overstated the case. Scientists are still debating the role of Indian fires in creating prairie landscapes — especially on the humid eastern tallgrass borderlands. Some vote for climate alone; some for human manipulation. But it seems obvious to me that Indian fires would have little effect without the overriding influence of drought.

I will tell you a story about the Sun's children. It is not my story, but Aesop's. In Greece, about six hundred years before Christ, Aesop was a Phrygian slave. His animal tales are rooted in an oral tradition older than written cultures. Aesop's fables still touch us because they are memorable narratives that caution or edify. They instruct us about how to conduct our lives.

Lewis and Clark noted: "a cloudy morning & smoky all Day from the burning of the plains, which was set on fire by the Minetarries for an early crop of grass, as an inducement for the Buffalow to feed on. . . "

Destructive as tornados are, they do not hold a candle to the environmental damage we have done. . . . Plows, not fires, destroyed deep-rooted grasses; plows ripped open the prairie's stabilizing sod skin, baring soils to constant drying currents. Whirlwinds of eroded topsoils that brought darkness at noon and drove thousands off the land were occasioned by human hubris, error, and greed.

Once upon a time the Sun was about to take to himself a wife. The Frogs in terror all raised their voices to the skies, and Jupiter, disturbed by the noise, asked them what they were croaking about. They replied, "The Sun is bad enough even while he is single, drying up our marshes with his heat as he does. But what will become of us if he marries and begets other Suns?"

Drought, lightning, fire, and wind may be symbolized as the offspring of Sun. Drought is a fact of plains existence. It comes to the prairies again and again. Corn is a domesticated tallgrass which, cultivated by European settlers, reigns supreme on the breadbasket plowlands of Midwestern prairies. Unlike big bluestem, corn needs care and constant moisture. Ask any farmer about crops and drought. He will look up at the sky and throw out his hands. Even if drought means famine, what can he do?

Lightning is another climatic commonplace on the plains. The Osage prairies of Oklahoma and the Kansas Flint Hills to the north are lightning country. In 1989, according to the U.S. Weather Service, this region drew the second highest number of lightning strikes in the United States. Add the elements of drought and lightning to grass, and you've got a recipe for fire.

"Every light against the sky told of a prairie fire," wrote one Kansas pioneer woman. "The direction of the wind, either from or opposite the direction of such fire, or sidewise, the unsteadiness of wind with possibility of veering so as to bring fire toward the home — all these were noted. . . . Many times, on awakening in the dead of night, the room was light with reflection from the sky, shining thru uncurtained windows from some fire ten or twenty or fifty miles away."

Wind, everblowing wind, is as crucial a force in plains life as drought, lightning, and fire. Constant winds, it is said, drove prairie women crazy. Wind in the extreme, together with electric storms and rain, means tornados. Plains people were, and still are, on alert during tornado season. Most dwellings and all schools have cyclone cellars. Weather-crossed Oklahoma — along with Missouri, Illinois, Kansas, and parts of Texas — is known as "Tornado Alley." Since 1950, the average number of twisters to hit down on Oklahoma has been 53 per year. Many more people die from tornados than from prairie fires. The most deadly swarm of tornados recorded in the U. S. swept through midwestern prairie country from Missouri into southern Illinois in 1924, squashing the lives of 689 men, women, and children.

In John Madson's *Where the Sky Began*, there is an account of a Kansas farmer — Will Keller from Greensburg — who claims to have looked up into a cyclone's eye. Keller reported:

> . . . At last the great shaggy end of the funnel hung directly overhead. Everything was as still as death. There was a strong gassy odor and it seemed that I could not breathe. There was a screaming hissing sound coming directly from the end of the funnel. I looked up and to my astonishment I

saw right up into the center of the funnel, about 50 to 100 feet in diameter, and extending straight upward for a distance of at least one-half mile, as best I could judge under the circumstances. The walls of this opening were of rotating clouds and the whole was made brilliantly visible by constant flashes of lightning which zigzagged from side to side.

Destructive as tornados are, they do not hold a candle to the environmental damage we have done, and continue doing, with our hands and minds. Plowing and farming exacerbated the conditions for the 1930s ecological Dust Bowl disaster in the wheatlands of Oklahoma. Plows, not fires, destroyed deep-rooted grasses; plows ripped open the prairie's stabilizing sod skin, baring soils to constant drying currents. Whirlwinds of eroded topsoils that brought darkness at noon and drove thousands off the land were occasioned by human hubris, error, and greed.

But plows and the people who use them did not create the wind itself, or the years of drought that dried soil to fine powder. It is reassuring to know that our species cannot control everything. With accelerating technologies, human beings have created dust bowls, deserts, and holes in the ozone. With our chemicals and fire-born inventions, perhaps we are warming the atmosphere, but we are not in charge of the wind, rain, or sun.

Science and an ethics of conservation can help us repair some of the damage our species has done. But we must recognize the limits of what can be preserved as we continue to destroy ecological systems created by millions of years of evolution. For no matter how lovely our rain dances, or how earnestly we pray for light, when cosmic forces take over, all we two-leggeds will be able to do is croak to Jupiter, hoping some all-powerful god will shield us from the Sun's fire-born children. In this, arrogant *homo sapiens* are riding the same precarious lifeboat with Aesop's lowly Frogs.

Bison in the Tallgrass

"Reader! listen to the following calculations and forget them not. The buffaloes (the quadrupeds from whose backs your beautiful robes were taken, and whose myriads were once spread over the whole country, from the Rocky Mountains to the Atlantic Ocean) have recently fled before the appalling appearance of civilized man, and taken up their abode and pasturage amid the almost boundless prairies of the West . . . and over these vast steppes, or prairies, have they fled, like the Indian, towards the setting sun."

GEORGE CATLIN

1 8 3 2

I N THE BISON PENS of the Ken-Ada Ranch just outside Bartlesville, Oklahoma, the ground is parched by the August heat. Dust blows behind the wheels of the all-terrain vehicle that transports us toward the shaggy beasts. We stop at a safe distance and proceed on foot. One bull raises his massive horned head, bends his forelegs under him and rises from the dirt. He gives us a spiritless lookover and ambles away.

The bison cows seem in worse shape than the bulls; their flanks are marked with red, open wounds. Later, I will learn that bulls nip cows in the rough game of mating, and at least some of the sores have arrived via sexual encounters. Which is what we are looking for as we trail through the bison enclosure following a film crew from the National Geographic Society.

"It's supposed to be rutting season," says Maryan Smith, the film's director — a tall, lovely, talented, and persevering young filmmaker. She shakes out her long brown hair. "We've been waiting and waiting all month . . . ."

"Maybe the bison are camera shy." I am anthropomorphizing, but cannot help feeling empathy with the bison. Very few of us relish being filmed in the act of procreation. It

occurs to me that the bisons' sexual energies are low because they feel depressed from summer heat and parched ground. Perhaps they hate the limitations of a freedom they were born to enjoy. Then again, perhaps, like us, they prefer to do it in privacy.

Maryan wants to record the dramatic summer rutting show that bulls enact in the wild. "There is, perhaps, not an animal that roams in this or any other country," wrote fur-trader Alexander Ross, "more fierce and forbidding than a buffalo bull during the rutting season."

To win the favour of his desired cow, a bull has to fight off rivals. The cow may not be sure this is the guy for her, and the bull will have to court for days, tending her, guarding her from competitors. Challenged, he will raise his plumed wisp of a tail, which engorges for this purpose. His hair bristles, his eyes bulge, and he utters guttural roars. On their natural stomping grounds, bulls in rut face each other, paw the earth, dig their horns into sod and toss up chunks of grass.

If bluff doesn't work, a courting bull charges, head to head, trying to bring an opponent to his knees. Only the mat of hair and thickness of bone beneath his brow keep a bull's skull from cracking on impact. If one bull falls, the other may rip his flank with sharp-pointed horns. A prime bull, say eight years old, can do fatal damage to an old giant. It is better for the oldster to turn tail and run. During the strenuous rutting season, a bull

Top, a bison cow with her calf and a visiting calf (bison rarely give birth to twins); facing page, a bison cow in autumn. Above, a "buffalo nickel."

Bison photos by Harvey Payne; nickel courtesy of Gene Dennison; photo by Don Wheeler

A mature bull stands about 6.5 feet, tall as a basketball player, and can weigh nearly 2,000 pounds.

may lose two hundred pounds. His bellow becomes a whisper. He sulks, panting, dragging his great blue tongue through the grass. Meanwhile, the cow remains calm, holds her weight, and when she is ready, the mating takes only a few passionless seconds.

In the summer of 1859, a western mule-skinner named Alexander Majors came upon two fighting bulls on a bluff above the Missouri River. They bellowed and charged. Both went down, then righted themselves. "The muscles on thighs and hips rose like huge welts. We could see the roll of their blood-red fiery eyes. They braced and shoved with terrible force. The froth began to drip in long strings from their mouths. They were both held panting, their tongues lolling out."

The fight-to-death Majors described ended by comic chance. After a second charge, one bull's legs crumpled. The other lunged, but before he hit his mark, the earthen cliff broke from its moorings and collapsed into the river, taking the astonished bulls with it.

MARYAN SMITH AND I have come to these pens to see bison in rut, but since they will not cooperate, we are content to study their faces and forms. Every

Bison herd in a March blizzard on the Tallgrass Prairie Preserve.

Photo by Harvey Payne

American who has held a nickel in her hand knows what a bison looks like. Bison images have become a ho-hum stereotype of the Wild West. But bison in the flesh are another matter.

Imagine seeing a wild herd for the first time — the legendary buffaloes of the New World, which few Europeans had ever seen. In his book *The Bison in Art,* Larry Barsness quotes a letter home to Spain by Captain Vincente de Zaldivar. The explorer said of the fabulous beast, "Its shape and form are so marvelous and laughable or frightful, that the more one sees it the more one desires to see it, and no one could be so melancholy that if he were to see it a hundred times a day he could keep from laughing heartily at it many times, or could fail to marvel at the sight of so ferocious an animal."

Bison in the flesh are awesome. Here are a few facts. Bison are the only bovine species with long hair — a thick, curling shoulder cloak, which is coarse and dark brown. A mature bull stands about 6.5 feet, tall as a basketball player, and can weigh nearly 2,000 pounds. Cows are a bit smaller. Both sexes have convex foreheads, shoulder humps, and heavy, curved horns, although the bull's horns are larger.

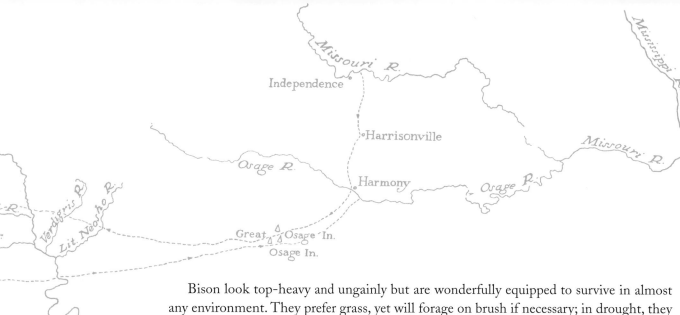

Bison look top-heavy and ungainly but are wonderfully equipped to survive in almost any environment. They prefer grass, yet will forage on brush if necessary; in drought, they can subsist for days without water while moving to wetter ground. Bison thrive in mountains as well as lowlands. They face into storms, and their heavy coats enable them to weather extreme cold. When the sun grows warm, they shed fur in ragged molting patterns. Bison run faster than most horses, are agile enough to scale heights with mountain sheep, and can jump over obstacles up to six feet high — standard height for bison fences.

The original extinct American species, *Bison antiquus*, ranged from Alaska to Nicaragua, and from eastern woodlands to Oregon and California. These are extinct, but they evolved into the species we know as "buffalo" or *Bison bison*, although some taxonomists have replaced the genus name *Bison* with *Bos* — the same genus as cattle. There were two varieties of bison in North America, the woods bison that were found in northern Canada and the predominant plains bison. Woods bison are larger and a shade darker than plains bison, with shorter beards adapted to brushy habitats. The woods bison live in small nomadic herds, a few of which have been preserved in their northern Canadian homelands.

Plains bison populations grew to astronomical numbers. Estimates run from 30 million to 60 million. The herds foraged all three types of prairie — tallgrass, midgrass, and shortgrass — but the largest herds seemed to gather in the middle. Bison populations grew to swarming numbers for many reasons, a prime one being longevity. Bison in wild or semi-wild environments live probably fifteen to twenty years, with cows giving birth to one calf each spring.

Because of their bulk, strength, and fleetness, bison could defend themselves against all predators except humans with spears and guns, or the occasional ravenous grizzly bear or risk-taking mountain lion. Grey wolves culled the old and sick animals, keeping herds prime. And the symbiotic relationships of bison herds to grass and fire kept food sources plentiful, providing constant new range.

When Europeans saw hills and plains black with bison in their thousands, they believed the animals migrated in season like wildebeasts or passenger pigeons. The French explorer Victor Tixier traveled the Osage country from Missouri to Arkansas and Oklahoma in 1839-40. His report is one of the few historical accounts that describe the

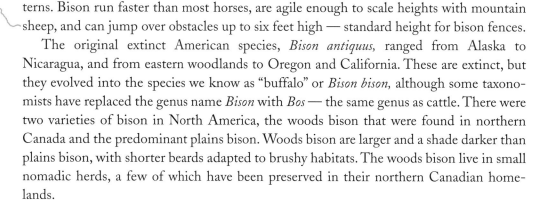

Tixier's route through Osage Country. Below, a drawing made by Tixier of Majakita, Head of the Osage.

The artist George Catlin (1796-1872) traveled the American West in the 1830s recording the native people and scenes he came upon. In these two paintings, the buffalo, like a small mountain in motion, is pursued and then turns on its pursuer. Top, *Buffalo Chase,* and below, *Buffalo Hunt, Chasing Back.* Both in oil on canvas.

From the collection of Gilcrease Museum, Tulsa, acc. nos. 0176.2177, 0176.2178

Osage country. By then, bison had been hunted out near the mouth of the Missouri, but he found plenty "beyond the Osage villages, one hundred and twenty miles above the Arkansas River." Tixier notes: "The bison has two main yearly migrations, which follow the seasons and the green grass. In the spring, it goes from Texas to Canada and returns when winter is near; thus it goes through the hunting grounds of the Osage twice a year."

Evidence shows that herds were nomadic rather than migratory. When the rut began, cows and yearlings scattered into the main herd. Separated from her primary group, a cow would be courted by outside bulls, thus her offspring would not be weakened by

A Snow Landscape with Buffalo, George Catlin (1796-1872), oil on canvas.
From the collection of Gilcrease Museum, Tulsa, acc. no. 0176.2169

Before horses and rifles enabled Indians to be more heedless, and before the calculated mass slaughter carried out by white traders, settlers, and commercial buffalo hunters, nature was the bison's worst enemy.

inbreeding. After rut, bulls tended to move off by themselves; cows with their young came together in small roving bunches.

Some plains tribes, especially after becoming horse cultures, hunted bison excessively. Tixier says, "The savages wage a merciless war on them; it can be said that they waste a great many. For instance, the Osage leave from one hundred to one hundred and fifty pounds of excellent meat on every carcass. In winter, there are periods of abundance during which they kill buffaloes just for their tongues and their skins. . . . It is impossible to make these improvident people understand that to kill buffaloes in such manner is to hasten their complete disappearance."

Before horses and rifles enabled Indians to be more heedless, and before the calculated mass slaughter carried out by white traders, settlers, and commercial buffalo hunters, nature was the bison's worst enemy. Prairie fires could burn and blind the beasts, or diminish the sight of already weak eyes. Spring blizzards might freeze hundreds of calves; and tornados could toss a bison into oblivion, just as they toss trees and houses. In 1854, on a hunting expedition with a group of Miamis in southwestern Kansas, Ely Moore and his party were surprised to discover two dead buffalo on a patch of tornado-tossed bare earth. The force of the storm had lifted sod in hunks, ripped the hides off the animals and crushed their bones.

During hard winters, herds crossed ice-covered waters with no problem. But a bison cannot know from the banks that the ice ahead may be thin from spring thaw. Once leaders begin crossing a frozen river, the herd will follow, even when ice gives way and pushes one after another under to drown. John McDonnell, a trader on the Qu'Appelle River in Canada, watched 7,360 shaggy carcasses float past him one spring day before he tired of counting. Alexander Henry, another fur trader, reported a steady line of drowned bison that floated by his camp on the Park River for two days and nights in 1801. Instinctual follow-the-leader behavior probably did more damage to bison than weather or fire.

Stampedes, the dramatic mass hysteria moviemakers love to portray, were deadly. Any chance alarm could start the herd moving, and once in motion it gathered its own momentum. Often, the massed bison could run safely over the plains, but when the front line met with obstacles such as quicksand or cliffs, the leaders were pushed so hard by pressure from the hordes behind that they might not be able to sidestep the danger or stop. In 1541, Coronado's southwestern explorers reported seeing a stampede run into a ravine. Some animals fell, then more fell upon them until the gap was filled to the brim. And still the stampede roared forward, the main herd running over the bridge made by the trampled bodies beneath their hooves.

Lewis and Clark, during their voyage up the Missouri in 1805, wrote about cliffs where stampeding buffalo had fallen to their deaths, but their party was lucky not to have encountered such turmoil first hand. Other explorers, settlers, and cattlemen were not so fortunate. Their stampede stories became part of western mythology. Here is one from Texas, reported in Wayne Gard's book, *The Great Buffalo Hunt*.

Buffalo Hunt Scene, Archie Blackowl (Cheyenne, 1911-1992), watercolor. Below, a buffalo herd running toward the camera, Haynes, St. Paul. Philbrook Museum of Art, 1986.5; Western History Collections, University of Oklahoma Library, Campbell, W. S. #1667

In 1878, on the high, wide Staked Plains of the panhandle, some surveyors were mapping grasslands that stretched flat and bewilderingly empty from one horizon to the other. A sound came from the north — a throbbing in the earth. Then a great cloud appeared, skimming the plains like a thunderhead come down from blue skies. As the cloud rushed toward them, the men saw it was dust, and in the dust they spied dark, moving objects. The cry went up: Buffaloes! Stampede!

With no time to escape, the men gathered in single-file. They had only one saddle horse, which they placed at the tail end of the line. Oscar Williams, the only surveyor armed with a rifle, manned the front position and began shooting when the bison came into range. He killed several of the leaders, whose bulky bodies formed a dam of flesh

channeling the bison around the men. Williams claimed that the safe ground was merely twelve feet wide. He could reach his rifle at arm's length on one side or the other and touch the hide of a racing animal. By his account, fifty thousand surged past. This is no doubt an exaggeration, but we do not expect accuracy when the ground is shaking and the air is windy with buffalo breath. When the main body had passed, the trembling men turned and watched the cloud of bison run across a tule-lined creek. For several minutes, according to Williams, the waters stood still.

THE 300 BISON I SEE gathered in the Ken-Ada Ranch enclosure is the start-up herd for the Tallgrass Prairie Preserve. These chosen ones will be documented on film, in articles and scientific studies. They are the latest stars in a story of extermination and rebirth through preservation — a much-told sad/happy story.

Like American Indians, settlers in the nineteenth century, wherever they roamed in the New World, could and did feed on plentiful bison and used their hides for shelter and clothing. But unlike native peoples who were primarily hunters and gatherers, whites sought control over the earth they claimed. Once a farm family cleared its homestead of trees and brush, plowed up the sod, built its house, barns, fences, and corrals, bison became a nuisance. The herds trampled crops, broke down enclosures, threatened any child or adult who ventured too close. So farmers shot bison to get rid of a pest, just as they eradicated competing predators such as wolves, eagles, and grizzly bears.

The folk wisdom that says bison were pushed out of their home ranges toward Catlin's "setting sun" is not necessarily true. More probably, bison, like elk and grizzlies, were killed off from south to north, from east to west when fur hunters, farmers, and towns invaded their home ranges. As frontiers moved toward the Mississippi, then hopped, skipped, and

The Hunt by Jim Red Corn
(Osage), watercolor, 1993.
Courtesy of Daniel Boone; photo by
Harvey Payne

jumped over the plains to Oregon and California, wagon-train pioneers noted huge herds on the move. They did not realize the bison were nomadic inhabitants like Indians, not emigrants like themselves.

James Shaw and Martin Lee of Oklahoma State University have been studying the numbers of bison on the grasslands of Oklahoma, Kansas, and the Texas panhandle during the years between 1800 and the Civil War. Their data is based on observations of explorers, traders, and surveyors, and though such firsthand reports cannot be exact, they are the best information we have. The researchers counted numbers of bison sighted during four historical periods: presettlement accounts from 1806 to 1820; journals and reports from along the Santa Fe Trail from 1821 to 1832; reports from military expeditions into Oklahoma and southern Kansas from 1833 to 1849; and boundary survey expeditions dating from 1850 to 1857.

They found that even in the earliest years, travelers came upon fewer bison on the tallgrass plains than on the midgrass and shortgrass regions to the west, where the large herds grazed. Some scientists attribute the relative scarcity to diet, claiming the coarse tallgrasses were less easily digested than the little bluestem of the central plains. Others believe that by the early 1800s most bison had been killed off in tallgrass regions because the land was moister, more populated, and better suited to agricultural production than the arid west-running plains. And while the Mississippi River offered close access to markets for robes and hides from the tallgrass herds, the south-central midgrass plains remained remote. Thus, it makes sense that the tallgrass plains would be hunted out first.

The folk wisdom that says bison were pushed out of their home ranges toward Catlin's "setting sun" is not necessarily true. More probably, bison, like elk and grizzlies, were killed off from south to north, from east to west when fur hunters, farmers, and towns invaded their home ranges.

By the 1830s, only a few scattered herds of plains bison remained on the tallgrass prairies that stretched from Iowa to Texas. Even in the set-aside Indian Territory of Oklahoma, nineteenth century adventurers rarely saw bison along the eastern tallgrass borderlands from Fort Gibson to the Arkansas River. When Washington Irving's party arrived in 1832, they saw no "buffalo" until they had crossed the river and ridden onto the fiercely contested hunting grounds of the Osage, Pawnee and Comanche tribes.

Irving's party wanted to participate in the great American buffalo hunt, which had become a national and international pastime. Every adventurous man-child on both sides of the Atlantic dreamed of tracking and shooting the wild buffalo. European noblemen and American leaders voyaged West with their entourages to test their skills against the horseback exploits of romanticized Red men. Young Count Albert de Pourtales was typical of this breed.

Pourtales came to America with Washington Irving. He was twenty years old and Swiss. In Geneva, when he was fifteen, Albert had seen six sideshow Osage Indians in feathers and beads and had become obsessed with the idea of going on an Osage buffalo hunt. His dream came true. "I am about to die of excitement," he wrote in a letter to his mother.

In St. Louis, the Count found appropriate attire. Somewhat amused, Irving described the costume: "a gay Indian hunting frock of dressed deer skin, setting well to the shape, dyed a beautiful purple, and fancifully embroidered with silks of various colors . . . . With this he wore leathern pantaloons and moccasons [sic], and a double barrelled gun slung by a bandolier athwart his back; so that he was quite a picturesque figure as he managed gracefully his spirited steed."

DECIMATION OF THE HERDS

40,000 buffalo hides, piled in yards of Rath and Wright, Dodge City, Kansas, 1877, ready for shipment. On the facing page, a buffalo hunter's camp in Western Oklahoma, ca. 1874 with hides staked on the ground to stretch and dry. Tongues, a favorite food, were dried on racks. A grindstone for sharpening knives is also visible. Facing page, bottom, four men skin a buffalo.

Western History Collection, University of Oklahoma Library, Rose Collection #1622; Phillips Collection, #3182; W.S. Campbell Collection #731

The exuberance of Pourtales' dress is mirrored in his journal entry concerning his first (almost fatal) buffalo hunt. Washington Irving and young Albert Pourtales, along with his friend and tutor Joseph Latrobe, chased and wounded a few bulls. One angry old giant turned and charged them. The hunters backed off, deciding it would be better sport to round up and shoot a few cows. Albert wrote of this chase:

> . . . in a few moments the herd, which had been skillfully turned, was gal-
> loping at top speed as it filled the air with its bellows of distress. It was won-
> derful to see that confused, compact mass running across ponds, jumping
> over brooks, and splashing in all directions, with the three of us, twenty steps
> behind them, moving as fast as our horses could go, loading our rifles, and
> gaining on the cows with each step, even though they are much faster than
> the bulls. . . .

Irving and Latrobe brought down a couple of fat cows, taking only their tongues as trophies. Pourtales rode on. "I was like a madman. My shouts terrified the herd as I gal-loped behind it at one moment and at its side the next, never more than ten paces away. . . . No Roman 'cavalcatore' was prouder of his herd than I was of the buffalo that ran before me."

After dashing in wild loops around the prairie, surrounded by racing cows, Pourtales finally decided to shoot one: "Aiming carefully at her heart," he writes, "I pulled the trig-ger — Oh, fury! Only the firing cap went off!

The frightened cow suddenly turned on me. My horse sidestepped wildly and almost threw me."

Discovering he had no more ammunition, the young hunter also discovered he was lost "on this immense prairie." Albert spent the night in an elm tree surrounded by howling wolves. Next day he was rescued by Irving's party. Momentarily chastened, Albert wrote in his journal, "I promised myself never to wander off too far from the hunters and also never to let the excitement of the hunt carry me off into the middle of a herd of buffalo."

A PARTY OF WHITE HUNTERS who killed bison for sport often left hundreds of carcasses to rot. This was an outrage to those traditional Plains Indians who revered Buffalo and depended on the sacred beast's body for life's necessities. In *The Osages, Children of the Middle Waters,* John Joseph Mathews describes the physical work of buffalo drives in times when hunters chased their prey on foot, armed only with spears and bows made of Osage orange, called *bois d'arc* because the wood was so tough.

A tribal hunt incorporated vital spiritual practices. It also embodied a political organization that ruled the tribe. "The organization of the tribal hunt," wrote Mathews, "was the organization of tribal economics, and there was no place for individual exhibitions of bravery or marksmanship, or other histrionics to which the young men, by their very nature, were prone." Show-offs like Count Pourtales would not be tolerated, for they endangered the economic life of the people.

Hunts were a communal undertaking, like war. Terrain, water, camping spots, the temper of the herd, animal and human competitors, strategy and escape routes had to be closely considered. Traditional lines of authority and divisions of labor maintained order; before setting out for the kill, clans performed rituals, offered prayers to powerful spirits.

"There must be perfect order, a reflection of the order of the sky," wrote Mathews, for The Little Ones on foot could be wiped out by the massive, unpredictable beasts they hunted. Possibilities for chaos loomed at every moment.

The hunt began with scouts looking for herds on terrain that held a cliff or ravine. Then, said Mathews, "There were certain men who must approach the herd down wind, so that the herd might scent the men even before seeing them, keeping the scent of the men in their noses, with their eyes for the down-wind front [they ran almost invariably into the wind]."

By the time the bison became aware of their hunters, they would already have been driven into the belly of a gourd-shaped pattern of enclosure picketed by men.

> Forming the periphery were men behind stone cairns which they had built or behind piles of broomweed or other available prairie weeds. These they set fire to at the exact moment when their yells and robe-waving seemed unlikely to veer the herd . . . The men in these positions did not wish

A tribal hunt incorporated vital spiritual practices. It also embodied a political organization that ruled the tribe. "The organization of the tribal hunt," wrote Mathews, "was the organization of tribal economics, and there was no place for individual exhibitions of bravery or marksmanship, or other histrionics to which the young men, by their very nature, were prone."

Buffalo Group by Cecil Dick
(Cherokee, 1915-1992),
watercolor.

Philbrook Museum of Art, Tulsa, acc.
no. 1946.25

to frighten the animals and perhaps stampede them, so they simply showed themselves and waved their robes, and if necesssary set fire to the weed piles.

As the bison were driven forward, they funnelled into a narrow man-lined passage that Mathews calls "the gourd's neck." The channel led to the edge of a cliff and ended in a drop-off.

> The men stationed along the neck were painted like demons, and at the right time they danced and waved their robes with demoniac yells, and lit their weed piles on a signal from one of the a'ki-da, and by this time the herd might have become panic stricken and lunged along the only way open to them.

Bison are not stupidly self-destructive. They would, of course, try to save themselves. But if the drive had been properly conducted, such awareness came too late.

As the leaders saw the escarpment, they would set their feet as hook brakes, lowering their heads. This was of no avail; the irresistible mass behind them pushed them over the cliff, and all of them the drivers had managed to keep within the boundaries of the gourd-shaped drive tumbled to the canyon floor, in clouds of dust, where the tribal members assigned to this special work began to cut the hamstrings and use lances and clubs, and

Shooting buffalo on the line of the Kansas Pacific Railroad in 1871. Woodcut by Berghaus.

The Bettmann Archive, Inc.

arrows when necessary, but the last were used only on those that seemed to be getting away. Arrows shot in excitement could be very dangerous.

The Osage rules for butchering were as precise and unvarying as rules for the buffalo drive. First, the skinners removed hides, using them as clean mats on which to place meat. And, as we have often been told in stories designed to awaken shame at our wastefulness, almost every bit of the creature had a use — even the intestines, which were run out on the canyon floor like a hose, squeezed until empty, and turned back on themselves in long tubes to be dried and washed.

Women, children, and old men carried the butchered meat, hides, innards, and bones back to camp. Women filled emptied paunches with tallow, buried them in clay molds, and fired them to form vessels. They stripped meat and dried it on racks over smoky fires. And, when the day's work was ending, everyone sat down to a fine feast of roasted ribs.

Fifty years after Catlin wrote his prophetic words, the sun set hard on the American bison. It was also setting on the no longer "boundless prairies" he had painted with such exactitude and love. Both of these near extinctions were the work of so-called civilized man.

Indian hunting — when augmented with horses and guns — as well as the much more destructive white man's habits of killing for sport or simply for its own sake, had reduced the huge herds that inhabited America's grasslands from about thirty million in the 1500s (some estimates claim sixty million) to about eight million in the 1830s. Then commercial traders in meat and buffalo robes enlisted Indians as well as mountain-man white hunters and made further inroads into bison populations on the Great Plains from Canada to Texas.

After the Civil War, railroads brought thousands of pioneers to settle the plains and the butchery accelerated. Travelers amused themselves by taking potshots at bison from railroad car windows. Many knew they were involved in extermination. For example, a settler on Montana's Tongue River called for his wife and children to witness the shooting of the last straggling bull in the county. Such ordinary men and women were the destroyers whom writer Larry Barsness calls "bloodthirsty frontier plinkers" in his engaging book *The Bison in Art*.

In the 1870s, Germans discovered an economical way to tan buffalo hides, and the last commercial slaughter started. Hide hunters armed with Sharps rifles would center themselves in a herd, shooting in precise killing patterns. They stripped hides off the dead animals, leaving the meat to rot. Granville Stuart, a Montana cattleman and the state's first official historian, was dumbfounded by the hide-hunter debauch during the 1879-80 season on the northern grasslands surrounding the Musselshell River.

The bottoms are sprinkled with the carcasses of buffaloes. In many places they lie thick on the ground, fat and the meat not yet spoiled, all murdered for their hides, which are piled up like cordwood along the way. Probably ten thousand buffaloes have been killed in this vicinity this winter. Slaughtering the buffaloes is a government measure to subjugate the Indian.

By the 1880s, travelers on west-bound railroads passed hundreds of piles of mouldering bones. Bone-picking became the final commercial bison resource, for the buffalo were gone. They had left indelible marks on the earth: wallows scooped into pastures, woodlands, and across every plain; foot-deep trails cut into the grasslands; tons of dried manure called "buffalo chips," which warmed settlers in sod houses on treeless prairies. A few small herds had survived, but to find them you would have to climb into remote valleys deep in the Rocky Mountains.

Indians starved. In 1872, the Osage went on their last successful buffalo hunt in the midgrass plains of western Oklahoma. A decade later, the Blackfeet in Montana ran out of bison in the shortgrass. Granville Stuart was correct. The U.S. government did nothing to stop the slaughter, for no matter how immoral, it was in the national interest to drive

THE END

A lithograph from the late 1800s entitled "The End 1883" shows a farmer plowing through buffalo bones while another man is gathering them up into a wagon. By 1875, the bones of thousands of buffalo lay scattered over the Great Plains.

Western History Collection, University of Oklahoma Library

Sunset on the tallgrass prairie;
a bison cow with her calf.

Photo by Harvey Payne

Indians off the plains by depriving them of food. The cavalry could defeat starved peoples,
force them onto depleted reservations, feed them with cheap spuds and lard, populate
their territories with settlers. With the buffalo and Indians gone, white conquerors were
free to restock the empty grasslands with domestic cattle and build a "civilized" country
for their kind.

CATTLE HAVE DOMINATED the
few remaining tallgrass prairies in Kansas, Oklahoma, and Texas since the 1870s. The
Ken-Ada Ranch where Maryan Smith and I stand mesmerized by 300 corralled bison
holds summer grazing leases for thousands of steers on the Tallgrass Prairie Preserve. But
it also raises bison, and this bunch will be the initial herd to return to tallgrass habitat in
Osage County.

The bison in their enclosure are better off than they look to my amateur, sentimental
eyes. Each one has been carefully chosen for bloodlines and health. Transponders holding

microchips have been inserted under their skins, giving each bison a unique alpha-numer-ic code corresponding to a coded computer file that includes breeding information, age, origin and place of the mother herd. Although soon the three hundred will roam the pre-serve's tallgrass prairies and creek bottoms in relative freedom, they are much-touched by humans and thus not quite wild. These animals will be tracked, herded, fenced in, studied, bought and sold like cattle. The bison we control — which means all bison on earth — stand between the true wild animals of the past and beasts bred for human uses such as horses, goats, cows and sheep.

This is how domestication begins. Put a creature of nature in a cage and its wildness seems to evaporate. I grew up in Chicago, with the Lincoln Park Zoo almost literally in my backyard, and I learned to love the amazing variety and beauty of animals by observ-ing polar bears and tigers, and Bushman, the famous gorilla, cavorting for tourists and pac-ing his tiny cell. The zoo was all I knew of wild animals until I hit the mountains and shores of the Pacific Northwest and the Rocky Mountains, where bears, mountain goats, and elk run, and even some buffalo roam in wide spaces.

The days of animals being truly wild are coming to an end with the management and manipulations of lands we like to call wildernesses. Wolves and grizzly bears wear radio collars so we can trace their movements and cull the ones who attack humans or the cat-tle and sheep humans consume. Even bull trout in my Big Blackfoot River have electron-ic markers planted under their skins and are tracked from the air by small planes with receivers. The bison of Yellowstone Park are shot when they leave its invisible boundaries to forage on private or B.L.M. grazing lands because ranchers fear they carry brucellosis. And in 1995, Montana Senator Conrad Burns submitted a bill to Congress that would force Yellowstone bison — some of the last free-ranging beasts of their kind — to be cor-ralled, tested, tagged, and managed like the much smaller herd on the much smaller Tallgrass Prairie Preserve.

Having observed animals in the wild, I cringe in zoos these days, look away from elk farms, feel disgust at bear parks and commercial roadside snake pits. But for many wild creatures on the verge of extinction, zoos are the last resort — the breeding grounds for future generations who might return to repopulate more natural environments.

We should be thankful for zoos. If it had not been for some forward-thinking preser-vationists in the early 1900s, such as Martin Garretson of the Bronx Zoo, and western col-lecters such as Buffalo Jones from Garden City, Kansas, or South Dakota's Scotty Philip, no one could see any American bison, anywhere at all. Michel Pablo of the Flathead tribe saved one herd and sold 600 head to the Canadian government to stock Wood Buffalo Park — the world's largest bison preserve. Texas cattle baron Charles Goodnight began penning wild bison in the 1880s and developed his herd until his death in 1929. Goodnight's breed line stocked the government-run herds in Yellowstone Park, and many more.

Indians starved. In 1872, the Osage went on their last successful buffalo hunt in the midgrass plains of western Oklahoma. A decade later, the Blackfeet in Montana ran out of bison in the shortgrass.

Bison are making a comeback. There are nearly 150,000 in the United States and their numbers are increasing. You can buy buffalo burgers at roadside stands near the Moiese National Bison Range in Montana's Mission Mountain Valley. You can eat succulent buffalo hump or grilled steaks in San Francisco, Chicago, New York. Buffalo robes are sold in specialty stores around the country, and skulls are at a premium in western-style interior decorating emporia.

Indian tribes, small entrepreneurs, and celebrity ranchers such as Ted Turner and Jane Fonda raise bison for meat and hides, as historical curiosities, for cultural reasons, for pleasure, and to entertain a tourist industry that prizes American lore. In national, state, and nonprofit preserves such as the Wichita Mountains Wildlife Refuge in Oklahoma, Wind Cave National Park in South Dakota, or The Nature Conservancy's preserves in the Dakotas, Nebraska, Kansas and Oklahoma, bison are bred for their own sake, and for scientific, educational, and ecological purposes. On grasslands and in mountain valleys that were part of their original range, bison again roam with deer and antelope, wolves and coyotes. There, we like to believe, they are almost free.

ALL THIS WAS FORETOLD in prophecies from plains tribes. The story I know best was told to Frank Linderman by Plenty Coups, a revered old chief of the Crow Nation. When he was a boy, Plenty Coups went into the Crazy Mountains of Montana on a vision quest. He fasted for four days and nights, yet no animal spirit spoke to him in dreams. Then he cut off the tip of his little finger, shook his blood on the ground, fasted and slept again.

The spirit who came to him in a dream that night was Buffalo — an animal who transformed himself into a man with a buffalo robe over his shoulder. The Buffalo-man led Plenty Coups into a dark cave in the mountain.

> I could see countless buffalo, see their sharp horns thick as the grass grows. I could smell their bodies and hear them snorting, ahead and on both sides of me. Their eyes, without number were like little fires in the darkness of the hole in the ground.

Plenty Coups followed his Buffalo-man through the massed bodies of the underground herd until he emerged into sunlight at a faraway place called Castle Rock by white men, "the fasting place," by Crows. The Buffalo-man shook a red-painted rattle, sang a strange song four times, and pointed to a cavern.

> Out of the hole in the ground came the buffalo, bulls and cows and calves without number. They spread wide and blackened the plains. Everywhere I looked great herds of buffalo were going in every direction, and still others without number were pouring out of the hole in the ground to travel on the wide plains. When at last they ceased coming out of the hole in the ground,

all were gone, all! The Buffalo-man shook his rattle again, and pointed to the magical cave, saying "Look!" Out of the hole in the ground came bulls and cows and calves past counting. These, like the others, scattered and spread on the plains. But they stopped in small bands and began to eat the grass. Many lay down, not as a buffalo does but differently, and many were spotted. Hardly any two were alike in color or size. And the bulls bellowed differently too, not deep and far-sounding like the bulls of the buffalo but sharper and yet weaker in my ears. Their tails were different, longer, and nearly brushed the ground. They were not buffalo. These were strange animals from another world.

The silent Buffalo-man shook his rattle a third time. Plenty Coups looked into the life-giving, life-taking opening and "saw all the Spotted-buffalo go back into the hole in the ground, until there was nothing except a few antelope anywhere in sight."

"Do you understand this which I have shown you, Plenty Coups?" asked the Buffalo-man.

"'No!' I answered. How could he expect me to understand such a thing when I was not yet ten years old?"

Plenty Coups grew up to see the last herds of wild bison replaced with spotted cattle on the open range. He led his people when they were free; and later was confined with them on a reservation that got smaller and smaller as white settlers came to claim the best land. Plenty Coups saw the earth change under his moccasins, but although he became very old, he did not live to see his people emerge from the hole of their adversity, or to witness the return of the buffalo.

Bison rolling in the dust-bath trough of a buffalo wallow.

Photo by Harvey Payne

~ ~ ~   B I G   B L U E S T E M   ~ ~ ~

The Last Free Lunch

"Go West, young man, go forth into the Country."

JOHN SOULE

TERRE HAUTE EXPRESS, 1851

TRAVELING THROUGH A NEW LAND, even a prairie that appears nearly empty of humans, awakens my curiosity. I start browsing the regional sections of bookstores, wander into museums, check out local attractions and curio shops, collect old postcards, drive back roads. The Osage is foreign as any faraway country and equally intriguing. I begin to delve into its layers of history. What I find confounds me. All my adult life I have steeped myself in stories of western settlement that make sense in Montana but are not relevant in north-eastern Oklahoma. Here, I discover an Indian country with no Indian reservations, a cow-boy country with no sagebrush or snow-white mountains. I see no false-front honkytonk towns, and as I drive along the Verdigris River, farms and hamlets have a lived-in, aged and leafy feeling. The people are multiracial, the population more dense and hidden than the familiar open-faced folk of Montana. I feel a southern leaning.

The first stage play I ever saw was the musical, "Oklahoma." My parents took me to the theatre in Chicago. I wore my best blue dress, with socks to match, and Mother had tied my black braids with blue satin bows. Romanticized Oklahoma, "where the corn grows high as an elephant's eye," was, I knew from the musical and later western movies, a land-rush frontier where women dressed in red-checked gingham and men looked like John Wayne. The Oklahoma of popular culture needed 1950s technicolor to induce such a false dream of the Wild West.

Then a second Oklahoma came to inhabit my more mature imagination. This was a serious region, black and white and stark as photographs by Walker Evans. I had read

A view of the Tallgrass Prairie Preserve.

Photo by Harvey Payne

Steinbeck, listened to the ballads of Woody Guthrie, and the images that haunted me were landscapes of earth denuded, portraits of defeated women, grim children, Model T's, unpainted shacks — Dust Bowl and Depression images more gritty than the old westerns but equally inadequate to the realities I eventually encountered.

Between such opposites was an actual Oklahoma of oil booms and busts, of Baptist fundamentalists, hucksters, red earth, green hills, Cherokee women who were not princesses, and Osage ballerinas who were. I had glimpsed that land in 1981, when I journeyed with my companion, Bill Kittredge, to Oklahoma City's Cowboy Hall of Fame to receive a Western Heritage Award for our movie, "Heartland." Next morning, we rented a car and drove to Tulsa through cone-shaped hills lime green with spring grass, vivid as the Catlin paintings we were heading to see in the Gilcrease Museum. On our way through Art-Deco Tulsa, we stopped to tour Oral Roberts University. We gaped at the faithfuls' glittering Disneyland architecture and stood dwarfed under a multi-story sculpture of praying hands. This, I thought, is enough Oklahoma for me.

Fifteen years later, I return with new eyes. I realize that to find connections among many tangled roots in the history of Osage County, I need to learn about the historical elements that have planted Osage prairie-dwellers so firmly in their land. To comprehend the evolution of this one particular place, I must try to comprehend the larger picture of the state. I was wrong to have made such facile judgments during my first visit, and I was ignorant. I did not know that Oklahoma held crucial keys to anyone's understanding of the American West, or that it was both the first and last of the Trans-Mississippi frontiers — unique in its patterns of settlement and older than the California gold rush, older than the Oregon Trail.

The Indian Territory of Oklahoma, like its weather, was a tempestuous American enigma. Here lay a temperate country with red rivers and big bluestem high as a man's head. Unplowed sod rolled to azure horizons. And all of that agricultural promise had been forbidden to white Americans

RED, WHITE AND BLUE

Red in the story of the American West symbolizes Native America — *Mounted Warrior,* by George Campbell Keahbone (Kiowa), 1946, watercolor. White, for pioneer life, is symbolized by the statue of the Pioneer Woman, located in Ponca City, Oklahoma. The conceptual ideals may be thought of as blue. Here they are demonstrated as Osage Indians sign the Declaration of Allegiance to the United States Government in 1913.

Pioneer Woman photograph courtesy of Oklahoma Historical Society (neg. no. 19584); photo of Osage signing courtesy of the Department of Library Services, American Museum of Natural History (no. 316554), photo by Joseph R. Dixon; Keahbone painting from the collection of Philbrook Museum of Art, Tulsa

~ ~ ~ BIG BLUESTEM ~ ~ ~

from the years after the Louisiana Purchase until the end of the nineteenth century. Although I had read in desultory ways about a place called Indian Territory, I never immersed myself in its stories and did not realize that the hills and oaks, rivers and prairies Bill and I had sped through had been confined within an invisible Chinese Wall. I was about to learn that from 1830 to 1906, most of Oklahoma had been set aside for the dispossessed native peoples east of the Mississippi. It was a ghetto, a Promised Land, an American experiment in the separation of races and cultures.

Oklahoma stands at the juncture of North and South, East and West, and its human history, like its natural history, may be seen as a crucible where disparate elements have met, mixed, and melded. The story I am about to weave is bounded in time, as it is bound to place. And, like the American flag, it may be imagined in three colors.

The red, of course, is the Native American story, woven here in three distinct threads. There is the Osage thread, which I will endow with special importance because it relates most directly to the tallgrass region that is, after all, the main story of this book. And there is the thread of the Five Civilized Tribes, who dominated the history of Indian Territory from its beginnings, enacting an idea with geographical boundaries called Indian Removal. And there is the story of the other tribes, indigenous and exiled, who lived in Indian Territory and also shaped its character and fate.

The white pattern is the pioneer story. It begins with the colonial forces of Spain, France, and England; takes shape in Washington, D.C., through Jefferson's Louisiana

The story I am about to weave is bounded in time, as it is bound to place. And, like the American flag, it may be imagined in three colors. The red, of course, is the Native American story. . . . The white pattern is the pioneer story. . . . Woven beneath the red history and the white are blue conceptual skies — slippery abstractions such as "civilization" and "democracy" and "free men."

Purchase and his articulation of the American Dream; and works itself out in the messy process of western conquest called Manifest Destiny. White settlers coveted Indian lands, and as is usual in America's history, what the white folks wanted, the white folks got. After the Civil War, the reunited federal government disassembled Indian Territory piece by shattered piece. No matter how hard they tried to abide by the rules of white civilization, the tribes lost again. The walls of their short-lived republics came tumbling down, and by the turn of the century, a whole lot of prime land was up for grabs.

Woven beneath the red history and the white are blue conceptual skies — slippery abstractions such as "civilization" and "democracy" and "free men." This heady blue mix of philosophy, policy, and outside forces diverse as grasshopper invasions or the War of 1812 creates a necessary background against which the drama of history occurs. Tracing some of these ideas will, I hope, help bring form to the intertwined stitchery of events. But now my metaphor runs out and the history begins.

THE EUROPEAN STORY of Indian Territory opens with the first whites who stepped foot in the region we call Oklahoma. Spanish explorers, governors, priests and soldiers began their long presence in 1541, when Coronado's conquistadors traveled north and west from Culiacan seeking the mythical treasures of the mythical Seven Cities of Cíbola. They were followed the next year by Andres de Campo, and later by Juan de Oñate in 1601. Then, in the eighteenth century came French explorers and fur traders: La Harpe on the Kiamichi and Arkansas rivers; Du Tisne on the Verdigris River in Kansas; the Mallet brothers, Pierre and Paul, exploring the Canadian River in 1740, with Fabry de La Bruyere on the same river in 1741.

The Spanish and French were imperialists looking for natural resources to exploit and send back to their kings and emperors. Except for some French traders and *coureurs de bois,* who married Indian women and created a congenial mixed-blood culture, most were not interested in settling in America's western wild lands. And, although the horses and dependence on trade goods which they introduced into Native American ways of life made significant changes, the Spanish and French did not restrict the movements of nomadic tribes or attempt to transform the hunting and gathering patterns that ruled traditional structures and daily lives.

Spanish and French traders were well acquainted with the tall, fierce, and imposing Osage Indians, who were a powerful force in the central plains region west of the Mississippi. In the early years of the fur trade, from home villages near the center of Missouri and other clan sites in Arkansas, Kansas, and Oklahoma, the Osages had dominated

Osage territory around 1775.

the flow of commerce up the Missouri and down its main tributaries. They grew rich, never doubting their dominance.

Women, who were gatherers, planted corn in the prolific bottomlands. As they planted, they sang a song of initiation that proclaimed their sacred, joyous connections to the earth.

Osage men were hunters and warriors who ranged freely over the prairies of southern Kansas and northern Oklahoma following bison, elk, and deer. They were also dreamers and politicians, and their leaders, the ones John Joseph Mathews calls The Little Old Men, had been successful in negotiations with French fur traders as well as Spanish lords and soldiers.

So when, on a cool June day in 1804, Lewis and Clark camped in the heart of their territory at the mouth of the Osage River, it was impossible for the Osage leaders to imagine how quickly their world would change. The French trader, Auguste Choteau, had sent a message to Makes-Tracks-Far-Away reporting the transfer of Osage lands from French control to American control by terms of the Louisiana Purchase. But the Osage leader burned the letter, not believing such a thing could happen.

He should have believed. For far away, in Washington, D.C., the philosopher/president Thomas Jefferson had signed a bargain that would determine the fate of the Osages, create a place called Indian Territory, and change American history.

TO TALK ABOUT JEFFERSON, we must also speak of the genesis of the United States and of the American notion of freedom. The Revolution was a revolt against colonial tyranny. It began as a protest against unfair taxation by a distant British ruler and ended in a representative form of government in which every white man of property would have equal voice.

The original colonies were populated in part by men and women from the British Isles fleeing religious oppression. In the New World they were determined to become "free men" in spirit as well as body, free to follow the dictates of conscience. Such citizens were the heart's blood of Jeffersonian democracy — an educated populace of yeoman farmers who owned land, produced wealth from their labor, and could rule themselves under a system of democratic representation set forth in the Constitution, with individual freedoms guaranteed by the Bill of Rights.

Jefferson knew the United States would expand and sought to protect its borders to ensure peaceful growth. Once the union was secure and functional, he took advantage of Napoleon's surprising offer to sell for a paltry fifteen million dollars France's huge empire west of the Mississippi. Through his Louisiana Purchase of 1803, Jefferson believed he had ensured the orderly expansion of the United States for time immemorial. He justified his act in a letter to Senator John Breckinridge of Kentucky:

OSAGE CORN
PLANTING SONG

I have made a footprint, a sacred one.
I have made a footprint, through it the blades push upward.
I have made a footprint, through it the blades radiate.
I have made a footprint, over it the blades float in the wind.
I have made a footprint, over it I bend the stalk to pluck the ears.
I have made a footprint, over it the blossoms lie gray.
I have made a footprint, smoke arises from my house.
I have made a footprint, there is cheer in my house.
I have made a footprint, I live in the light of day.

The future inhabitants of the Atlantic and Mississippi States will be our sons. We leave them in distinct but bordering establishments. We think we see their happiness in their union, and we wish it.... God bless them both....

The letter continues, articulating ideas that would lead to the establishment of Indian Territory and prepare the ideological ground for forcible Indian removal:

The inhabited part of Louisiana, from Point Coupee to the sea, will of course be immediately a territorial government and soon a State. But above that, the best use we can make of the country for some time, will be to give establishments in it to the Indians on the east side of the Mississippi, in exchange for their present country, and open land offices in the last, and thus make this acquisition the means of filling up the eastern side, instead of drawing off its population.

With Indians shunted off to a distant, cloistered territory where they could be gradually weaned from "primitive" hunting and gathering ways and could peacefully learn the advantages of agricultural "civilization," Jefferson believed the United States had room to grow along a path bounded by reason and moderation.

When we shall be full on this side, we may lay off a range of States on the western bank from the head to the mouth, and so, range after range, advancing compactly as we multiply.

Of course, the settlement of the West would not adhere to any theory of order or reason. As every mule knows, the grass always seems greener on the other side of the fence. Lewis and Clark, Freeman, Pike, and other early explorers returned from the unknown West with glowing reports about its natural resources. The good news spread. During the next two decades (even before the Oregon Trail and the California Gold Rush) a steady trickle of disgruntled settlers left homesteads on the Ohio, Illinois, and Kentucky frontiers in search of trade, riches, and lands west of the Mississippi. Merchants and adventurers rode their horses and wagons into the rich Osage lands of Missouri, or across Oklahoma on the trail to Santa Fe through the gateway city of St. Louis.

An increasing number of Anglo-Americans who emigrated West throughout the nineteenth century had vastly different purposes than the fur-traders, mountain men, and explorers whose paths they followed, or the Spanish and French conquerors who came before. These folks wanted more than imperialistic ownership of Indian lands. They want-

Courtesy of the Museum of Northern Arizona Photo Archives, 2642/H425. Photo by Gene Balzer ed to make homes in Indian country and eventually create new states. They were colonizers who believed "wild" Indians were threats to soul as well as to body — and to property, which in their cosmology represented individual identity and freedom.

These American settlers wanted to transform native peoples in the name of God and civilization. Jackson's invention of zones called Indian Territory (and the later creation of smaller confinements called reservations) answered the needs of conscience as well as conquest. By sequestering Indians, then opening their huge western bison ranges to settlement, American "Fathers" could force native "Children" to subsist on trade goods, agriculture, and government handouts. Thus, they might control the Indians and appropriate their lands with few moral qualms. As the nineteenth century progressed, the Osages (as well as all other western tribes) found themselves beseiged by a swarm of white folks who did not want only furs or trade. These people wanted the Indians' sacred homelands.

Many early settlers on the Missouri frontier were honorable, law-abiding, and hard working — the kind of yeoman bourgeois that Jefferson admired. But along with them came a ragtag stream of men (and I do mean men) who were poor, violent, adventure-seeking and mostly illiterate. These wanderers trekked West with no regard for treaties or laws, expecting bonanzas. Following heroes such as Daniel Boone, they moved from frontier to frontier, took what they could by force or, as many would have it, what they were free to take by right of being "free men."

Ruffians felt unlimited freedom because they knew that in the wilderness west of the Mississippi, no army or strong arm of government could stop them. Outlaw means outside the law. And in the early 1800s, land-seeking outlaws moved into the prairies and woodlands of the central and southwestern plains — a region that had been since pre-Columbian times the domain of the Osage, Wichita, Pawnee, Comanche, and other plains tribes.

Wealthy and powerful as they were, the Osages were no match for the unstoppable, insatiable new hordes. John Joseph Mathews in his history of the tribe, describes the onslaught:

> The Anglo-Saxon invaders had a tribal memory . . . . It was a racial memory of British kings who could have you hanged from a cross-road gibbet if you killed a deer or a partridge. . . . Not only did they have racial memories of suppression by princes and parliaments and hierarchies, but they might even have had fresh memories of the class distinctions in the Thirteen Colonies. These free men were not scholars and gentlemen from the Atlantic Seaboard, but many of them, perhaps most of them, were refugees from the law and were men more savage than those whom they called "Injuns."

His voice gathers passion, as he continues:

Jackson's invention of zones called Indian Territory (and the later creation of smaller confinements called reservations) answered the needs of conscience as well as conquest. By sequestering Indians, then opening their huge western bison ranges to settlement, American "Fathers" could force native "Children" to subsist on trade goods, agriculture, and government handouts.

A team of government surveyors assesses the Osage land in 1866 in preparation for settlement by non-Indians.

Osage land cessions between 1808 and 1825

It was these barbarians who shouted of their freedom from kings and strong governments and princes of both worlds, in the wilderness, and raped and murdered and stole horses . . . and took away their [the Little Ones'] "remaining days."

Traditional Osage lands in Missouri, Kansas, and Arkansas were also being invaded by displaced tribes from east of the Mississippi. To protect as much autonomy as they could, the Osages agreed to abide by a series of treaties that narrowed their range into smaller and smaller circles. In 1808 they gave up most of their lands in Missouri. Soon after, in an 1825 treaty, they gave up the rest, ceding "all lands lying within the state of Missouri and Territory of Arkansas," as well as much of the plains country to the south and west. In exchange they received a fifty-mile wide reservation in southern Kansas — tallgrass prairie country with sections of rich, deep soil more suitable to farming than the rough grasslands across the Oklahoma border that would become the tribe's final home.

WE WILL DROP OUR OSAGE THREAD here and backtrack to an equally important motif in the warp and weave of Indian Territory. South of the Kansas border, in the

woodlands of western Arkansas and eastern Oklahoma, a wholly different pattern of migration had emerged as Jefferson's policy of Indian removal became the shaping force in the history of the region.

The Cherokee, Creek, Choctaw, Chickasaw, and Seminole tribes of the American South, later called collectively the Five Civilized Tribes, had earned this label by adapting to European notions of civilization. Always agricultural societies, they gradually abandoned the hunting and gathering elements of their traditional cultures. Some, especially mixed-bloods, owned cotton plantations and black slaves. These tribes developed complex constitutional governments modeled on the American Constitution; they established schools; and a good portion learned English and converted to Christianity.

Florida Seminole Daily Life, Fred Beaver (Creek/Seminole), 1911-1980), watercolor.

Philbrook Museum of Art, Tulsa, acc. no. 1926.7

Government officials believed that such enlightened peoples would be opportunistic as white entrepreneurs, that they would seize the chance to trade endangered old homes and lands for protected new ones. But despite their accomodations to Anglo-Saxon ways, the five southern tribes remained culturally distinct from the prevailing white society and from one another. They were alike, however, in one crucial respect: all were connected to their home grounds in deep and sacred ways that rootless white Americans could not imagine. In the preface to his landmark book *Indian Removal,* the Oklahoma historian Grant Foreman says:

> They were not nomads like some western Indians; they were less inclined to wander to strange places than white people. They loved their streams and valleys, their hills and forests, their fields and herds, their homes and firesides, families and friends; they were rooted in the soil as the Choctaw chief Pushmataha said, "where we have grown up as the herbs of the woods."

Speculators and settlers lusted for the lush, productive countryside of the Five Civilized Tribes in Mississippi, Alabama, the Gulf coasts, and Appalachia. And after rumors of gold provoked a wild rush into the Georgia hills, the state's legislature bypassed federal treaties, annexed Cherokee lands, and opened them to settlement. Violent land-grabbing became commonplace on Indian farms and estates throughout the South.

In the first decades of the nineteenth century, some far-sighted Cherokees, Choctaws, Creeks, and members of the other tribes (especially enterprising mixed-bloods) cut their losses by exchanging southern estates for holdings in Arkansas and Oklahoma Territories. When they arrived, they found that some of their new lands . . . were still used as traditional hunting grounds and village sites by Osage clans. Officials back East never realized this would be a problem.

Prairie in summer in early morning fog.
Photo by Harvey Payne

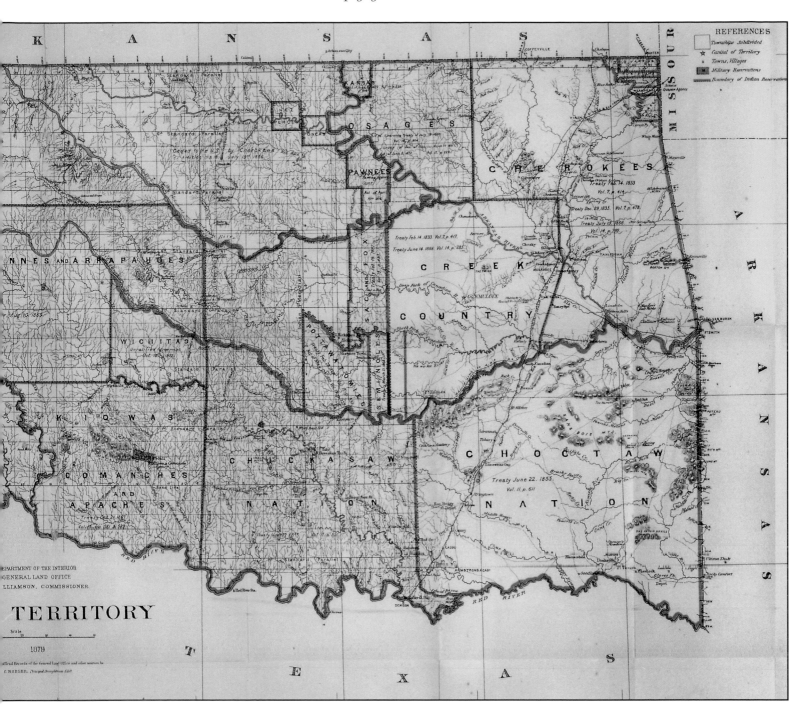

A J o u r n e y I n t o t h e T a l l g r a s s

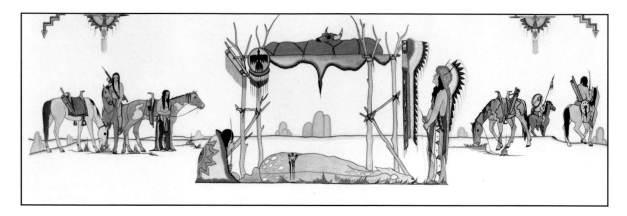

Cheyenne Burial, Archie Blackowl (Cheyenne, 1911-1992), watercolor.

Philbrook Museum of Art, Tulsa, acc. no. 1945.25.1

NOT ALL MEMBERS of the Five Civilized Tribes chose to stay home and fight. In the first decades of the nineteenth century, some far-sighted Cherokees, Choctaws, Creeks and members of the other tribes (especially enter-prising mixed-bloods) cut their losses by exchanging southern estates for holdings in Arkansas and Oklahoma Territories. When they arrived, they found that some of their new lands in the northeastern section of Indian Territory were still used as traditional hunting grounds and village sites by Osage clans.

Officials back East never realized this would be a problem. To them, Indian Territory held ample room to accommodate any number of Indians. After all, an Indian was an Indian — pretty much all alike. Thus, the Fathers in Washington promised Cherokees and Creeks possession of the tallgrass prairies, the blackjack hill country and fertile lands along the Verdigris, Arkansas, and Canadian rivers that the Osage considered theirs.

It is easy to understand the frustration and anger of the Osages. The Oklahoma hunt-ing grounds they had fought to protect for hundreds of years had been given away. This they could not accept. Plagued by Anglo land-seekers coming in from the north and east, now they were surrounded from the south by agricultural slave-owning tribes alien as any white farmer. In the chaos before the removal acts of the 1830s, there was no clear title to much of the contested land, and battles raged.

In 1817, a small army of Cherokees augmented by some Choctaws, Chickasaws, and a group of white men described by Major William Bradford, newly arrived at Fort Smith, as "a set of the most abandoned characters ever disgraced a gallows," attacked an Osage village on the Verdigris River. The Osage men had gone off on their autumn hunt and the village was filled with old people, women, and children. According to John Joseph Mathews, as they tried to escape to limestone bluffs and timbered mounds, 14 old men were killed, along with 69 women and children. On one mound, a group of older boys was castrated. The marauders took 103 prisoners to be sold as slaves to eastern Cherokees.

"It has been said," wrote Mathews, "that the Verdigris turned red with the blood of women and children, and the mound to which many of them fled and on which the young boys were emasculated and the girls raped is called Claremore Mound, and the slaughter is called the 'Battle of Claremore Mound.'" The hatred and rivalry of Osages and Cherokees began in such incidents — the Osages being equally guilty of violent attacks — and lasted for generations.

Meanwhile, back in Georgia, Alabama, Mississippi, and the Carolinas, traditional full-bloods and some militant mixed bloods such as Chief John Ross resisted removal. Groups of embattled Indians chose to hide in the hills and fight for their last bits of sacred land. They refused voluntary exile, avoided capture, and many of their kin still live in the ancestral lands.

General Andrew Jackson was an Indian fighter and a populist. He had no sympathy with the Indians of the South or anywhere else. Indian removal had been a major plank in his platform and in 1830, after becoming President, Jackson helped push through the Indian Removal Act. This legislation gave the policy of removal the force of law and left

The Endless Trail, Jerome Tiger (Creek/Seminole, 1941-1967), watercolor.

Philbrook Museum of Art, Tulsa, acc. no. 1995.7.105

its enactment to the Executive Branch. I will not go into the tragic details that top one another in horror. During the next few years, over sixty thousand resisting Indians, often in chains, freezing and starving, were marched on five long "Trails of Tears" into Indian Territory.

By then, the federal government had narrowed the confines of Indian Territory to what would become Oklahoma. Surveyors divided the ground into swaths running from north to south between Kansas and Texas, and from Arkansas borderlands in the east, westward across the plains. The northeastern corner became Cherokee land and included a long west-running stripe along the Kansas border called the Cherokee Strip. The central part of the territory on both sides of the Canadian River became the domain of Creeks and Seminoles. Chocktaws and Chickasaws inhabited the southern third down to the Red River.

Although their treaty-lands extended westward into the bison and game-filled Oklahoma grasslands, the Five Civilized Tribes never settled there in any numbers, preferring to cluster around villages and cultivate farmsteads in their eastern and central holdings. Part of the reason for such close gathering was fear — fear of the nomadic indigenous tribes who lived and hunted bison on the plains. The Comanches, Apaches, Pawnees, Wichitas, Kiowa, and especially the Osage were horseback warriors, more fierce than the southern exiles, and determined to fight for access to food, clothing, shelter, and land that was the source of the sacred stories that defined their cultures.

Tired of war, once they found secure dwellings, survivors of the trails of tears began to rebuild their lives. Their task was made easier because this new domain seemed familiar. The Arkansas/Oklahoma borderlands were hilly, wooded, well-watered, mild in climate, and reminded the Indian immigrants of their lost homelands in the South. Wealthy families planted cotton, built log manor houses with verandas like southern mansions, and housed black slaves in one-room shacks. Small farmers plowed gardens and planted corn, squash, melons. Many imported hogs and cattle. Soon the Five Civilized Tribes had colonized the eastern half of Indian Territory into communal agricultural societies based on the ones left behind.

Osage Death Song

A-he the he, Ah, the he.
It is I who cause them to lie
blackening on the earth,
A-he the he, Ah, the he.
It is I who take from them
their remaining days.

FROM THE REMOVAL ONWARDS, white squatters and outlaws tested the patience of the Five Civilized Tribes in Indian Territory, but they were fleas on a big dog rather than a swarm of killer bees. White settlers pressing in on the Osage on their Kansas reservation were much more deadly. Their presence brought large-scale suffering.

During the 1830s, hunger swept the Kansas Osage clans as bison and other large game were hunted out for trade and to feed increasing populations, both red and white. The new immigrants brought death with them in the form of diseases such as smallpox, measles, and cholera. Mother Nature heightened the hard times with floods followed by drought.

By 1834, the women's planting-corn song of hope had been put aside for songs of mourning. Every village resounded with the wailing death song.

The crisis waned. By mid-century, a certain balance of power brought relative order and peace to the Osages in Kansas and the Five Civilized tribes in Indian Territory. But then came the Missouri Compromise, the Kansas and Nebraska Acts, John Brown's revolt, and other intrigues that created turmoil in the West as the Civil War approached. Dark times returned. In their Bicentennial study, *Oklahoma, A History*, H. Wayne Morgan and Anne Hodges Morgan sum up the situation:

> On the eve of war, Indian Territory felt the passions that tore the nation apart. On the southern border, Texas was strongly proslavery. Arkansas, on the eastern flank, was secessionist, and a divided Missouri pressed the northeastern corner. To the north, bloody violence convulsed the ardently Unionist new state of Kansas. And the lonely, unsettled, western and northwestern reaches of Indian Territory seemed a vacuum waiting for disorder.

Appealing to their southern heritage, agents of the Confederacy convinced the Five Civilized Tribes to become allies. However, during the conflagration only the Choctaws remained true. The other tribes split into factions and fought their own civil wars on their own ground. Union forces, Confederate forces, and guerilla bands also plundered Indian Territory, leaving villages and farms in ashes. When the damage was assessed after the war, "the three northern tribes lost almost one-fourth of their people," according to the Morgans. "And nineteen thousand Indians were homeless, crowded into refugee camps at Fort Gibson, in Kansas, or scattered through the Choctaw and Chickasaw nations."

As punishment for the Five Civilized Tribes' alliances with the South, the federal government declared their old treaties invalid and repossessed the western half of Indian Territory. During the next decades, American military aggression turned west to subdue the still free-ranging plains Indians, and Oklahoma's western lands became reservations for people who had always lived or hunted there, such as the Comanche, Kiowa, and Apache, as well for displaced midwesterners such as the Peorias, Iowas, Kickapoo, Sac, and Fox. Other portions of the old bison range would serve as reservations for newly-defeated Cheyennes, Arapahos, and for the survivors of our last astounding Indian war — Chief Joseph's band of Nez Perce from far-away Idaho.

The Osages, on their Kansas reservation, survived the war and its aftermath with fewer losses than the Five Civilized Tribes. During the conflict they, too, had been divided. Some clans sided with the South, others with the North, but ultimately they joined forces with the Unionists and came out smelling sweet as a prairie rose. "At war's end," writes John Joseph Mathews, "the Little Ones were lucky that they had suffered nothing more than smallpox, measles, and constant harassment during this barbaric period in American history."

Appealing to their southern heritage, agents of the Confederacy convinced the Five Civilized Tribes to become allies. However, during the conflagration only the Choctaws remained true. The other tribes split into factions and fought their own civil wars on their own ground.

Osage Treaty, now in the collection of the Osage Tribal Museum in Pawhuska.

Courtesy of the Osage Tribal Museum, Library and Archives; photo by Harvey Payne

Kansas had become a state in 1861. After the Civil War, the land-hungry new citizens exerted unceasing pressure on Congress to dissolve the Osage Reservation. In an 1865 treaty, the Osages were forced to sell a 30-mile hunk of prime farmland, the proceeds and interest of which would be held in trust by the U.S. government at five percent interest. Kansans, however, wanted all the Osage land. Lobbying gained force, and in 1871-72, Congress and the tribe finally agreed on terms for permanent removal. The Osages sold their rights to 8 million acres at $1.25 an acre. With some of that money they purchased a reservation carved out of Cherokee lands in Oklahoma Indian Territory.

The place they chose for a new reservation was familiar — nearly a million and a half acres in the north central portion of the Cherokee Strip. The price was 70 cents an acre. Foregoing better agricultural land, the Osages repossessed the tallgrass prairies and blackjack hills that they had been forced to cede to the enemy Cherokee Nation under the treaties of 1825 and 1839. They believed they would be left in peace there. In *Wah'Kon-Tah: The Osage and the White Man's Road,* John Joseph Mathews quotes the decisive speech of an Osage leader, Wah Ti An Kah. "White man will not come to this land," said the chief. "White man cannot put iron thing in ground here. . . . This will be good place for my people."

Blessed with a hard-nosed but honest Quaker Indian agent, Isaac T. Gibson, the tribe arrived at its new reservation depleted in population (down to 3,956 people by Gibson's count), but more wealthy than most other tribes that had been evicted from their lands. According to Mathews, the Osages rode into Oklahoma with twelve thousand horses. Many people were sick, hungry, despairing, and unwilling to relocate, but the tribe would be able to buy supplies and food with annual interest payments of $15,000, plus additional interest payments allocated for educational purposes. Agent Gibson, together with an eloquent leader named Pawne-no-pashe (Not-Afraid-of-Longhairs), had also convinced Congress to include provisions in the treaty that ensured communal ownership of the reservation — an act of foresight that would reap benefits in the long run.

The Osage Reservation, ca. 1900.

The Osage Agency in
Pawhuska, Oklahoma, ca.
1880s.

Osage County Historical Society

The first Oklahoma years were tough. During the dislocation and acclimation period from 1877 to 1884, the Osages lost about one-third of their population to disease and starvation. The plains, which had provided protein and skins for time immemorial, were barren of big game. When the men, women, and children went on their last great buffalo hunt in 1876, they returned empty-handed. The bison were gone, but proud Osage hunters and warriors believed the "civilizing" occupation of farming demeaned them. As Mathews explains, "tradition still held them. They planted in the Planting Moon, April, but even if they didn't go on the buffalo hunts, they did not cultivate their crops. Rations were stopped since they refused them, saying that 'they were fed like dogs.'"

In 1879, under duress from starving Indians, another agent, Laban J. Miles, agreed to allow the Osages to receive annuity payments in cash as well as beef, thus giving them means to honorably feed themselves. He also leased 350,000 acres as grazing lands for Texas herders driving cattle to Kansas, which brought more cash to the tribe. As means of survival changed, the old ways of tribal organization disintegrated. To deal more effectively on their own behalf, in 1881, at the Osage Agency named Pawhuska after the tribal leader, White Hair, the two main branches of the Osages joined under a written constitution based on the Cherokee model. They had become, officially, the Osage Nation.

We have been talking and talking about the Native American history of Indian Territory, but what, you may ask, about the Wild West saga celebrated in songs, dime novels, and western movies — the pioneer past that most of us know and love?

I am going to skip ahead of the cowboy part of that story — Texas trail drives, rodeos and cattle barons. The cattleman's story will be the subject of our next chapter. Here, we will speak of railroads, outlaws, land rushes, and towns.

White settlement arrived late, hard, and fast in Oklahoma. Any story about place and people is strange and unique in its particularities but, like every aspect of Oklahoma's history, its pioneer story is more sudden, more dramatic, more peculiar than the common tale. That's because the era centers around the grand land giveaway I have called "the last free lunch." In less than twenty years — from 1889 to 1907 — this remote and sparsely inhabited Native American reserve became a populous white state.

One way to see the quick and drastic transformation is to look at demographics. Just after the Civil War, Indian Territory held some 50,000 Native Americans, 8,000 former African American slaves, and perhaps 2,500 whites. By 1900, with the Native American population remaining about the same, there were 109,400 whites and 18,600 blacks. The non-Indian population had increased 12-fold. Indians became a minority in their land.

Railroads were a major factor in the immigrant upsurge. Under the Reconstruction treaties of 1866, the U.S. government gave railroad companies the rights to build lines across Indian Territory. This they did, usually starting from St. Louis with lines running from northeast to southwest. By 1905, Oklahoma held 5,231 miles of track. Railroads spurred the creation of towns, created market access for timber, coal, and cattle, and brought laborers, black and white, foreign-born and Anglo-American, into the region.

The newly-opened territory also attracted a more dangerous gathering of frontier exploiters — gamblers, prostitutes, whiskey merchants, thieves, and outlaw gangs. Eastern society's rejects found fat cities in railroad tent-camps called "Hells on Wheels." While the Five Civilized Tribes scrambled to create order during the chaos of Reconstruction, outlaws ran wild. Law enforcement was a laughable concept, and the motto of the territory might well have been, "take care of your own damn self."

Some of the freed slaves set loose in the region created another source of disorder. With no land, possessions, food or jobs, many turned to stealing from their former Indian masters. In retribution, The Five Civilized Tribes formed vigilante patrols who roamed the night, whipping and lynching suspected thieves. The newly enfranchised African-Americans gathered in all-black communities for self-protection and survival, forming towns such as Red Bird and Boley.

More notorious were the myth-making gangs: the James Brothers, the Younger Gang, the Daltons. Indian Territory offered such easy pickings that it earned the name, Robber's Roost. Unable to deal with the influx of outlaws, the Five Civilized Tribes called for help. In 1871, the United States set up a court at Fort Smith, Arkansas, with jurisdiction over Indian Territory. The infamous hanging-judge of that court was Isaac C. Parker, who tried 9,000 cases (including the bandit Belle Starr), and sentenced 160 felons to death, with 79 actually executed. To arrest outlaws, the government brought U.S. marshals into the territory. Lawmen such as Bill Tilghman and the black marshal, Bass Reeves, were paid by the head, but only if their prisoners arrived in court alive so that Judge Parker could enjoy the satisfaction of seeing them quickly hung.

Although frontier justice helped to quell outlaws, the federal presence undermined the jurisdictions of tribal courts and the governments of The Five Civilized Tribes. But such incursions were nothing compared to what was happening and about to happen in the heartland of the territory, on a passel of plains called the Unassigned Lands.

"BOOMING" was an old and natural sound on the grasslands: the booming of male prairie chickens in their strutting mating dances; bellows of bull bison; thunder from the skies; the beat of Osage drums. But the new Boomers were two-legged and white and they received their name because of the loud and insistent message they drummed in newspapers all over the nation. Boomers incited a media blitz that called for Congress to open homestead lands in the heart of Oklahoma Territory.

After the Civil War, when the U.S. appropriated most of the western area of Indian Territory from the Five Civilized Tribes, one prime parcel had been left free for new reservations, but remained uninhabited except by a few nomadic plains tribes who still wandered through it on the lookout for scarce game. This chunk, called Unassigned Lands or the Oklahoma District, had been owned by the Creeks and Seminoles, and its center was what is now Oklahoma City. Freed slaves wanted to settle there, claiming it was public land available in 160-acre parcels under the Homestead Act. But the government said, no, these were definitely not public lands.

In the 1880s, with a national publicity campaign started by the mixed-blood Cherokee promoter, Elias Boudinot, the pressure to open Indian Territory to settlement gained steam. Drought, grasshoppers, hard winters, and bad management had produced a horde of failed pioneers still looking for the agricultural paradise promised by their American Dream. Many of the disappointed gathered on the Kansas/Oklahoma border, eager to penetrate the only free land left open on the central plains. They were captained by a professional squatter, Charles C. Carpenter, who had led an invasion of settlers into the Black Hills of South Dakota — sacred Sioux lands forbidden to whites.

Carpenter tried again in Oklahoma, leading a charge from headquarters in Independence, Kansas. But his group was turned back by the 10th Cavalry, an all-black unit who had earned respect as "Buffalo Soldiers" during the Indian wars, and were now defending red lands from white trespassers.

Carpenter failed, but his successor, David L. Payne, "Prince of Boomers," advanced the cause by invading Oklahoma with his motley followers in 1880 and again in 1881. Payne got arrested, convicted, but not punished by Judge Parker, who obviously approved of Payne's crusade. Publicity increased as newspapers carried stories about the never-say-die farmers who strengthened their political force with allies such as railroad promoters, business entrepreneurs, and just-plain adventurers. Finally, in 1889, Congress caved in. The federal government paid a small sum to the Creeks and Seminoles for clear title to two million acres of Unassigned Lands, and surveyors divided the earth into quarter-sections and townsites. On April 22, the whole kit and kaboodle would be open for settlement.

We know "the rest of the story." Thousands of frantic seekers lined up at the borders of the Oklahoma District, on horseback, in buggies, jumping off railroad cars. Most came from Kansas, but some arrived from Texas and the South. Historians Morgan and Morgan give a glimpse of the oddity of the scene:

In the 1880s, with a national publicity campaign started by the mixed-blood Cherokee promoter, Elias Boudinot, the pressure to open Indian Territory to settlement gained steam. Drought, grasshoppers, hard winters, and bad management had produced a horde of failed pioneers still looking for the agricultural paradise promised by their American Dream.

A mural in the Oklahoma
State Capitol Building by
Oklahoma artist Charles
Banks Wilson captures the
color and motion of the land
run.

Courtesy of Charles Banks Wilson

The typical frontier family consisted of a big-boned, shaggy father with
a determined wife and several small children. Their prairie schooner bulged
with chickens. . . . Next to such a family might be a span of prancing bays
with a fine carriage, all shiny wheels and polished brass . . . . One man rode
an ox. A girl in a billowing pink dress sat astride a spirited thoroughbred.
But four circus midgets riding a single horse toward destiny surely provoked
the most comment.

With the Unassigned Lands settled, the next step would be the dismantlement of reservations where Indians actually lived. The 1887 Dawes Act made the taking legal. It provided for the division of Indian reservations into allotments, with tribal members receiving 160 acres of fee-simple lands and the remainder available as homesteads. Soon land runs and safer, more orderly land lotteries became the most popular sports in Oklahoma Territory, for once opened, the playing fields could never be closed.

And so it came to pass that the second land run divested the Iowa, Sac and Fox, and Shawnee-Potowatomi tribes of their reservations, which became absorbed into Oklahoma Territory; and a third run brought 25,000 settlers into more arid Cheyenne and Arapaho lands — an area devoted to cattle grazing until Russian Mennonite immigrants turned it into a profitable breadbasket with their hardy, imported Turkey Red wheat.

The newly coined word "Sooner" joined "Boomer" and "Nester" in the lexicon of pioneer Oklahoma. Sooners were unscrupulous people who would sneak into land about to be opened, stake illegal claims, and settle in. Sooners, when found, were evicted, and the name was an insult to honest settlers. But Sooners, Boomers, and Nesters all came together during the wildest, most lawless, and largest land rush of all when, in 1893, on a hundred-degree September noon, 100,000 stampeding pioneers battled for claims in the 58-by-100-mile strip of delectable grasslands called the Cherokee Outlet.

WHILE FREE-LAND MADNESS dominated the western half of the territory, the Five Civilized Tribes were able to tether their treaty holdings in the east for a few extra years under a special provision of the Dawes Act. Aware of their precarious position, they sent delegates to Washington and argued eloquently for permission to create a separate Indian state, to be called Sequoyah in honor of the great leader and scholar.

They failed, of course. No politician in Washington, D.C. would allow a bunch of Indians to control a rich territory as large as Indiana. And so, the old, powerful, and independent governments of the Five Civilized Tribes lost their Promised Lands. Their people had been marched to Oklahoma as the first participants in Indian removal and now they would be absorbed into the united territory called Oklahoma.

The first train leaves the line north of Orlando for Perry carrying settlers to the opening of the Cherokee Outlet, September 16, 1893. In the lower image, settlers gather and wait on the line for the signal to start the run.

Western History Collection, University of Oklahoma Library, Phillips Collection #2043, #2040

It was a tragic time for the Cherokees, Creeks, Choctaws, Chickasaws, and Seminoles. When the communal lands that created the tribes' base of wealth had been broken apart, grafting court-appointed "guardians" robbed them of most of what was left. Whole societies that had been conceived in hope and promised freedom in perpetuity, fell into hopelessness and poverty. In a replay of their tribes' original great loss of southern homelands, many fullbloods hid in the woods, unwilling to sign allotment papers or agree to the new terms of their existence. Eufala Harjo, a Creek woman said:

> We are pushed out of all that we had. The full-blood Indian people are pushed out today, and they have left their homes and taken what they have, and everything, and are camped out in the woods today. . . . It is going to be cold weather after a while, and there is the women and the little children and the old people, and we don't know what to do with them or where to get a house to put them in. All the property such as cattle and hogs and horses — it's all gone, we have not got anything left. We used to have plenty and more than we wanted and now we haven't got anything.

Up north, in their remote and unplowable tallgrass prairie, the Osages fared better. After they had sold their Kansas reservation and bought a hunk of Oklahoma, the Osages were left with a surplus of $8,500,000. These funds, held in trust by the U.S. government, accumulated interest at 5 percent. As early as 1889, the Commissioner of Indian Affairs noted that the Osages received "The largest regular annuity paid to any tribe . . . about $160 paid to each man, woman, and child." This seemed like a fortune to the poor whites of the region, and many white men married Indian women for the money. Others bought and bribed their way to inclusion on tribal rolls.

The result was a great swell of mixed bloods whose interests were more in line with the dominant white culture. The mixed-blood population soon equalled the traditional full bloods, and the Osage Nation split into competing factions. In 1894, an official U.S. commission urged the tribe to allot its lands into the usual 160-acre parcels. Anti-allotment fullbloods refused, claiming 500 white people had cheated their way onto the tribal roll. The tribe called an election, which the fullbloods won by a small majority. Luckily for all concerned, the reservation remained communally owned.

The urgency for allotment increased after 1897, when Kansas banker Edwin Foster discovered oil on land originally leased by his deceased partner and brother, Henry. A couple of years later, Edwin Foster and his son, Henry V., started shipping out barrels of black gold. More whites moved into the Osage country on the hunt for easy riches and by 1904, according to historian Frank W. Porter, "the non-Indian population had expanded to between 10,000 and 15,000, far outnumbering the 2,200 Osage."

Beseiged tribal leaders with their lawyers and agents negotiated in Washington, D.C., and in 1906, the Osages finally accepted terms for allotment designed to suit their needs.

At left, the tallgrass prairie in summer. Above, a view of the run into the Cherokee strip, Sept. 16, 1893.

Photo by Harvey Payne; photo this page from the Western History Collection, University of Oklahoma Library, Cunningham Collection #184

Each of the 2,229 enrolled members received a 160-acre homestead, as well as an additional 498 acres of "surplus" land — often in a different part of the reservation. In this way, all reservation land remained in the hands of Osage enrollees, at least in the short run.

More important, the tribe retained communal ownership of the mineral rights under the land. These mineral rights could never be sold. Income from oil, gas, or precious metals would be distributed among enrollees according to their shares. This was a major coup, for the Osages would become the wealthiest tribe in the United States. But wealth created its own terrors, which we will discuss in the chapter on oil.

The 1906 Allotment Act also stated that the tribe could keep communally owned quarter sections of land to provide homes for members who wanted to continue living in traditional village style. These small reserves sat beside the Agency in Pawhuska and at trading-post settlements in Hominy and Grayhorse. As sop for the mixed-bloods, the treaty granted railroads passage through the reservation and permitted five town sites to be platted for future growth.

In 1896, these members of the Osage Tribal Council signed a lease with Henry Foster. That lease amazed the oil world: oil rights for 10 years for the entire 1,500,000 acres of Osage land. Left to right, front to back: Saucy Chief, Charles Prudon, Mo-she-to-moi, Jules Trumbly, Black Dog, O-hah-walla, Chief Claremore, Ne-kah-wah, She-tunkah, John Mosier, Chief Jim Bigheart, Chief of the Osages (hatless), White Horn and Pete Big Heart.

Osage County Historical Society

~ ~ ~ BIG BLUESTEM ~ ~ ~

Settlers in western Oklahoma
ca. 1890.

Western History Collection, University
of Oklahoma Library, Forbes Collection
#73, #68

One year later, in 1907, when Oklahoma entered the Union as
its forty-sixth state, the reservation was dissolved and became
Osage County, one of the largest counties in the nation. The old
Agency in Pawhuska evolved into the county seat, and the prairie-
sprouted towns of Hominy, Fairfax, Foraker, and Big Heart (later
Barnsdall) grew fast and bright as sunflowers in the tallgrass.
Merchants, bankers, ranchers, teachers, lawyers, carpenters, oil-rig
crews, cowboys, farmers, outlaws, and adventurers came into the
country and made it their home.

Some inhabitants of Osage County today are descendants of its
original settlers. There are French/Osage families that run back to
French traders such as Auguste Choteau, and pioneer settlers from
the Midwest, and the great grandchildren of African slaves; also fullblood Osage Indians
and a host of mixed-blood everybodies. There are oil people, and cattle people whose
Texas ancestors drove herds across Oklahoma to feast upon the big bluestem and
Indiangrasses. Ranchers, more than any group, shaped the destiny of the prairies. They
dominate the small human enclaves and give the Osage country its character.

Soon after statehood, the Osages, the Five Civilized Tribes, and all the dispossessed
and defeated peoples who once owned Indian Territory were granted American citizenship. They became part of an Oklahoma stew of races and ethnic cultures, which you can
see as you travel across the state from the cities, hamlets, and farms of the eastern hill
country and out into the cross timbers, bluestem prairies, and mountains of the southwest.

Soon after statehood, the Osages, the Five Civilized Tribes, and all the dispossessed and defeated peoples who once owned Indian Territory were granted American citizenship. They became part of an Oklahoma stew of races and ethnic cultures, which you can see as you travel across the state from the cities, hamlets, and farms of the eastern hill country and out into the cross timbers, bluestem prairies, and mountains of the southwest.

✣

Near the Texas border, you will see Chickasaw and Choctaw Indians along with black and white immigrants from the South who settled in an area called "Little Dixie." Out on the western and northern plains, you will run into descendants of Midwestern pioneers called "Jayhawkers." In Tulsa, Oklahoma City, and more rural enclaves, you may encounter some of the black population that once lived in 26 segregated towns. And all over the state, you will find cultural reminders of Germans, Russians, Poles, Italians, Jewish merchants, and other Europeans who came to Oklahoma because it offered a chance to start over, a chance to be free folk in a free land.

FREE FOLK, free land are concepts not so simple as they seem. On April 19, 1995, I was in Montana at my word processor and looking out my bedroom window at weather that whirled from sleet to rain, then a glow of blue skies, when the phone started ringing from Chicago, from Boston.

"Thank God you're safe," said my mother. "I was afraid you were there," said my sister. Oklahoma City is a far way from Pawhuska or Tulsa, where I might have been. But a bomb, perhaps set by "free" militiamen protesting big government, had just exploded 168 innocents into death in the Federal Building. I was my kin's only link to Oklahoma, to tragedy, to history.

The outmoded myths of the Wild West die hard. In some of America's most isolated communities, angry, renegade white folks are hiding out in compounds and proclaiming their independence from a repressive government bureaucracy. Mirroring gun-toting outlaw heroes of the Trans-Mississippi frontiers, they refuse to pay taxes. They are heavily armed. They are often anti-Semitic and racist, and yet it is not by chance that many such groups call themselves "Freemen." They trace their brand of radical libertarianism to Thomas Jefferson and other leaders of the American Revolution.

Didn't Jefferson suggest it would be a good idea to have a revolution every 19 years or so to keep government from tyranny? "I hold it," he said in a letter to James Madison, "that a little rebellion now and then is a good thing, and as necessary in the political world as storms in the physical."

Didn't Jefferson own slaves and believe Indians were "primitive," and didn't he champion small government, minimal taxes, armed militias? In a letter to Elbridge Gerry, he wrote: "I am for a government rigorously frugal & simple, applying all the possible savings of the public revenue to the discharge of the national debt; . . . I am for relying, for internal defence, on our militia solely, till actual invasion . . . ."

The American fear of big government has deep and justifiable roots. Unfortunately, the current brand breeds conspiracy theories that blame dark or swarthy-skinned minorities for the failures of white Christians. Like the minorities they despise, a growing number of white Americans feel disenfranchised. They want to fight any group that prevents them from accumulating the power and riches they believe should be theirs by right of

A Prairie Preserve landscape.
Photo by Harvey Payne

being "free men." Racial and ethnic hatred is the dark side of our old revolt against tyran-
nical kings — the violent pay-off of our society's elevation of individual freedoms above
values leading to the common good.

Fifteen years after visiting three of Oklahoma's cultural icons — The Cowboy Hall of
Fame, the Gilcrease Museum, and Oral Roberts University — I step into a tallgrass prairie
that looks like virgin land but is no more virgin than the logged forests of my Montana
mountains. When I take off my tourist shoes and put on my walking shoes, I find myself
deep into a story that is heart-breaking and complex in its revelations of American dreams
and American nightmares. Then, in the midst of my research, a contemporary Oklahoma
tragedy leads me to understand that the explosive, double-hearted notion of freedom that
rules populist politics at the turn of the twentieth century goes back two hundred years to
Thomas Jefferson, the Louisiana Purchase, the death of Indian Territory and the unful-
filled promises of the American West.

Cows and Cow People

"You was free, and you was doing something you liked — I guess I was born to be a cowboy."

DALLAS POTEET

I N THE BRIGHT AUGUST MORNING, Mary Barnard Lawrence takes me for a prairie ride in her maroon Lincoln Continental. The sky is pure washed blue, the air crisp and fragrant as a sheet hung out in last night's rain, then dried by sun. Horseback would be more appropriate, I think. But Mary is over seventy, and a knee injury has kept her off horses for years, so the Lincoln is her steed. Dust rooster-tails behind our wheels as she steers us up a hill along a rutted track through the tallgrass.

We park the car and walk to the top of the dome. A yellow-breasted meadowlark sings to the morning. Mary stands tall and gray-haired, the breeze riffling her long safari skirt as she studies the rise and fall of land and grass — her domain. She is the daughter of this ranch, its devotee, and she has sold her birthright to The Nature Conservancy, sold it with a glad heart.

"This is my favorite spot because you can see so much." Mary points to the north. "That's my Sand Creek pasture."

Sand Creek was Mary's land, promised to her by her father, H.G. Barnard, after James Chapman died and the ranch was split between the two families. She remembers H.G. gathering up his four children and showing them which pieces of the prairie would be theirs. Mary never got to control her parcel, however, for when H. G. passed away, the ranch was run as a whole by hired managers with proceeds divided among the heirs.

"I used to see so many wildflowers." Mary's tone is wistful. "We'd ride out in the spring before the cattle ate them." Below us a straggling cottonwood bends toward a small stock-watering pond. "Spring trap," says Mary, referring to another small pasture near head-quarters.

Cattle on the Chapman-Barnard ranch ca. 1940s

Photo courtesy of Bob McCormack, Tulsa, Oklahoma

Trap is a common word out here, meaning a place to catch some running thing —
horses, cows, bison, or in this case spring waters. Memory is also a catching place for the
bittersweet stories of a family's life on the land. Mary's family story, like many of the cow
people's stories in the Osage, begins in Texas. It is grounded in a larger story about the
cattlemen's frontier, which again begins in Texas.

A chuck-wagon scene on the trail.

Western History Collection, University of Oklahoma Library, Frank Dale Healy Collection #7

AFTER THE CIVIL WAR, farmers and ranchers in Texas returned from battlefields east of the Mississippi and found their lands unmolested. Their main crops were cotton and corn, but most Texas farmers also ran herds of longhorn cattle. During the war years, with young men gone off to be soldiers, longhorn cows and calves ran loose on the open range and, untended, multiplied. An Iowa cattle buyer came to the Brazos in 1866 and described a typical scene: "[the] prairie," he said, "was literally covered with tens of thousands of cattle, horses, and mules."

Demand for beef-on-the-hoof in Texas towns or in river ports along the Mississippi could not keep up with the burgeoning supply. But the population of the United States had also grown (the decade from 1860-1870 saw a 22 percent increase); the fertile Midwestern prairies were filling up with farmers tilling the soil; and as range became scarce, the usual sources of beef were inadequate to meet the demand. Prices rose to new heights.

Missouri market towns such as Sedalia and Kansas City were destinations for some of the earliest Texas cattle drives along what was called the Shawnee Trail, which wound north from the Gulf of Mexico through the lands of the Five Civilized Tribes in Indian Territory. Although these difficult cattle drives had begun during the 1850s, they increased in size after the war and continued along the Ozark route until 1866.

Longhorns are a tough, venerable breed whose ancestry goes back to wild Spanish bulls, descendants of the great extinct aurochs painted in prehistoric European caves. Longhorn bulls sported knife-sharp curved horns that could gut a bullfighter, or a careless cowhand in a cattle chute. Ernest Staples Osgood, in *The Day of the Cattlemen*, gives this description:

> They were of light carcass with long legs, sloping ribs, thin loins and rumps, and a disproportionately large belly. In color they were nondescript, yellow, red, dun, and black, with often an iron-grey stripe along the back. Their meat was coarse and stringy, "teasingly tough." They were almost as wild as the buffalo that they supplanted on the plains, for behind them were generations of untamed ancestors.

Texas cowhands called drovers herded the longhorns for hundreds of miles through river bottoms and swamps, cross-timbered rough country, forests, canyons and plains — a dangerous business beset by nature's own booby-traps: quicksand, snakes, tornados, and the unpredictable surprises that could turn a placid herd into a stampeding mass of furious energy with a thousand legs and a will of its own. The imagining of those early cattle drives became an American mythological exercise. Here is Osgood again:

> To all those who saw that long line of Texas cattle come up over a rise in the prairie, nostrils wide for the smell of water, dust-caked and gaunt, so ready to break from the nervous control of the riders strung out along the flanks of the herd, there came the feeling that in this spectacle there was something elemental, something resistless, something perfectly in keeping with the unconquered land about them.

Drovers crossed the Red River at Colbert's Ferry and rode north to Fort Smith, Arkansas, then continued through the Ozarks to Sedalia, Missouri, or branched west into Kansas. Longhorns were impossible to control in the hills and hardwood forests of eastern Indian Territory. They scattered among the trees, running wild. Only a portion reached markets. The rest became meat for Indians, settlers, wolves, coyotes, eagles, and crows. Man-made troubles upped the ante. In the wake of the Civil War the territories of the Five Civilized Tribes had fallen into lawless chaos. Outlaw gangs raided the herds; hungry Indians stole passing cattle; and passage was not free. By the Indian Act of 1834, which set the rules of access to Indian Territory, drovers had to obtain consent from tribes in order to cross their lands, or pay tolls, or be penalized a dollar a head. In 1867, the Cherokees set a toll at ten cents a head, and the other eastern Oklahoma tribes soon did the same.

Even after tolls were paid, troubles continued. The Five Civilized Tribes ran their own herds and did not appreciate an invasion of Texas longhorns into their pastures. Cowboys

The Texas longhorn.
Photo courtesy of Mary Lawrence

Noon stop on the Chisholm
Trail, above, and cowboys
posed along the trail, below.

Western History Collection, University
of Oklahoma Library, Phillips
Collection #1932, #1934

had to keep their cows moving, and on specified trails, rather than letting them range widely and slowly, fattening on the lush tallgrasses. And when the herds reached Kansas or Missouri, the drovers had to deal with the wrath of pioneer farmers whose fields the longhorns trampled, whose fences they busted.

At the end of the trail, the Texans faced quarantines, for Midwestern stockmen feared a disease called Texas fever, carried by ticks from Texas that attached themselves to the cattle. Longhorns were pretty much immune to the fever, but not the northern European Shorthorns, Angus and Galloway breeds, or the Herefords that would come to stock the tallgrass plains. By 1867, both Kansas and Missouri had passed quarantine laws limiting the period of longhorn entry to winter months when the ticks were dormant.

Oklahoma's central and western grasslands offered country better suited to Texas longhorns. The open land held only a few disenfranchised Plains tribes who were nomadic hunters in need of income and more similar in culture and spirit to Texas cowboys than the Choctaws, Creeks, or Cherokees. At journey's end, the scattered pioneers in western Kansas and Nebraska proved more eager for business with Texans than the long-settled straight-laced farmers to the east.

Cattlemen from the huge breeding ranches in north central Texas soon began to trail their herds on western routes through Indian Territory. Drovers could keep their longhorns in better control as they ambled across unpopulated meadows of big and little bluestem grasses, fattening steers as they traveled north. Then, with the new, west-winding railroads heading across the continent and looking for cargo, they had easy access to eastern markets. By 1867, the Kansas Pacific had built a railhead in the raw town of Abilene, complete with loading pens and chutes. And three years later, three hundred

miles further north, the Union Pacific extended to Schuyler, Nebraska, and was making tracks for Ogallala. From western railheads such as these, longhorns could be shipped to stockyards in Omaha, Kansas City, and Chicago.

During the next twenty years, the cattle business exploded all across the West, for beef was profitable from on-the-hoof to T-bone, especially for entrepreneurs whose investment in nearly wild longhorns reaped the benefits of free range with little expense except for a cowboy's meager wages. The Texas way of producing cattle was not capital or labor intensive like more conservative Midwestern practices that depended on property, fencing, feeding hay in winter, and careful husbandry. Texans believed longhorns could take care of themselves. Just put them on good grass and watch them grow.

Some of the most famous Texas cattle drives ran north and west along the Chisholm Trail or the Great Western route through western Oklahoma's Indian Territories. Although ranchers continued to ship steers east from cowtowns in Kansas and Nebraska, they also shipped them west to growing markets in the Rockies through the new terminus in Denver. But shipping to market was only part of the enterprise. As the boom swelled in the 1870s, cowboys drove bulls, cows, and calves further west and north to stock the nearly empty shortgrass high plains of Colorado, Wyoming, Idaho, and Montana.

The careless days of free-range Texas longhorns, cowboys and cattle kings were short-lived. By the 1880s, competing Kansas ranchers, whose open western range was being taken up by settlers, were also driving their shorthorn herds westward. Texans suffered another setback when, in 1885, under pressure from Boomers who also wanted access to Indian lands, President Grover Cleveland ordered all southwestern cattlemen to push their herds out of the Cheyenne and Arapaho reservations in Oklahoma.

During this era, cattle prices went up and down with the nation's economy, but the cattle drives continued unabated. In a few years the western shortgrass plains, from south to north, reached cattle-grazing capacity. At the same time, an increasing stream of homesteaders began to move into the northern grasslands and the foothills of the Rocky Mountains. Their claims to land and water, their barbed-wire fences and plowed fields touched off the legal and gunfight battles between Nesters and cowmen that are the stuff of popular westerns.

Ultimately, climate and economics had the last word when, in the 1880s, a depressed market left too many cows on the over-grazed ranges, and then summer droughts and Arctic winters killed off thousands of the starving cattle. Reminiscing about free range days and the slaughtering winters that ended them in 1886-87, Montana's rancher/historian Granville Stuart wrote, "A business that had been fascinating to me before, suddenly became distasteful. I never wanted to own again an animal that I could not feed and shelter."

Like Stuart, cattlemen throughout the plains either quit the business or realized they would have to fence pastures, breed stock better suited to northern climes, feed hay in

~ ~ ~ BIG BLUESTEM ~ ~ ~

winter, build barns, own property, and care for their stock. The lines between cattle-king, small rancher, and nester dimmed, and the cattle boom waned as wheat and other crops became profitable.

OKLAHOMA'S STORY, AS USUAL, did not quite follow the pattern. During the Texas cattle-drive period, and after the end of free range when homesteaders were claiming their quarter sections, fencing and plowing up the grass, the Oklahoma plains remained a cattleman's paradise. Some of the last best tallgrass and midgrass prairies stood untouched in north-central and western Indian Territories, where white settlement had been prohibited until the land rushes at the end of the century.

The Oklahoma grasses were taller and richer, the climate milder than the northern ranges. Here, from the 1870s into the mid-1880s, Texas cattlemen and Kansas ranchers bought grazing leases from Indian agents of the Cheyenne, Arapaho, and Osage reservations, and also from the Cherokees for prime grasslands in the Cherokee Outlet. The lease laws in Indian Territory were confusing, contradictory, and unenforceable, leaving cattlemen responsible for guarding their herds. For protection, many ranchers set up permanent camps and fenced leased land where they could fatten cattle on plentiful bluestem grasses before shipping them out to Kansas railheads in the winter.

To negotiate land and water rights leases with tribes, to protect their cattle from rustlers, to promote better breed stock, and to keep political control of the grasslands, the stockmen formed cattlemen's associations. Producing and selling cattle had become big business, often run by faraway corporations or absentee landlords and operated by hired hands. Cattlemen's associations were powerful forces in Oklahoma and the Rocky Mountain West, and their descendants have continued to influence the policies that govern western politics.

The Oklahoma grasses were taller and richer, the climate milder than the northern ranges. Here, from the 1870s into the mid-1880s, Texas cattlemen and Kansas ranchers bought grazing leases from Indian agents of the Cheyenne, Arapaho, and Osage reservations, and also from the Cherokees for prime grasslands in the Cherokee Outlet.

Tallgrass prairie in summer with cattle in the distance and a sandstone boulder in the foreground. Immediate left, evening meal at the camp, Townsend and Picketts Ranch, Indian Territory.

Prairie photo by Harvey Payne; historical photo, Western History Collection, University of Oklahoma Library, Robert E. Cunningham Collection #270

Roundup in the Cherokee
Strip, ca. 1885.

Western History Collection, University
of Oklahoma Library, Cunningham-
Prettyman Collection #97, Forbes
Collection #129

The Cherokee Strip Livestock Association was exceptional because it was a joint
arrangement run by cattlemen and the Cherokee Nation to sidestep restrictive lease laws.
This powerful group kept exclusive control of the six million acres that brought its members wealth. But the ranchers and Indians lost their private
kingdom when the government forced the Cherokees to
sell them the land, then opened it to settlement during the
Cherokee Outlet land rush of 1893. Boomers and Nesters
won again. According to H. Wayne Morgan and Anne
Hodges Morgan in their history of Oklahoma:

> Farmers especially disliked the cattlemen, who,
> in their view profited handsomely from grazing the
> Indian lands that they wished to make into family
> farms. . . . By the beginning of the twentieth cen-
> tury, this historic tension had matured into a suspi-
> cion of big or complex business enterprise and a
> corollary bias toward the small farmer that became
> the core of political attitudes as Oklahomans
> looked toward statehood.

The Osage Reservation adjoined the Cherokee Strip,
and its tallgrass prairies were also sought as grazing land
for Texas cattle. In the early 1870s, the Osage Indians had
resisted the Texas invasion, fearing longhorns would
deplete grasslands where their thousands of horses grazed.
But their agent saw an opportunity for needed income and
authorized grazing leases for several Texas shippers and

their drovers, as well as for nearby Kansans. The leased grasslands in the western and north central portions of the reservation would eventually evolve into the great ranches of Osage County.

Never an agricultural people, the Osages adapted to the presence of cowboys and cattle trailing through their prairies and reaped the benefits. They discovered that cow people were a less intrusive presence than the Boomers who clamored to disband the reservation and farm its grasslands, or the horse thieves and whiskey merchants who snuck in from across the Kansas border. Government agents missed a bet when they insisted that Osage men learn farming rather than herding, for cowboying was an activity much closer to traditional male roles, and ranching would have enabled many more Osage people to hold onto their lands.

Before allotment broke up the Osage prairies, many of the cow camps on leased land had become de facto working ranches feeding a multitude of cattle, horses, and some sheep. Most fullblood Osages preferred to live in small communities sheltered in forested hills and watered by creeks and lakes. They were not opposed to leasing the unpopulated grasslands in the central and northwestern portions of the reservation. After allotment in

Cowboys branding a calf.
Western History Collection,
University of Oklahoma Library,
Phillips Collection #1931

*The cattleman's
frontier in
Oklahoma, as in the
rest of the West, lasted
for only two-score
years. When it ended,
Nesters created a
more stable and
egalitarian agrarian
culture. But the
romance of the Texas
cowboy remained the
region's dominant
mythology.*

1906, large and small ranchers bought what lands they could from Indian freeholders or continued to lease grazing lands, not from the tribe, but from allottees who lived in the Indian Camps at Pawhuska, Hominy, and Grayhorse. Some Osages, especially mixed bloods, became ranchers themselves; others worked as cowhands. In this way, the great bison prairies evolved into cow country populated by Texas cowboys, Midwestern cowboys, a few Indian and black cowboys, and a hardy bunch of ranch wives and cowgirls.

In 1887, the Santa Fe built a railroad line into Elgin, Kansas, near the Osage's northern boundary. Paul McGuire, an Osage County historian, claims that on its busiest day, the Santa Fe carried 43 trainloads of Texas cattle into the country during a 24-hour period. Because of the Kansas quarantine laws, huge dipping vats were constructed at Elgin to rid cattle of the Texas fever ticks. Longhorns unloaded from railroad cars had to swim through the vats to reach the stockyards. Also, fenced lanes from the Osage County border to the railroad yards kept Texas cattle from mixing with local herds. By 1928, the region was declared tick free, but by then the romantic cattle-drive days were long gone.

The cattleman's frontier in Oklahoma, as in the rest of the West, lasted for only two-score years. When it ended, nesters created a more stable and egalitarian agrarian culture. But the romance of the Texas cowboy remained the region's dominant mythology. Historians Morgan and Morgan describe the cattlemen's "Grass Empire" as an American counterpart to Europe's chivalric feudal times:

> Bridging the disappearance of the nomadic Plains Indian civilizations and the coming of modern white culture, these years were the middle ages of the frontier. A curious feudalism sprang up, strongly reminiscent of the feudal order of medieval Europe. Wealthy ranchers became "cattle barons" in the penny press and local politics. Rodeos and roping contests replaced jousts and tournaments of old. Brands were the frontier's heraldry. And cowboys arrayed in their colorful costumes, including high-heeled boots, broad hats, jingling spurs, and special trousers, were as splendid as Lancelot or Gawain.

OSAGE COUNTY never lost its feudal cattleman's heritage. Because much of the land was cloaked with thin sod over rock beds, it could not be profitably plowed for cotton or wheat, and for this reason the Osage prairies remained mostly off-limits to farmers. Its northern and western grasslands became a haven for huge ranches modeled on the Texas ranching tradition. Here, thousands of

A J o u r n e y I n t o t h e T a l l g r a s s

Tallgrass
Prairie
Preserve
Drive

cattle could graze on private pastures and then be shipped to markets. The Oklahoma climate was mild enough to overwinter stock, native bluestem grasses were richer and more plentiful than imported grasses, and with no federal grazing lands, government regulations would not limit what a man could do. With no one to account to but themselves, the market, and God, the ranch folk of the Osage believed they had been set down in cowboy heaven.

Any visitor will see that the county's culture is still indelibly imprinted with the cowboy's nomadic, adventurous way of life — a style that melds well with the warrior/hunter horse-loving Osage Indian culture that is native to the land. Locals dress in boots and jeans, drive pickups, wear Stetsons, and enjoy cowboy occasions such as rodeos.

Rodeos are a favorite sport, although not so dominant as they were in the 1920s and again in the 1950s, when oil money produced large prizes. Pawhuska, according to local historian Paul McGuire, became "the steer roping capital of the world," breeding champions such as Henry Grammer, Ben Johnson, Sr., and Ben "Son" Johnson, Jr. The roping arena in Pawhuska is named after Ben Johnson. Nearby Claremore was home to a much greater western star, Will Rogers, the great humorist sage. Rogers was a mixed-blood cowboy, raised on a ranch overlooking the Verdigris River, who got his start as a trick roper known as the Cherokee Kid. There is a college in Claremore that bears the name Will Rogers, and a museum where you can watch his exploits in Hollywood westerns or chuckle at his earthy wisdom.

Although not as celebrated as its western stars, the region's ranch dynasties retain a high status. Most locals know who the Drummonds are and can name owners of other large spreads — the Mullendore Ranches, the more recent Boots Adams Ranch, and, of course, the Chapman-Barnard Ranch. Which, as you may have guessed, brings us back to Mary Barnard Lawrence.

"Dad was from a struggling ranch family from around Gainesville, Texas, on the Red River," Mary tells me as we drive around the preserve's perimeter. "He told me the hardest work he ever did was picking cotton in the fields."

Horace Greeley Barnard was born in 1883. His father, who had fought in the Civil War on the Confederate side, went to Oklahoma Territory during the 1889 land rush and staked out some land near Norman, then got sick and was taken home in a wagon. He died soon after. Barnard's widow was left pregnant, with five boys and four girls to care for. Ida, the oldest, married a banker named Robert McFarlin and bore a girl, Leta, at the same time that Mrs. Barnard gave birth to her tenth child, Mabel. Soon afterward, Mrs. Barnard died. "Aunt Ida nursed two babies, her own and her baby sister," says Mary.

Times were tough in Texas, so the Barnard clan decided to search out the land their father had claimed in Oklahoma. H. G. crossed the southern plains in a mule-drawn wagon. "The mules, their only future security, got away," Mary explains, "and the older children had to search for them for days, leaving Horace and his teen-age sister, Cora, to fend for themselves in the Territory."

The Chapman-Barnard
Ranch, in the 1940s. Below,
Ben Johnson, Sr., and H. G.
Barnard in front of the Ranch
Headquarters.

Courtesy of Bob McCormack

When they reached their father's property, the Barnards discovered squatters had claimed the land. Some of the family settled in Norman. There's a McFarlin Memorial Church there, and a Barnard Memorial Church in Holdenville, where the family eventually moved. "Aunt Ida and Bob McFarlin took Dad in," Mary continues. "It changed his life."

Horace G. Barnard's life was enriched in two ways because of his close association with the McFarlins. First, it caused him to meet his future wife, Mary Frances (Frankie) Prothro. Frankie was best friends with Horace's youngest sister, Mabel. Frankie had a crush on nineteen-year-old Horace, and many afternoons she would entice Mabel to promenade with her past the Barnard's Holdenville Livery Stable so she could "peek at Horace." The young folks courted for four years, and when Frankie reached 18 and graduated from high school, they married. It was 1907, the year Oklahoma became a state.

The second way the McFarlin connection changed H. G. Barnard's life was by starting him in the oil business. Bob McFarlin's nephew, James (Jim) Chapman, was Horace's best pal. Soon after Frankie and Horace married, Jim Chapman moved in with them. Chapman was becoming a successful oilman. "Uncle Jim had a talent for striking oil," says Mary. She laughs. "I swear he could smell it!"

Horace became involved in the McMan Oil Company, in which McFarlin and Chapman held principal interests. The McMan grew into one of the largest independent oil-producing firms in the country at that time. It was bought out in 1916 by the Magnolia Oil Company, which eventually became the Mobil Oil Corporation. By then, Jim Chapman had married his cousin, Leta McFarlin, and the tightly bound Chapman and Barnard families moved to Tulsa.

Although oil provided wealth, Chapman and Barnard were Texans with ranching in their blood, so in 1915, they purchased 1,200 acres in Osage County to start the Chapman-Barnard Ranch. By 1920, the ranch had grown to 60,000 acres; and by the 1950s, the partners held more than 100,000 acres of Osage grasslands.

Mary Barnard Lawrence and her brother Bud Barnard vaccinating cattle, ca. 1940s.

Courtesy of Mary Lawrence

MARY AND I drive along the western edge of the Barnard portion of the old ranch, which is now part of the preserve's bison units. Our road loops south across a patch of private land toward the extinct Midland Valley railroad station called Blackland. I wonder at the name. Some people claim the place was named for soil that was blacker there than elsewhere, but to my eyes, this land does not look particulary black.

Mary is too young to remember the origins of Blackland. I would discover some of its history from stories told by one of the most well-known and respected oldtimers who had lived on the Chapman-Barnard Ranch. Ollie Johnson Rider was 12 when the railroad was

built. Bred on the prairie frontier, Ollie was the first wife of the ranch's foreman Ben Johnson, Sr., and mother of its most famous offspring, the movie star Ben Johnson, Jr., who locals still call "Son." In a mother-son interview with Marty Marina of The Nature Conservancy, 92-year-old Ollie recalled the excitement of a railway coming into the country in 1904 and 1905.

"All that dirt work and everything was on mules. There wasn't such things as an automobile or a truck. Or a dozer or anything like that. It's all done with wheeler slips. And they'd have these gangs. Camps, they called them. One of 'em would be Irish people — all Irish in that one. And then down here a few miles they'd have another one — they'd all be black people."

"They was a little primitive at that time," Ollie continued. "They'd fight and raise cain, you know, kill one another. They didn't have a big funeral or anything; they'd just put him out there in that dump [near Foraker], and run a wheeler slip over, and that's it. . . ."

"But where the black people were they had white men, overseers, bosses," Ollie remembered. "And he was on a horse — McCullough, this boss was. And he carried a bullwhip on his saddle. 'Course a pistol . . . And he got into an argument with this one big old black man, and McCullough told him he was gonna put 'im in the dump."

According to Ollie's story, the big black man stayed tough: "He says, 'Cully, I'll put you in the dump!' And I don't know how they settled that, but . . . neither one got in the dump."

The railroad is gone now, rails pulled up and only the hand built roadbed left to mark its existence. But Blackland is on the map — a name that I will always associate with the pick-axe labors of ex-slaves and Irishmen. A place where men were killed whose bones lie buried in the detritus of a ghost town dump.

Today, Blackland is an old station building, some holding pens and corrals, and a modern ranch house across the gravel road. Mary perks up as we approach the corrals. The stories this place holds for her are happy ones. "More cattle were shipped from here during World War II," she tells me, "than from any other place in the United States."

Chapman and Barnard were not the only ranchers who received and shipped cattle at Blackland, but they were the most ambitious. In addition to their Osage land, they held renewable ten year leases on ranches in Texas, south of San Antonio, an operation Mary describes as three times larger than the 88,000 acres they owned and leased at that time in Osage County. The partners wintered steers in Texas, then brought them by rail to Oklahoma in April. "Usually in rainstorms," says Mary, with a chuckle.

Mary was never part of the unloading crew, but Cecil "Raisins" Rhoads surely was. An oldtime Chapman-Barnard cowhand, Raisins had earned his moniker as a young man because of his huge appetite for chuck-wagon dessert — at that time mostly gobs of plump, soaked raisins. "The good Lord knowed when they was a-comin'," said Raisins, speaking of cattle, not dessert, " 'cause it rained every time."

Carloads of cattle would arrive before dawn and the hands would have to drive the

By 1920, the ranch had grown to 60,000 acres; and by the 1950s, the partners held more than 100,000 acres of Osage grasslands. More cattle were shipped from the station at Blackland than from anywhere else in the U.S. during World War II.

COWHANDS

Facing page: Top left, Frankie and H. G. Barnard; in the cowhand group are (back row) Bill Mills, Gay Harris, Henry Grammer, Ben Johnson, Sr., Red Carter, Jack McCaleb, Snook Jones, and Lewis Allen; (front row) Eddie Burger, Floyd Schultz, Red Sublett, Roy Quick, Guy Schultz, and "Oklahoma Curley." The photo below shows cowhands at the Chapman-Barnard Ranch. Pauline Walter (center) and Leta Chapman (right) stand with the women in the background. At center left and right, seated, are Clyde Lowry and Ben Johnson, Sr.

Courtesy of Mary Lawrence; cowhand photo courtesy of the Osage County Historical Museum

The Chapman-Barnard Ranch in the 1940s. Above, Ben Johnson, Sr. in the late 1930s. Johnson was ranch foreman and world's champion steer roper.

Ranch photo courtesy of Bob McCormack; Ben Johnson photo courtesy of Mary Lawrence

spooky steers to the ranch through the pitch-black night. Raisins Rhoads recalled one vivid ride, with blue light running across the backs of cattle and horses:

> We was getting in a whole bunch of King Ranch Brahmers. And we was just starting to leave, and all of that lightning playing across them horns. I never seen it but once or twice in my life, but that was the prettiest thing I ever seen in my life. And the most scariest.

A lot of cattle ran through the Chapman-Barnard Ranch. Ben Johnson, Jr., grew up there. When he was a boy, as many as 18 to 20,000 head grazed the place each year, he told Marty Marina in their interview. If a bunch of steers didn't fatten up enough to ship, they'd winter them over, then sell them the next summer. There were winters when the cowhands fed from 3,500 to 7,000 animals. It was a hard, seven-days-a-week job, scattering cattle along creeks for shelter, cutting water — meaning chopping open the iced-over streams with an axe so the cattle could drink.

Mary did not break ice, ride fence, or tame broncs, but she put in her share of hard, dirty work. "Summers," she recalls, "we'd work pastures on Thursday and Friday, work pastures and ship on Saturday and Sunday." Horseback hands would round up the fattened cattle, sort them by size and drive them to the roundup grounds. The work would start at first light because it was cool then. "Cattle," says Mary, "get increasingly hard to handle with intense heat and pesky flies."

When the cattle had been gathered, foreman Ben Johnson and a second foreman, Clyde Lowry, or Mary and her father would cut out the fat cattle to be shipped. "Of course my eldest brother, Jim Bob, was there too, after he moved to the ranch from Texas," Mary continues. "I think I loved all the work I did on the ranch, but there was something about cutting cattle that topped it all."

"They'd get to market on Monday morning. Dad would call Monday to see what the price had been. During the war, buyers came up here. Scales were built at Blackland and the buyers would ride into the pastures. Sometimes they bought whole herds to be shipped through the summer as they fattened. Everyone came at shipping time. All the neighbors.

They'd bring food. Help out. Eat in."

Mary parks the Lincoln in back of the squat frame building at Blackland that once was a store, then a shipping depot and cake house — cake being the pressed cottonseed plants fed to cattle in stockyards. She yanks at the large sliding door, but it is locked. "This is where we ate those great dinners after the work was done," says Mary. "We had such good times. I was so sad when they took up the tracks."

Across the way is a modern house and some outbuildings on recently-purchased Chapman land. Oil pumps are scattered in a swale and empty miles of grass sweep to the horizon. But what Mary sees in her memory is the little house at Blackland where Dee Martin and his wife lived with their cowgirl daughter, June, nicknamed Cotton — one of ten children.

Dee Martin worked 30 years for Chapman and Barnard. He wintered cattle, feeding them with a team and wagon, and took care of the west side of the ranch — about forty thousand acres. He also kept track of all the brands on the place and, with June, worked the stock pens during shipping. "June and I often worked together in the pens," Mary tells me. "I loved old Dee. He really taught me a lot — patience for one thing."

June Martin Finn is an older woman, now, and enjoys the comforts of modern ranch life. But she remembers the old days, and the hardships her mother, Goldie, faced. In a letter about the life of a cowboy's wife, she writes:

Hands from the Chapman-Barnard Ranch at Blackland in 1928. In the front row are Max Johnson, Norris Brown, Tucson, Peeley Mills, Ben "Son" Johnson, Jr., George Bowman, Homer Mintar ("Red Gravy"), and Dee Martin. In the back row are Jim Bob Barnard, Don Moore, Shorty Layton, John Barham, H. G. Barnard, J. D. Martin, a railroad man, and Wiley Evans. Ben Johnson, Sr., is in front.

Courtesy of Mary Lawrence

Handling cattle in the 1940s at the Chapman-Barnard Ranch. Chapman and Barnard lean out of the cake house at Blackland on the facing page.

Courtesy of Bob McCormack, Tulsa, Oklahoma

It was always lonely and sometimes very frightening. The wife of the cowboy who lived on the outlying ranch often saw no one but her husband for a month at a time. Her husband left before daylight and often wasn't back until dark . . . They didn't have electricity, so they usually didn't have a radio and very few could afford a car . . . she often washed on a wash board and ironed with a flat iron. They didn't have running water, they burned wood for cooking and heat and used coal oil lamps for light. If they ran out of wood during the day, they also had to chop wood. . . . Daddy would borrow a pickup from the ranch and he and Mama would go to town for groceries once a month. The rest of the time she just made out with what she had. The only time we got mail was when I would [ride] the 8 miles to Foraker, horseback to get it.

Mary Barnard Lawrence prizes the experience of being part of cowboy life — working at a job she chose to do with all her heart. Mary was her father's favorite hand, and proud of the honor. She worked cattle on the ranch for three summers during high school while her girlfriends spent their vacations beside the pool at the country club in Tulsa. And then, during World War II, when most of the cowboys had been drafted or enlisted as soldiers, she quit college at Sarah Lawrence to work full-time on the ranch. "In the winter, that was one of the times I loved the most — feeding cattle."

Mary has sweet memories of those ice-edged days. "Nuck or Roy would blow the horn on the pickup and the cattle would come to the horn. They followed along as I dumped feed from gunny sacks off the back of the truck. One winter morning during calving, they had to boost me up on my horse, I had so many clothes on."

Mary's older sister, Ann, was more interested in riding good horses than tending cows. She rode English style, with English tack and gear. Their brother, Bud (H. G., Jr.), a noted Tulsa architect, also helped out on the ranch during the war. Mary took after her much older brother, James Robert (Jim Bob), who lived in San Antonio and worked the Texas

end of the cow business until the leases there were not renewed. After a divorce, Jim Bob moved back to the Osage and built a Spanish-style stucco house designed by his brother, Bud, near the headquarters. He brought a black cowboy named Clyde up with him from Texas, who rode with him and cooked for him until Jim Bob remarried.

Mary tells me, "The family had assumed for years Jim Bob would be taking over the operation of the Chapman-Barnard Ranch someday, but he never got the chance." The business end of the ranch operation was always run from the Chapman-Barnard-McFarlin office in Tulsa. In 1966 James Chapman died, and his half of the ranch passed into the hands of trustees.

As Mary recalls:

> On his return to the Osage, Jim Bob's job became what I think was known as the ranch manager. Even after Uncle Jim Chapman's death, the ranch continued to be run as a whole out of the original headquarters. Dad continued to stay involved at both the ranch and the Tulsa office until his death in 1970.

It's an ancient story — the difficulties of a father handing his power to a son. H. G. Barnard continued to control the operation at a time when he might have been expected to hand over more responsibility to Jim Bob. No one knows for sure how much this disappointment contributed to Jim Bob's deepening unhappiness, which became a source of worry to his sisters and brother. "We knew he was in emotional trouble and he was drinking too much," Mary remembers, "but we didn't know what to do."

The trouble ended tragically, when Jim Bob committed suicide at the ranch. "His premature death prevented his proving himself in the job he had worked for most of his life," Mary says. "This tragedy had an irreversible effect on the future of the ranch. After Dad's death two years later, nothing was ever the same. Those two events, followed by the years of the ranch's being run solely from the office, subsequently led to our need to sell the land."

Now Mary returns in memory to the happy summers of her youth when the family worked together, shipping cattle at Blackland. "My job was to bring cattle down the chutes from the pens to the holding pens." Mary smiles. "It was either all mud or all dust."

Emerging from a cloud of dust at the center of the swarming herd in Mary's memory is the tall, handsome, horseback hero of her youth, foreman Ben Johnson, Sr. "Ben would yell, 'roll 'em jockeys!' The horses knew his yell. They'd rear back and start. It'd be a great surge to get the momentum going. People came from all over to watch that."

In their 1992 interview, Ben Johnson's ex-wife, Ollie, and his son, Ben, Jr., shed a different light on the ranch experience, telling their tales from the perspective of hired hands.

Ollie came to the ranch around 1917, when she and Ben were newly married and he was still a working cowboy — a long ways from the exalted and better-paid position of foreman that he would hold after their divorce. The Chapmans and Barnards had recently bought the ranch and, although they lived in Tulsa, they wanted to clean up the original two story ranch house to be their living quarters during visits. The house had been built for an Indian family, then sold to the previous owner, who had let it molder.

"There's two bedrooms downstairs, and one great big room, living room and dining room together. And a huge kitchen. The filthiest thing I ever saw," said Ollie. "But the house was old — smoked and ugly."

The owners had hired a black cook, "a great big man," as Ollie described him.

Frankie Barnard (just arrived in her touring car, wearing a new silk dress from a shopping trip to Kansas City), Leta Chapman, and Leta's mother, Ida McFarlin, along with Ollie, herself, set about to clean up the place.

"We had him [the cook] to set a tub on the stove, wood stove they cooked on, filled it full of water, and we poured some lye in it…. And the black man, he wasn't very happy about it. In fact, he was mad at us. He told us 'too many cooks spoil the broth.' [But] we couldn't take it anymore, so we just went and cleaned it. Can you imagine millionaires cleaning the kitchen?"

Ollie and Ben lived in an upstairs room infested with bedbugs. Next door was a bunkroom with cots for the bachelor cowboys. "They had a lot of cowboys at that time," said Ollie. "They had some old blankets, old, kind of like an army blanket now, it was gray, and they had some old quilts. I don't even like to talk about it, it's so nasty. . . . And when the bosses' families come, they got a big tent and set it up out in the yard — that's where they stayed."

Ollie tried to rid her bed of bugs. "I had Ben take the mattress out in the yard," she said, "and I poured boiling water on that to kill the bedbugs. Then I got me some cans — I imagine it was tomato cans or something like that — and I put kerosene in that, and set the bed legs in it, pulled it out from the wall so they couldn't get off [the walls] on the mattress."

When the owners left, she and Ben escaped to the tent. Ollie loved the tent. She was young and childless, with a little time to spare between chores. "I liked to hunt and fish, and I roamed up and down Sand Creek there pretty good."

Photos by Harvey Payne

Soon, Ollie and Ben moved from Headquarters to living quarters in the old store building in Blackland. The cake house Mary showed me was where the store used to be. That was 1918, the year of the great flu epidemic. By then, she had given birth to Ben, Jr. ("Son"). When both of her loved ones took sick in the middle of winter, Ollie set a fire in the cookstove, settled the baby and his father on a pallet beside it, and raced to town to get medical advice and medicine. Of course she went horseback.

"He was just a colt," said Ollie, "and I was ridin' him with a hackamore. And I come in to a place where the tallgrass had blown over, and snowed over it, and of course I had him in a long lope; he jumped a coyote out of that. Oh, could he go fly! I was afraid to fall off so I rode him. I could have froze to death out there."

Danger was an everyday occurrence. "We don't know any better," said Ollie. "That's the way we was raised, all of us."

Ollie and Ben eventually divorced. Son lived with his mother in town during school time, and worked on the ranch during the summers. When he was 11, his father put him on the payroll.

"My situation was a little different from most," he said, " 'cause my dad ran the ranch, and he never gave me the short way of any time. 'Cause he'd always give me the long way around, or if there was a dirty job to do, they'd always give it to me. They didn't want to give me any of the best of it in front of everybody else, you know. So consequently, when I'd get off and get out of sight, I might take a little nap, or I might go fishin', or I might rope something. . . . I kind of had the name of being maybe a little bit lazy. But I was just protecting myself a little bit."

Coming to Ben's defense, Ollie said, "I've never seen Son do something he didn't do it right."

Ben agreed. "If I say so myself, I've always been a good cowboy. And I never

Ben Johnson, Jr. Below, Ben Johnson, Sr., and Frankie Barnard at the Blackland shipping pens in the early 1940s.

Photo of Ben Johnson, Jr. by Harvey Payne; photo of group courtesy of Mary Lawrence

— there's never been a cowboy that ever done what I've done. That's won the World Championship in the rodeo, and also won a couple of Oscars. . . . I'm in the Cowboy Hall of Champions in Denver, and I'm also in the Cowboy Hall of Fame in Oklahoma City. So I've gone about as far as I can go. I've got to help somebody else to get in there now."

Ben Johnson, Jr., went to Hollywood in the days when westerns were the most popular entertainment in America, and like Gary Cooper and other westerners who became stars, he went as a cowboy, not an actor. At that time, he had reached adolescence and no longer rode under the strict supervision of his father. Son was working on a ranch near Dewey when director Howard Hughes came to Oklahoma looking to buy horses for his western, *The Outlaw,* starring Jane Russell.

"I showed these horses to him," said Ben, "and they seen I could ride a horse pretty good, so they hired me to take the horses to Hollywood. That's how I got to Hollywood — in a carload of horses. And at that time I was making $35 a month [as a cowboy]. And the first week I was on Howard Hughes's payroll I made $175. I wasn't very smart, but I knew that was more than 35. So I stayed with it."

Years later, when the Chapman part of the ranch was up for sale, Ben Jr. and his friend John "Duke" Wayne wanted to buy the place. But the deal could never be worked out. Chapman's estate manager, a prominent Tulsa lawyer, would not hear of it. He "wouldn't let us get within a half a mile of nobody," said Ben Jr. Now Ben Jr. has passed on — a passing that marks the end of the colorful cowboy era at the Chapman-Barnard Ranch. As we enter a more complex, politically-charged and ethically ambiguous era, we should keep his voice alive in our inner ears. He worked hard, stayed tough, laughed at himself. He was not afraid to look past, present, or future straight in the eye.

THE NATURE CONSERVANCY'S purchase of the Barnard Ranch was originally opposed by some ranchers in Osage County. But the multi-generational Drummonds — who own some of the largest spreads in the region — were not among them. Fred A. Drummond, the eldest rancher, lives in an imposing white-columned house in Pawhuska. He is a rotund, rosy-cheeked, white-haired man, courtly in the way of oldtime cowmen. When I come to visit, he is alone, his wife, Ruth, gone to visit relatives. The mansion was his compromise with Ruth, a former schoolteacher. "My wife was a city girl," he explains. "Never did like the country."

The Drummonds are one of the oldest white families in Osage County. One of their forebears was a Scots trader, also named Fred, who ran the trading post in Pawhuska in the late 1880s before settling permanently in Hominy, where he bought a store and, eventually, a bank. Known for his fair dealings with the Osage, his reverence for education and devotion to family, the first Fred seems to have passed on these values to his latter-day kin.

We sit in leather chairs in Fred's study and talk about cows and cowboys. Fred started ranching in 1928, when he was fourteen. He borrowed money to buy his first hundred heifers.

"In the old days," he says, "oldtime cowboys liked to ride a horse. Get up at 2 a.m. to ride to the other end of the ranch. Get 'em at daylight before it got hot. Each cowboy rode eight horses. Now they only get three. Don't need three. Most of the young cowboys'd rather ride in a pickup. It's just a change of times."

⁂

"In the old days," he says, "oldtime cowboys liked to ride a horse. Get up at 2 a.m. to ride to the other end of the ranch. Get 'em at daylight before it got hot. Each cowboy rode eight horses. Now they only get three. Don't need three. Most of the young cowboys'd rather ride in a pickup. It's just a change of times. We don't like it, but we gotta accept it."

Ranching has also changed with the times. Fifty years ago, Fred explains, most ranchers ran cow/calf operations. These days they mostly fatten steers. "The reason we got rid of our cows is it takes three acres to feed a steer; eight acres for a cow/calf unit. This grass, as it becomes more scarce, you got to run yearlings. The cattle business is a gambling business. Right now it's been tough. I'm not selling cattle on my ranch," says Fred, "I'm selling grass through my cattle."

Grass range is getting scarce on the Osage prairies because a number of large, out-of-state outfits are buying the land for a high price. Recently Lee Bass from Texas bought about 35,000 acres of the old Chapman Ranch; and in 1988, the Mormon Church bought some 67,000 acres in Osage County from the Adams family. "They don't make any better land," says Drummond. "Steers put on 300 pounds in the summertime, three pounds a day from April to June. July, two pounds a day. August, not over one pound."

According to Fred A., some small ranchers were opposed to the Conservancy's purchase of the Barnard Ranch because they hoped to lease that land themselves. "They were jealous." Fred A. believes in the preserve. "I thought it would help our county, and our state, and our town. The town needs rejuvenation."

The business office of the Drummond Ranches occupies a storefront building in Pawhuska's old red-brick downtown. Except for the western art, wildlife paintings, and old photos on the walls, the office could be a stockbroker's place of business. One wall holds a state-of-the-art computer linked to the commodities exchange in Chicago.

Frederick Ford Drummond, called Frederick — not Fred — runs the complex buy-sell operations of the ranch business from this office. He is a wiry, upright, neatly dressed man who earned a master's degree from Stanford University's Business Administration program.

Frederick, a board member of the Oklahoma Nature Conservancy, is one of the most articulate advocates of the Tallgrass Prairie Preserve. When the possibility of buying land for a preserve came before the board, says Frederick, "I made the motion that they should buy the Barnard Ranch. It's a beautiful ranch that needed to be preserved for posterity."

Among local ranchers, the Drummonds were more the exception than the rule in their support of the preserve. Other ranchers opposed the preserve because the Barnard Ranch was prime land, and good grazing lands at affordable prices have become hard to find in Osage County. Desirable large holdings are being broken up through family squabbles, Frederick explains, and government inheritance and gift taxes, as well as state taxes, can run up to 63 percent of a ranch's market value, which makes it difficult for owners to pass their properties intact to heirs.

"Some small ranchers are afraid of being priced out of the market," says Frederick, and other locals are suspicious of tax-exempt landowners such as the Mormon Church buying and holding onto large parcels of land forever. But the spectre of government land ownership is even more fearful.

"Ranchers are a very independent lot," Frederick continues. "They don't like government interference." When the federal government tried to establish a tallgrass national preserve in the region, some ranchers feared that their properties would be condemned. They joined with other interests to oppose the park, and won. They believed the fight for a preserve here was over.

Our conversation is interrupted when a lean young man in jeans and a baseball cap walks into the office. This is Tim, Frederick's 26-year-old nephew and Fred A.'s grandson, who has taken on the task of managing his father's 70,000 acres. Tim went to Texas Tech in Lubbock, where he majored in Agricultural Business. He represents a new ranching generation, so I ask if he will take me to see the operation that he runs.

We climb into Tim's 4 x 4 pickup, which is equipped with a two-way radio and a cellular phone. Tim keeps tabs on fifteen cowboys and talks to buyers and other business people from his headquarters, which is the pickup. We drive north through Shidler to the Drummond Ranch, which spreads for miles through open grasslands to the Flint Hills at the Kansas border.

"We ran 17,000 head of cattle this summer," says Tim. "Market about 25,000 in a twelve-month period. Sold 4,000 cows last fall, leaving us with 1,100 cows. Cows are too high now. We'll wait for the cycle to bottom out."

Frederick Drummond and Ole Gray, August 1989.

He pulls onto a dirt road on a bluff overlooking large meadows, a meandering stream, barns, and a huge horse-training ring. As a sideline, Tim and his father Charles R. (Chuck) Drummond raise quarter horses and train cutting horses. "Dad was a great trainer," says Tim, "until he got hurt."

We drive to the family's modern ranch house on a tree-shaded knoll. Tim grew up here with his two brothers. Ladd, the younger brother, is his partner on the ranch; his older brother Todd was killed a few years ago in a car accident — a "real hand," says Tim, almost reverently. I ask about his mother, thinking about her sorrow. Tim avoids the emotional response. "She sure felt outnumbered," he says.

Tim is independent of his parents. He lives the bachelor life in a small, old, white frame house that sits exposed on a flat prairie. His only companions are several wag-tail dogs, who greet us with enthusiasm. I ask about his social life. "I've got no social life. Can't be boss if you're following."

The Cowboy Reunion at the
Chapman-Barnard Ranch in
1991.

Photo by John Lusk

It's a spartan road for a young man. I am impressed with Tim's work ethic, his single-minded devotion. He is no sentimentalist about the land. He does what he feels is most productive for the cattle business. Tim has planted non-native brome grass for winter feed; he sprays herbicides in May to kill weeds; spreads three to four tons of fertilizer a year. To him, big bluestem is "prairie hay," and the Tallgrass Prairie Preserve is a mixed blessing. "There's an awful lot of good grass just sitting there," he says.

Tim believes ranchers are usually the best stewards of the land. "We're in the business to fatten cattle. Can't fatten cattle if we abuse our prairie." Like his elders, he does not welcome outsiders who are buying up the land, driving up prices. Tim worries about people his age who would like to carry forward a tradition of family ranching. "Not many young people are able to come back to the land," he says. The future looks lonely.

COMING BACK TO THE LAND is what we love about cow people. They live amid grass, in wind, sun and snow, tending animals. They remind us of our hunting and gathering beginnings. We admire their weathered faces, their work-tempered bodies. And although most of us live in cities and would not give up our comforts, we are glad that cowboys still wander open spaces and choose to live close to weather and earth.

The "cowboy values" that govern this outdoor way of life are not based in politics or religion, but on a code derived from learning how to live hard on a hard land. Jim and Jeanne Ronda are historians who have been interviewing old-time hands during the annual cowboy reunions at the preserve. The list of values they gleaned from those interviews includes: hard work and perseverance; family, community, neighborliness; camaraderie; integrity and fair play; simplicity. But the values we most associate with the cowboy life are independence, self-reliance, solitude.

Helen Christenson is a prairie woman who helped arrange the annual cowboy reunions at the Tallgrass Prairie Preserve. She is attractive, dark-haired, about 50 — the daughter of Ben Johnson, Sr. "I missed those old boys," says Helen. "I love oldtime cowhands because what you see is what you get."

Helen's mother was Ben Johnson's third wife — a young nurse who died shortly after

giving birth to their second child, who also died. Her heartbroken father did not feel up to raising a young girl, says Helen, so she came to live on the edge of the ranch in the small town of Pearsonia with a kind family who had six grown daughters. She spent weekends with her father.

"Dad took me to the movies on Saturday afternoon," says Helen. "Saturday was a big day in town. Everyone went." Ben would hand Helen a ten dollar bill and tell her to treat her friends at the drugstore after the movies. "Dad wanted me to buy cake and candy and ice cream for all the kids. I'd say, 'Dad, I don't need this much.' He'd say, 'You never know, you might get into a Coca-Cola storm.'"

After Ben, Sr., died of cancer at 56, Ben, Jr., took his 15-year-old half-sister to live with him in North Hollywood. Helen hated California. "I cried every night," she says. "I swore if I ever got back to Osage County, I'd never leave it again."

Helen has been true to her promise. She grew up on the Osage prairies and lives there still, on a 1,400 acre ranch in Pearsonia, where she was raised. The town is long gone, returned to prairie grass, but Helen is happy to reside in familiar country with her husband and sons. She worked as Court Clerk in Pawhuska for some years, coming home to the tallgrass every evening. When I ask her to tell me how she feels about the place, her words express the sentiments of every resident I talked to — newcomers as well as oldtimers.

"It's heaven on earth," she says. "That's how I feel about it here. I wouldn't trade it for anything at all."

It was a good place to work. Good beds.

DINK TALLEY

Osage Oil

"Hit her like you live. Hard."

PIPELINE BOSS TO CREW

IF YOU WERE TO COME TO THE TALLGRASS PRAIRIE PRESERVE on an Indian summer afternoon, you might look up to indigo skies, or down to sunflowers at your feet. You might stand reverent before a herd of humped bison, so recently restored to native ground, or glory in a red-tail hawk swooping into a swale, the glow of light through his fan-tail repeating the russet colors of ripened seedheads. You might inhale the musk of grass and squint toward the many-rayed sun and be blinded.

Reveling in a spectacle of nature such as this, we tend to focus on what we want to see, and only in a kind of peripheral vision do we notice the black machines flocked in the tall-grass, pecking like unrelenting crows. We hear the buzz of insects, the hawk's scream, but ignore the soft insistent mechanical pulse of heartbeat pumps going down, down to what we cannot see — the black oil locked into porous rock reservoirs called pools, the pockets of gasses that lie under the grass, under the folding hills of limestone, under the terra cotta sandstone outcropped on ridges mantled with blackjacks and post oaks.

But there it is, the underground wealth of this prairie — a primordial energy that changed everything for the people of Oklahoma. The pure environmentalist in me would love to see the prairies as they were before oil wells, derricks, and access roads scarred the landscape. The social idealist in me wants more oil royalties for the tribe, prosperity for the workers and depressed towns of the Osage Hills. The realist in me knows that the pumps and roads, holding tanks and oil trucks will remain until the resource is used to its

Sunset on the Tallgrass Prairie with a pump jack. Inset: Activity at the Prairie View Church, 1923. The church is in the middle of an oil field.

Pump photo by Harvey Payne; inset photo, Western History Collection, University of Oklahoma Library

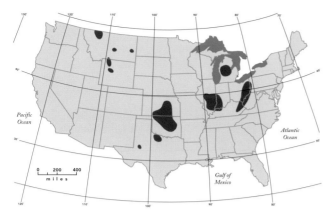

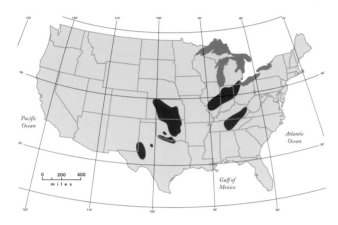

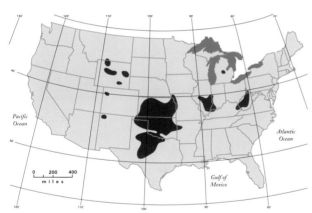

Locations of oil- and gas-producing rocks. Top, Mississippian age; middle, Ordovician age; bottom, Pennsylvanian age. Concentrations of rich producing rocks from all three periods are clustered in the area now known as Oklahoma. At right, a sketch of the western part of the Cherokee Sea of the Pennsylvanian age, which covered part of what is now Osage County, Oklahoma. The map shows present-day counties.

Maps by Chris Mitchell

practical limits. I also know that in time this, too, will pass — as all natural resources in the West are passing — used up, like the timber and gold and pristine waters. Meanwhile, we must learn to care better for what nature has given us.

The process of diminishment is well started. Everywhere on this prairie you can see the remains of ghost boom towns: Whizbang, Pearsonia, Nelagoney, Webb City, Foraker. A century ago the gumbo streets of those rough towns, their false-front hotels and brick banks did not exist, and now they are returning to tumble-down shacks, cement foundations, sod and grass. But the history of Osage oil does not begin with wooden derricks and the first gushers, it goes back to bedrock some 450 million years ago during the Ordovician age, and to limestone layers formed 300 million years ago in the Pennsylvanian age, when the Kansas and Oklahoma plains were a shallow, fairly level trough covered with warm-water seas.

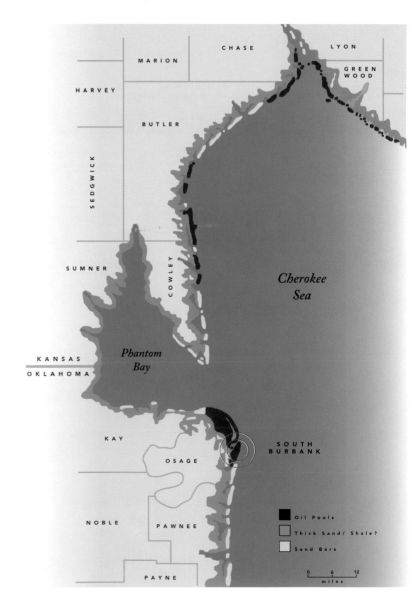

It is hard for us to imagine time in such magnitude, the minute accretion of muds and ancient forms of water-bred life slowly sinking to sandy bottoms. Sand upon sand, seas rising and receding and rising again over millions of years, life compressed into fossils, into layers of rock — that's what geologic history is. And we in our thronging population are just one of those layers, soon to be fossils, dust to dust, as the Bible tells our story.

Well, eventually, the crust of earth rose, and the sedimentary layers of limestone, shales, and sandstone also rose up and were folded into synclines and anticlines forming the characteristic domes and mounds and outcroppings of the south central Great Plains. Under such pressure, some rich swamps and sandy fossil beds liquified into huge deposits of oil, their vapors compressed into volatile gasses. In the unselfconscious poetry of geology, oil-bearing sands are called horizons. Strange to think of a horizon say 3,000 feet under the grass.

Wild Hog Creek at the Tallgrass Prairie.

Photo by Harvey Payne

The road between Oilton and Cushing. Below, the Magnolia Petroleum Company moving oil equpiment across the Cimarron.

OSAGE COUNTY is divided into two distinct topographies. From a rock-ribbed escarpment near the center of the region the land falls gently eastward in alternating belts of sandstones and shales. The Caney River, which courses along the Kansas border at the northern edge of the county, runs southeast and empties into the Verdigris River, as do the parallel slanting Sand, Bird, and Hominy Creek watersheds. West of the central escarpment are rolling prairies underpinned by a series of limestone layers and beds of shale. The watersheds of western Osage County — Buck, Grayhorse, Salt, and Drum creeks — flow in a southwesterly direction and drain into the Arkansas River, which marks the county's western and southern borders. In a swath down the central corridor that divides the two landforms rise the timbered Osage Hills, a southern flank of the Flint Hills of Kansas.

Pawhuska, the county seat and Osage Agency, sits astride Bird Creek just east of the center of the county. The Tallgrass Prairie Preserve lies northwest of Pawhuska in the Sand Creek drainage, and includes both limestone and sandstone formations. Bartlesville, the home of Phillips Petroleum, stands outside the northeastern corner of the county, and Tulsa, its commercial kingdom, sprawls to the south.

The watersheds that break the land into discreet strips running on angles from north to south helped to keep pioneer land seekers from overrunning the Osage country. Scores of gorges and gullies restricted travel in the old days to a few roads and trails that offered good fords for crossings, and even today you will not find many paved throughways in the county's interior hills and prairies. The creek bottoms were also where oil made itself manifest. It was at seeps, springs, and outcrops along the waterways that travelers in this solitary corner of Indian Territory discovered signs of black gold.

For ages, Osage Indians and other local tribes knew the locations of oil seeps on the tallgrass plains of Missouri, Kansas, and Oklahoma, and used the oozing black substance as homeopathic cure for rheumatism and other ailments, as well as for animal medication. When European explorers and travelers first crossed the prairies, they also came upon mineral oil and tar springs and used the natural oils to treat sick stock or to grease their wagon wheels.

But as early as the mid-nineteenth century, the Osage Indians discovered that white people demanded large amounts of oil for commercial purposes beyond occasional personal needs. Unfortunately for the hunters, planters, and gatherers, their homelands lay above the great Mid-Continent oil fields that extend from Missouri south into Oklahoma. In 1860, the first oil wells were drilled in the Osage's home territory in Missouri; and after the Civil War, production expanded to Fort Scott, near the center of their Kansas reservation. Soon, the Neosho River country that had been the Indians' ancestral land was transformed into a center of energy production. So, when the Osages moved to their new Oklahoma reservation in the 1870s, they were already aware of oil's potential worth, and the dangers development posed to tribal sovereignty and stability.

As Indian Territory opened to settlement, oil exploration also expanded along its eastern borders in the domain of the Five Civilized Tribes. Those nations looked to oil as a new source of income. The Cherokees allowed two wells within the city limits of

For ages, Osage Indians and other local tribes knew the locations of oil seeps on the tallgrass plains of Missouri, Kansas, and Oklahoma, and used the oozing black substance as homeopathic cure for rheumatism and other ailments, as well as for animal medication.

◈

Joe Beck, 1912, shooter for the Independent Torpedo Company
Osage County Historical Museum

Muskogee, and Oklahoma's first oil firm, the Chickasaw Oil Company, was a partnership between that tribe and a white doctor. Then, the Choctaws authorized their own Choctaw Oil and Refining Company, and the Creek Nation sold a 200,000 acre lease for oil exploration around Tulsa.

In the 1870s and 1880s, transportation and marketing to and from oil fields in remote Indian Territory posed huge problems. But by the 1890s, major companies had built pipelines around the edges of Oklahoma that tied Kansas and Texas production into a national network. Promoters knew they could build similar pipelines into the still-virgin country, extending the network. And the federal government had finally given railroads permission to cross the lands of the Five Civilized Tribes, which created a practical vehicle to transport workers, equipment, and tankers.

As cattle barons rode off into history's mythological sunset, the era of oil kings and mega-corporations was gathering steam. America entered the Automotive Age following Henry Ford's application of mass production techniques and demand for crude oil rose steadily. In 1900, 8,000 motor cars were registered in the U.S.A. By 1912, the number increased to 902,000. By 1927, Ford alone had sold 15 million Model T's. After World War I, when automobiles became common means of transportation, demand for oil and gasoline rose to fantastic heights. What a strange turn of fate for grasslanders in remote Osage County — Indians, cowboys, farmers, small-town settlers — to see their fortunes rise and fall throughout the 20th century with discoveries of oil and gas, the revolutionary technologies of energy industries, and the vagaries of international markets.

FOR A NUMBER OF YEARS, the Osage Indians and their agents sat back and watched the oil fever rise. Although several entrepreneurs pressed for permission to lease and explore for oil on Osage lands, the tribe held tight, but only by a slim margin. Blood politics divided tribal government — mixed bloods favoring development, fullbloods being especially wary.

The most persistent voice in the quest for Osage oil was John N. Florer, a trader who operated out of Grayhorse. An Indian friend had taken Florer to see a rainbow on the waters of Sand Creek, near Okesa, just west of Bartlesville. Florer knew what such a find promised, but he could not convince the tribe to sell him a lease. Even if they did, Florer would not have had the financial resources to take on the expensive business of drilling test wells. Seeking financial backing, he became acquainted with brothers Edwin and Henry Foster, bankers from Independence, Kansas, who were interested in expanding their holdings from cattle to oil.

From 1891 to 1896, the Fosters negotiated with the Osage National Council and with the Commissioner for Indian Affairs in Washington, D.C. for permission to secure a lease. Finally, after many political intrigues and the death of Henry Foster, Edwin Foster got what he wanted. His "blanket lease" allowed Foster exclusive rights for "prospecting and mining for oil and gas upon the Osage Reservation" — all of its 2,286 square miles. The

An oil well gusher at the Burbank Field, April 4, 1923, by Phillips Petroleum Company. Facing page, an oil well just brought in at Cushing.

Osage County Historical Museum; Cushing photo, Western History Collection, University of Oklahoma Library

lease would run for 10 years, and would be renewable for another decade. In return, the Osages would receive 10 percent of the value of all oil and $50 annually for each gas well.

Foster's first two wells in the northeastern corner of the Reservation were duds. But in 1897, just outside Bartlesville, Cudahy Oil struck oil at the Nellie Johnstone No. 1. The strike inspired Foster to try again along Butler Creek, just inside the Osage boundaries, five miles from the Nellie Johnstone. This time Foster hit pay dirt. His Wilkey No. 1 and Wilkey No. 2 were the first producing wells in the Osage. But Wilkey No. 1 had to be abandoned when attempts to "shoot it" with nitroglycerin produced a spurt of salt water instead of oil. Wilkey No. 2 produced 20 barrels a day, but Foster had not built adequate storage tanks, so most of the oil ran onto the ground. Indians scooped up what they could in buckets to use for home fuels.

Foster built wooden tanks for storage, but shipping his crude to markets posed difficult and expensive obstacles. His money was running out, so he formed a new company called Osage Oil to attract new investors. The company drilled eleven wells and struck oil in seven of them, but marketing remained an overwhelming problem. The wells were capped.

In 1899, the Atchison, Topeka, and Santa Fe Railroad reached Bartlesville, offering an accessible method of transportation for oil from that corner of Oklahoma. By May of 1900, the first tankers from the Osage region were steaming to Standard Oil's refinery in Neodesha, Kansas. Thus, according to oil chronicler Kenny A. Franks in his book *The Osage Oil Boom*, Bartlesville became the first oil boom town in Oklahoma. Then, during the first six years of the new century, Prairie Oil and Gas, a subsidiary of Standard Oil, expanded its pipeline system into Osage country. These first pipelines allowed the region's increasing production to flow north to Kansas, then clear to Standard Oil's huge refineries in Whiting, Indiana, or further east along the network to Brooklyn, New York. In another twenty years, metal pipe would criss-cross most of Oklahoma like a huge artery system, transporting oil and gas to Gulf Coast refineries as well to the north and east.

With these new means of transportation available, in 1903, Foster merged his previous companies into a larger organization called the Indian Territory Illuminating Oil Company (ITIO). When he died, his nephew, Henry V. Foster took over. Henry V. financed the growing venture by sub-contracting the huge Foster lease to 55 other companies. By 1904, production of Osage oil had swelled from 10,536 barrels annually to 1,868,260. Oil was discovered all over the county, in fields near Barnsdall, Avant, and Cleveland. Word spread, and other wildcatters and companies, large and small, protested Foster's monopoly. In 1906, when Foster's lease came up for renewal, the Osage National Council granted ITIO only 680,000 acres. The rest of the county would be up for grabs, leases sold to the highest bidders.

INDIAN VILLAGE - PAWHUSKA

Pawhuska as Indian village.
Drawing courtesy of the Osage County
Historical Society.

BEYOND THE EXCITEMENT OF OIL, the first years of the century were years of drastic political change for the Osage Nation. Although their reservation had remained intact while others in Indian Territory had been dispersed through allotment under the Dawes Act, the Osages knew they could not hold out forever. So when the terms of their own allotments were being negotiated in Washington, D.C., the Osages under the leadership of Chief James Bigheart and his son, Peter Bigheart, demanded communal ownership of all mineral rights lying under their lands.

James Bigheart had played a crucial role in Osage land policies from the time of the tribe's purchase of the Oklahoma reservation through the writing of its constitution and later negotiations with Congress concerning allotment. An educated Catholic who was mustered out as a lieutenant in the Union Army during the Civil War, Bigheart was a full-blood, but not a traditional or "blanket" Indian. A member of the Osage National Council, he believed that the salvation of his people would occur through capitalism — a kind of corporate ownership and management of tribal assets, which lay in and under the land. Bigheart was ahead of his time in such thinking, a smart and eloquent leader. The policies he fought to achieve enabled his people to become for a while the richest tribe in the United States.

The Osage Allotment Act, which was passed by Congress in 1906, ordered the principal chief to prepare an accurate roll of all tribal members. The magic number of that final roll totalled 2,229 Osage people: 926 fullbloods; 1,303 mixed bloods, including non-Indian adoptees such as a white woman who had lived with the tribe for years. In addition to individual allotments of tribal lands, the enrolled members would soon receive a "headright," which made them and their heirs equal shareholders in royalties derived from tribally-held mineral rights. Children born after the tribal roll was closed in 1907 were members of the tribe, but could not own a share of tribal headright income unless they inherited it from a relative. This divisive policy split the tribe forever after into wealthy "haves" and unlucky "have-nots."

A portion of energy income was set aside for the education of Osage children, and an additional amount served as an emergency fund for the tribe. The remainder would be paid to the tribal government to distribute among the 2,229 headright enrollees and/or their heirs. Under the 1906 act, no individual Osage allottee could sell his or her headright without approval of the U. S. Secretary of the Interior. All minerals and mineral rights were reserved to the tribe for 25 years, or as otherwise determined by Congress. Proceeds of those mineral rights would be distributed among headright holders. In 1931, the prohibition was renewed by Congress for another 25 years, and continues to this day, insuring the continuity of the headright system.

The original Osage oil boom lasted more than a quarter of a century. Between 1901 and 1928 Osage County oil fields produced nearly 475 million barrels of crude oil. Prices ranged from around half a dollar a barrel in 1915 to a high of $3.50 in 1920. Prices plunged in the depression of the early 1930s, dipping below 25 cents a barrel at one point in 1931 but not before pioneer oilmen such as J. Paul Getty, E. W. Marland, and Frank Phillips gleaned huge fortunes from their Osage holdings. They had been helped in 1916 when Henry V. Foster's lease expired and all of Osage County became available for speculation.

In the beginning, the tribe auctioned its mineral leases by sealed bid. A change of rules in 1916 allowed leases for Osage oil fields to be available to anyone who wanted to bid on them during periodic public auctions at the old Agency in Pawhuska. Before long, auction days in Pawhuska became great events, more entertaining than circuses because huge fortunes changed hands.

Several times a year, bankers, speculators, wildcatters, independent producers, and buyers for big oil corporations would gather under the "million dollar elm" on the grounds of

An Osage camp in Pawhuska, Oklahoma Territory, March 3, 1906.

Osage County Historical Museum; Osage Tribal Museum Archives and Library

The million dollar elm, under which auctions of the Osage mineral rights were held. The house of the Osage agent is in the background.

Courtesy of the Archives & Manuscripts Division of the Oklahoma Historical Society

An Osage woman prepares food next to her automobile, ca. 1926-1927.

the Osage Agency on the hill overlooking town. There, ace auctioneer Colonel E. E. Walters (Colonel was his first name) worked his magic. Sales began at 10:30 a.m. and continued until dark, with breaks for lunch and dinner. By nightfall the haul might reach three million dollars. A record was set in February 1920. This was just after the giant Burbank oil field in the western part of the county had been discovered, and everyone wanted in on the bonanza. Colonel Walters worked the crowd for $6,056,950 and the thankful Osages presented him with a diamond ring. That record was topped in 1924, when a one-day lease sale garnered $10,888,000.

Suddenly Osage headright owners found themselves rich. Like most folks who strike gold, they embarked on a flamboyant, all-stops-out party. The rush to spend money was highest during quarterly distributions of headright royalties at the Agency in Pawhuska. Disbursements lasted about five days, with fullbloods paid first, then the mixed bloods. Traditional Indians would arrive at the Agency, as one witness described it, "in their gypsum-rubbed leggings, their moccasins, silken shirts, wide beaded belts, wampum necklaces, silver arm bands and otter-tail pieces, the traditional scalplocks protruding from their shaven heads as they visited among themselves."

During their glory days on the prairies, the Osages had measured wealth by the number of horses a family owned. Now, they bought new cars. The Osages loved fancy cars. There were possibly more Pierce Arrows in Pawhuska than on Wall Street. For a time, Pawhuska had the largest Buick dealership in the U.S.A. But often the new owners did not know how to drive their shiny vehicles, so they hired white chauffeurs. Or they treated cars that would not run as they might have treated a broke-down horse. Local legend has it that if an Indian ran out of gas, he or she might abandon the car, hitch a ride to town and buy a new one.

The Indians also bought into European ideas of luxury — mansions, diamonds, fur coats, imported china, travel. Some Osages rode steamships to France, where they visited long-lost relatives who had gone there with Buffalo Bill's Wild West Show. In 1919, one group rented an entire Pullman car to take them on a Colorado vacation. Some Osage families owned ample brick homes but preferred to live in traditional huts on their lawns, right next to their new grand pianos. Kenny Franks, in his book about the Osage oil boom, says: "In a single day in 1927, one Osage woman spent $12,000 for a fur coat, $3,000 for a diamond ring, $5,000 for a new automobile, $7,000 for furniture, $600 to ship the furniture to California, and $12,800 for some land in Florida." Such items might be more for show than for actual use.

Seeking profit, fortune hunters arrived. Business people, lawyers, and hustlers flocked to Pawhuska, which was the banking and trading center, the place where money flowed. Most had no scruples when it came to bilking Indians. In those days, many Osages were easy targets. They did not speak English and could not read or write, signing credit vouchers with x's, running up huge debts. Prices for Indian buyers were jacked up to five or six times their value. Even ordinary items such as a pair of one-dollar silk stockings would be

The Osage Tribal Council at Frank Phillips's ranch, March, 1931. Phillips purchased mineral leases from the Osage. He is shown in a Plains-style war bonnet given to him by the tribe. The traditional Osage headdress was a beaver bandeau like the one worn by Chief Bacon Rind, (front row, second from left).

Courtesy of Woolaroc Museum, Bartlesville, Oklahoma. Photo by Griggs Studio

sold to an Osage woman for five dollars; five-dollar shoes might sell for twenty-five dollars.

Becoming alarmed by lavish spending habits of the Osage headright owners and the fraudulent practices of traders and business people, courts appointed white "guardians" (usually lawyers) for "incompetent" enrollees and minor children. "Incompetent" was a legal term used by the government to stipulate Indians of certain "blood ratios": over fifty percent Osage blood would need a guardian; under fifty percent would not. Such rules had been set in 1906 to protect Osage allotment holders in the selling of their lands. Extended to include management of oil royalties, the arrangement offered new opportunities for corruption.

Many guardians abused their power. They held the purses, and so were free to mismanage estates, charge exorbitant fees, and steal from their charges. One guardian sold his ward a car worth $200 for $1,250, pocketing the difference. Another charged an annual fee of $1,200 to manage his ward's $4,000 income. Still another mismanaged his client's $100,000 estate so badly that despite an annual headright income of $12,000, the hapless ward discovered he was not only broke, but $20,000 in debt. By 1925, a group of 600 legal guardians had milked over eight million dollars from the Osages they had been hired to protect.

THE STORY OF OSAGE HEADRIGHTS is complex and often violent. White people married headright owners for their money, then left them, receiving huge alimony payments. The Oklahoma Supreme Court aided the process of diluting Indian ownership of headrights in 1917, when the judges ruled that only legal marriages could be recognized in headright litigation. Thus, many traditional Osages who had been married in tribal ceremonies found that their marriages were invalid with regard to passing on headrights to their spouses or children.

The abuse accelerated beginning with the murder of Anna Brown, a wealthy headright holder from Grayhorse, in 1921. More and more unexplained murders took place in the Grayhorse and Fairfax areas and then throughout the county in what came to be called the Osage Reign of Terror. Before it ended, at least 22 innocent men, women, and children had been killed, although some researchers believe the murders ran into the hundreds. The story is long and convoluted, but at its heart were a group of white outlaws who would do anything to get hold of Indian headrights. The conspiracy involved white men marrying into headright families, then hiring thugs to murder every other eligible heir so that they could inherit the royalties.

It was a chaotic, lawless mess, but one trail of evidence led to an improbable chief conspirator — a popular Fairfax cattleman, businessman, and banker named William Hale. Hale had covered his tracks by hiring new outlaws to murder his original hired guns, but he did not count on his nephew and co-conspirator, Ernest Burkhart, turning state's evidence in a confession. The F.B.I., which had entered the case, finally brought the men to trial in federal court. In 1929, Hale and his cowboy associate John Ramsey, as well as the hapless Burkhart, were convicted of murder. Ironically, Hale served only eleven years of his ninety-nine-year sentence, paroled through political connections in 1947 despite protests from the Osage Tribal Council. Ramsey was paroled four months later, but Burkhart spent twelve more years in prison. Even after this conviction, scores of Osage murders remained unsolved.

In 1925, in an attempt to remedy unscrupulous manipulations of headright ownerships, the federal government made it illegal for persons who were not descended from the original 2,229 Osage enrollees to inherit headrights. However, this restriction applied only to tribal members of fifty percent or more Osage blood. In the meantime, several Protestant churches and a few large oil companies had finagled headright ownerships, and the way was left open for transfer of mixed-blood headrights. Thus, according to Sean Standing Bear, the young Osage/Sioux director of the tribal museum in Pawhuska, Osage wealth was distributed to such unlikely headright holders as the peroxide-blonde movie star Jean Harlow, rather than to disenfranchised Osage people.

Portraits of the Osage.

Courtesy of the Osage Tribal Museum, Archive and Library

OLD AND NEW

An Osage family with a new Euro-American style house and traditional Osage structure in the background. Below, a studio portrait of an Osage woman and her two daughters in western dress.

Osage Tribal Museum Archive and Library, Pawhuska

By 1978, Congress mandated that non-Indian headright owners could inherit only a life estate in the tribe's mineral rights. This remedy came late in the game, at the peak of the OPEC-instigated worldwide energy crisis, which began in 1973 with the Arab oil embargo, then recharged in 1979 during the Iranian hostage situation. Those events touched off another oil rush and soaring prices, putting headrights at a premium, for during the late seventies and early eighties, royalties rose from $8,000 to $12,000 per quarter and everyone wanted in on the bonanza.

Since 1983, however, Osage oil production and prices have been in a steady decline. If you were to chart the fortunes of Osage headright holders over time, you would see a mountain range with peaks and valleys. According to oil historian Franks, "after the initial Osage oil boom the average monthly income of a headright dropped to $50." And following the second Osage oil boom in the 1950s, oil income dropped again. Since the latest boom, says Geoffrey Standing Bear, "there has been a ten percent a year production curve downward."

Geoffrey Standing Bear, Sean's older brother, is a lawyer. When we talked in his well-appointed office in Pawhuska, he explained that the old tribal constitution set up a governing body representing headright holders only. "If you had two headrights you were twice as human as someone who did not have a headright. It got property and political rights confused."

This oligarchical system lasted until 1994, when the Standing Bears and other reformers led the tribe to adopt a new, more democratic, one-person, one-vote constitution. But serious social problems created by the nearly one-hundred-year-old headright division of mineral wealth remain. Many headright owners and their heirs invested wisely, managed their estates, moved to California, Florida, or Tulsa, became educated professionals — lawyers, ballet dancers, business people, ranchers — solid citizens of the American middle and upper classes. Some, who had lost their headrights or who had never been included on the original roll, remained poor, landless, and powerless.

Nevertheless, most Osages are proud that the tribe held onto mineral rights on their former reservation lands. That decision brought more than $300,000,000 in royalties and bonuses to the tribe and its headright owners. It is also true that beyond the injustices and family tragedies caused by the great flow of riches from the energy horizons under their prairies, the Osage people retained their ancient status as one of the most wealthy groups of American Indians.

THE FIRST OSAGE OIL BOOM cast wealth in all directions. It helped to create oil kings and huge corporations such as Frank Phillips and Phillips Petroleum, E. W. Marland and Continental Oil (Conoco), William G. Skelly and Skelly Oil Company, and J. Paul Getty of the Getty Oil Company. It also created work for a host of skilled and unskilled laborers who found hard, challenging, and often good-paying jobs in the oil fields.

Out in the country, the first professional to sniff out a possible oil pool was a geologist, known as a "rock hound" or "pebble pup." Then came explorer/drillers and entrepreneurs called "wildcatters," who would drill a wildcat well in a farmer's hog pen or a rancher's pasture. Oil scouts and curious locals would gather around the wooden derrick if a strike seemed imminent. Word of a gusher spread fast. Soon neighbors would be playing host to more oil company geologists who gathered data to verify the area's potential before their employers would bid on a lease.

Once a lease had been secured by the company's landman or "lease hound," the land above the oil well location had to be cleared and burned — a nasty, dawn-to-dusk job, especially if the place was thick with scrub oaks and brush. Unskilled laborers who cut and burned were paid about $120 a month.

Then came the teamsters called "mule-skinners" or "mule peelers," who hauled lumber and machinery to the site so that derricks and drills could be built. Teamsters drove wagons, and later trucks, day and night through rough terrain, and were well paid for their labors. Kenny Franks reports one skinner who says he made $100,000 one year — a sum rarely reached by any worker, even when the boom was in high gear and competition was hot.

The earliest drilling structures were wooden cable tool derricks, built on the spot under the supervision of a foreman called a "tool pusher." These structures rose 72 feet above the

... most Osages are proud that the tribe held onto mineral rights on their former reservation lands. That decision brought more than $300,000,000 in royalties and bonuses to the tribe and its headright owners. It is also true that beyond the injustices and family tragedies caused by the great flow of riches from the energy horizons under their prairies, the Osage people retained their ancient status as one of the most wealthy groups of American Indians.

⚮

A view of Cushing fields. At right, capping a well six miles east of Henryetta, Oklahoma. Middle of facing page, the nitro wagon beside a wooden derrick, Cushing.

Western History Collection, University of Oklahoma Library

ground, were usually 22 feet wide at the bottom and narrowed to 62 inches at the top. Rig-builders raced to get their derricks up, doing everything from digging cellars for footings to sawing and nailing. One rigger named Charlie Storms spoke about the brutal pace: "I've seen rig-builders . . . [urinate] while they was working. They didn't have time to take out to the brush, and they was so damned tired they just couldn't control themselves anyway." Wages for riggers ran about $12 a day.

When the derrick was up, a drilling crew arrived. A cable tool derrick drove a metal line with a bit attached at its bottom end deep into the ground. In the early stages, the bit would be about 18 inches wide. "The bit rises and falls," explained an old-time driller, and "it keeps turning, striking at a different angle each time. It pounds a hole, it doesn't bore

one." Throughout the process, the workers pumped water into the bottom of a drill hole, which turned the pulverized earth into mud. Then they replaced the bit with a sand pump or bailer, which lifted the mud and rock cuttings to the top of the hole before drilling recommenced.

To keep the well open, crews lowered casings into the hole, starting with pipe 18 inches wide and reducing diameters as the cavity plunged to 2,000 feet or more. As the hole deepened, the size of bits also got smaller to fit within the pipe. Before the advent of gasoline engines, all of this up-and-down work was powered by steam-run engines attached to boilers. Exploding boilers and high-pressure steam hoses were among the main hazards of the always-dangerous work of drilling. With no medical insurance, no workmen's compensation, old-time drilling crews worked 10 to 12 hour "tours" for wages of from $6 to $9 a day.

By the late 1930s, most wooden derricks had been replaced by pre-cut steel towers called rotary rig derricks, which lowered a rotating metal drill instead of the pounding bit. During the transition, competition among "jarheads" (cable drillers) and "swivelnecks" (rotary drillers) often ended in drunken street fights in the ramshackle boom towns where oil workers lived.

The work-inspired lingo of the oil fields included men called "roustabouts," who repaired and maintained wells, and "pumpers," who kept the pumps running, and a tough bunch of hand laborers called "pipeline cats."

Not all oil-field hands were men. Women worked in service roles — cooking, providing housing, cleaning, sewing.

Laying underground pipelines to transport crude from the huge oil fields to storage facilities and refineries was no job for softies. This was back-straining, rock-busting manual labor: digging ditches; screwing together heavy pipejoints; burying pipe — everything done by hand in mud, frost, and summer heat. Pipeline cats were the peons of the oil field workers, but a muscle-bound bunch respected by other more skilled and high-paid workers. "It takes a real man to be a pipeline cat," said Billy Bates, who had been a cat himself for many years. "The work would kill the average man. They can't take it."

Billy explained the job and its special language. "A stabber is the man who runs the pipelaying gang. He stabs the new joint of pipe into the joint just laid, and gives all the orders to the cats." But before any jointlaying took place, a right-of-way gang had to clear the brush, and a ditch-digging gang had to open a trough, and then other men would paint and wrap the pipes so they wouldn't rust quickly and leak oil into the ground. After the screwed pipe was down and ready, the ditch-diggers would have to take up their shovels again to cover it.

Like chain gangs or Marines on the march, the pipeline crew labored to a steady beat, the stabber singing out his orders:

> All right, cats, lets get going and roll some pipe. You pipe-hustlers, bring up the next joint. Come on get the lead out. All right, cats, up in the round eye. There she is. Catch her there, jack. She's loose as a goose. Wrap your tails around her, cats, and give her an honest roll . . . . Take off your tails, cats, and put on the hooks. Deuce and four. Ace and three. Now all together. Hit her like you live. Hard.

Eventually, backhoes would replace ditch-diggers, and welded pipe replaced hand-screwed pipe. Machines made work easier, but the singing stopped. "You don't have no stabber singing out the orders," said Billy Bates with a touch of regret. "No laughing, proud of their work cats."

Not all oil-field hands were men. Women worked in service roles — cooking, providing housing, cleaning, sewing. They were a tough-skinned and hard-laboring bunch. You can taste these women's voices in the words of an Oklahoma oil-field cook named Sadie Duggett, quoted from Anne Morgan and Rennard Strickland's anthology *Oklahoma Memories:*

> Lots of people act like they think I'm off my nut when I tell 'em I'm in the oil game, kind of. They got the idea that the only thing there is to oil is a bunch of guys drilling a well, cussing and hollering and getting drunk on payday. But it ain't. One of the most important things 'bout oil or anything else, far as that goes, is eating, and I kind of made it my job to see that all the guys 'round the oil field get enough to eat. These smart punks that think eating ain't connected with the oil game and that the field ain't no place for a woman can go to hell as far as I'm concerned.

Workers these days, complained Sadie, don't eat like they used to, don't eat enough to keep a grown man going. "They could set down and eat a half-dozen eggs, a side of bacon apiece, four cups of coffee, and push all of that down with a loaf of bread and a couple of pieces of pie." I guess if work was going to kill a guy anyway, Sadie's food would help him die happy.

OSAGE COUNTY never experienced an agricultural land rush like the opening of the Cherokee Outlet. Even after allotment, the big bluestem prairies remained nearly empty of humans. There were great herds of cattle to be sure, and cowboys, and some farms, and ranching towns, and Osage Indian encampments. Life remained simple, seasonal, and slow, but only for a few years. Then the oil boom transformed the quiet world.

Ramona, 1906. Prior to statehood many small towns in the Indian nations had saloons even though they were illegal. This one in the Cherokee Nation at Ramona had a fairly large stock of bottled goods as well as a patronized bar.

Western History Collection, University of Oklahoma Library

Most large-scale ranchers in the Osage felt threatened by oil people invading their domain. They did not benefit from the oil business except for damages collected from road building or oil and salt-water spills on their properties. But the commerce associated with oil was a godsend to many small farmers and ranchers as well as to business people in the boom towns. In a local history, *Osage County Profiles,* several old-time country people fondly remembered their share of the bonanza.

A drawing of the oil fields by Oklahoma artist Doel Reed, 1928.

Collection of Kent and Jeanette Young

Whizbang, Oklahoma, in its
heyday. Below, the Tonkawa
Oil Field with Three Sands in
foreground.

Western History Collection, University
of Oklahoma Library

"Practically all the work in the Shidler oil field was done by horses and the demand for hay, oats, and corn was insatiable," recalled Naomi Custer Maze. T. W. Price was struck by "the beautiful work horses used in those days to move oil field equipment, such as steam boilers and steam engines to drilling locations. I remember seeing eight large Percheron horses decked out in the most elaborate harness with tassels on their bridles pulling one steam boiler past our house east of Hominy."

Beginning about 1905, whenever a major oil field was discovered, a town grew up nearby. Boom towns usually followed the spur lines of railroads, gathering helter skelter around stations where oil and equipment were shipped in or shipped out. During the boom years from 1906 until 1928, more than a score of new towns spread like exotic weeds in Osage County under an artificial forest of derrick towers and refinery smokestacks.

The towns housed thousands of itinerant workers and provided necessary services. Before autos and pickups, wagons hauled materials from the railroads to the oil fields. You needed livery stables for work horses and mules, and feed stores, and hotel rooms for teamsters, drillers, bosses, and the supply salesmen who kept the machinery coming. Carpenters and cooks, grocers and bootmakers, saloon keepers and gamblers, school teachers and ladies of the night — all found at least temporary homes and employment in boom towns such as Whizbang.

Whizbang exists no more. Once it mushroomed at the edge of the wondrous Burbank oil field, near Shidler, not far from the southwestern corner of the Tallgrass Prairie Preserve. Whizbang was the wildest of the wild boom towns. Some say its name was inspired by a girlie magazine called Captain Billy's Whizbang. Others say the town earned its name because it "whizzed all day and banged all night." Another person claimed it was named after a Kansas City prostitute known as "Whizbang Red."

During the boom years from 1906 until 1928, more than a score of new towns spread like exotic weeds in Osage County under an artificial forest of derrick towers and refinery smokestacks.

A dim photo in the archives of the Osage County Historical Society shows the bleak beginnings of the town: an open sloping grassland from which about sixteen derricks rise; a series of curving dirt tracks that circle the derricks; a small, brush-lined stream with a line of cottonwoods along its banks; seven shotgun shacks and one tent lined up behind the cottonwoods. Soon there would be a Phillips Petroleum plant and a bunkhouse for its workers. Ghost-town chronicler John Morris tells us that Whizbang had a railroad station and large oilfield supply houses, and, by the early 1920s, "more than three hundred business buildings ranging in size from the very small hamburger shacks to two moderately large hotels."

By that time, the town had changed its name to DeNoya because U.S. Post Office officials would not handle mail for a place with the indecorous name of Whizbang. The new name honored a wealthy Osage Indian rancher and member of the National Council upon whose allotment the town sat.

"Many people living in DeNoya were not connected to the oil companies," says Morris. "Shootings were more frequent in DeNoya than in other towns in the Burbank area. The bank was robbed twice, and it wasn't safe for a woman to be on the streets of Whizbang after dark."

Housing was at a premium in boom towns — especially when a worker needed shelter for his wife and family. Kenny Franks relates one story, told by an oil field worker named

BOOMTOWN
ENTERTAINMENT

Left, a frame-and-tent saloon
in Lawton soon after the 1901
land opening. Below, a saloon
in Anadarko in 1901. Facing
page, the Buckhead Saloon in
Norman, 1901. Business was
brisk enough for two
bartenders.

Western History Collection, University
of Oklahoma Library

George Overmyer. George and his wife, Brenda, bought a boxcar shack in Whizbang, next
door to the Pettigrew Theatre where Brenda played piano to accompany silent movies.
Brothels surrounded their home, but the Overmyers felt lucky to have a place at all. One
day, an oil field tough guy came over and claimed he owned the house. The Overmyers
refused to budge. Then the
guy stomped into the theatre
where Brenda worked and
threatened her with an axe.
Spunky Brenda persuaded
some professional wrestlers
who were performing there to
help her hold the guy at bay
until her husband returned
from work. George fought the
man in the middle of Main
Street, knocked him out, and
told him to leave Brenda
alone. Instead, the guy pitched
a tent across the street from
the Overmyer's, and after
George went off to work,
shouted threats at Brenda. So
George bought Brenda a pistol and gave her shooting

lessons for all the world to see. "After that," said George, "there was no more problem."

Communities such as Whizbang had no water wells, no sewage treatment, no doctors or churches. Typhoid and flu epidemics were constant threats. Makeshift schools had a hard time finding teachers, especially because teachers' contracts stipulated that they must comport themselves as moral models for their students. Young school marms could not play cards or dance. They were forbidden to cut their hair short, like flappers, and could not marry. Weekends were to be spent in town, so everyone could see that they were behaving themselves. But on Friday nights, even schoolteachers could go to the movies. In Whizbang, that was not a far walk, for during the day, the theatre was the school, with benches for seats and boards for desks, until enough tax money was collected to build a four-room frame schoolhouse.

For entertainment, decent townfolk held dances, attended boxing matches, waited for circuit-riding magicians, singers, animal shows, and Chautauquas to pass through. Once, Rudolf Valentino stopped off in Pawhuska. And a touring dirigible offered a glimpse of aviation-age technology. Often children ran from classrooms to watch the latest gusher blow in. More often they played hookey for the sport of it.

"A kid can't study books in a boom town," said one old hand. "Us oil-field kids played hookey every day; we fought like wildcats just for the fun of fighting; we stole everything we could get our hands on to sell for junk to get money for shows, chewing tobacco, cigarettes, and whiskey. We'd even pool all our money together and get a whore."

Vice and violence ran together like bootleg liquor and blood. The largest population in any oil boom town were young, unmarried laborers who worked hard and itched to spend their wages on equally hard play. Although liquor was banned in the region while it was still a reservation, and continued to be banned under the Oklahoma constitution after statehood, bootleggers thrived and rum-runners came in from west of the Arkansas River, stashing their barrels in caves along its limestone banks. Many bootleggers were women, who cooked up a brew made of 120 proof alcohol, with chewing tobacco or creosote for color, and a bit of sulphuric acid for an added kick.

Dancing girls were available for a quarter a dance, fifteen cents going to the dancehall owner, a dime to the girl. If you took a girl to a room in back, she and the owner split the fee.

Every boom town had at least one brothel, and although some madams and prostitutes were professionals, many camp followers were poor farm girls looking for money to survive, or hoping to escape the loneliness and daily grind of arduous work on isolated prairie homesteads. Such girls were easy pickings.

"I can pick one out just by looking," said one madam. "Shuffling their feet and slobber all over their mouths, they're so hungry. . . . Some lady eases up to her and gets acquaninted and feeds her . . . and she'll follow her around like a damned dog. Get her in bed once, and she's with you from then on. Can't go back then and wouldn't if she could."

The largest population in any oil boom town were young, unmarried laborers who worked hard and itched to spend their wages on equally hard play.

BUSINESS of both the legal and shady kind was extremely profitable for boom town entrepreneurs. It was also dangerous. Hijackers roamed everywhere, and some roads, such as Pistol Hill between Shidler and Whizbang, were avoided by any smart person carrying a pocketful of gold. A businessman got awful nervous in the process of shipping his money to the bank. Gun-packing railroad agents charged extra to guard money until it was shipped, and one notorious agent used funds deposited with him to invest in oil leases. Lucky for his depositors, he struck oil and paid them all back.

Banks were robbed often, hijackers raided the U.S. mails, and bandits even went out to oil rigs and stole what they could from workers on the spot. Although some criminals were amateurs who figured stealing was more fun than sweaty labor, others rode in profession-al gangs with leaders like Elmer McCurdy, a train robber who was killed in a 1911 shootout.

The story of McCurdy's body is one of the most bizarre I have heard. The corpse was purchased by a street carnival show, then mummified and exhibited for 14 years. Later, covered with wax, it was used as a dummy, then stored in a warehouse, and finally bought by Spooney Sing for his Los Angeles wax museum. Sing rented some of his dummies out to be used on television shows. McCurdy's body ended up in an episode of the "Six Million Dollar Man," where it was hung from a gallows. The arm fell off. Inside it the astounded prop man found a bone. McCurdy's body is now buried in Guthrie, back home after 65 years.

If criminals in the boom towns were bad, the wandering class of lawmen who also fol-lowed the booms could be even worse. Many were arrogant, quick to use their guns, and tended to live by their own laws. Whizbang's peace officer, José Alvardo, for example, murdered at least two people, was tried and acquitted twice, maybe shot his girlfriend, and eventually was arrested in Texas for bank robbery.

The Ku Klux Klan tried to scare order into some towns; vigilante lynchings also took a toll. But the Wild West of shootouts withered as the oil business settled down. Companies built their own camps to house workers; refineries imported middle managers, who arrived with respectable families; and laborers with steady jobs grew older, got mar-ried and sedate. According to Kenny Franks, "Preachers and churches followed the women and children," and communities demanded responsible governments. As the middle class rose, boom towns declined.

Of course, they would have fallen anyway, for after 1928, oil and gas production glut-ted depressed national markets, prices took a dive, and the single-industry boom towns folded. In 1931, huge new Texas oil fields out-produced Oklahoma's by large margins, but the Oklahoma wells kept pumping until prices fell to nearly nothing. Then Oklahoma's governor, Johnston Murray, closed the fields until prices would become more stable. Jobs for nomadic oil workers disappeared and many took the trail to California, dispossessed along with Okie tenant farmers. Overwhelming forces such as drought and the Great

Depression had joined with human greed and ignorance to create a situation where the natural resources of soil and oil could no longer support the laborers of Oklahoma. Will Rogers, who knew Oklahoma and California better than most, quipped that the 1930s Dust Bowl exodus raised the calibre of culture in both states.

In the mid-thirties demand for oil began a slow rise, and with leadership from Oklahoma's oilman-turned-governor, E. W. Marland, the southwestern oil-producing states joined in an interstate compact to stabilize prices. By then, both farmers and oil producers realized the dangers of unchecked boom-and-bust resource extraction. Many farmers turned to soil conservation, and some powerful oilmen attempted to regulate their industries.

During the shift from boom to bust, and then toward a more stable economy, some of the older and larger trading centers in Osage County, such as Pawhuska, Hominy, Barnsdall, and Fairfax, settled into viable centers of civilization and trade. Others, like Wynona, slowly shrank, or like Foraker and Pearsonia, became outposts for a few, lone, holdout families. Nelagoney, Webb City, and scores of deserted hamlets simply crumbled in the prairie winds. Whizbang/DeNoya, perhaps because it was so ornery, held on until 1942.

Facing page, sunrise on the Preserve in late summer. Below, an outline map of areas of Kansas, Oklahoma, and adjoining states shows the major structural features.

Photo by Harvey Payne

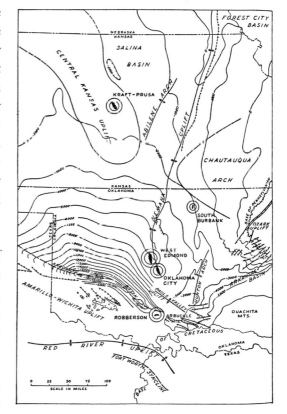

THE STORY OF OSAGE OIL encompasses one more boom in the 1950s, then a long, slow decline, and a third boom in the late 1970s and early 1980s. The discoveries of the 1950s were motivated by increased demand following severe gas rationing during World War II, but new technologies rather than exploration were responsible for the surge in production. In 1949, Stanolind Oil developed a method of oil recovery called the fracturing process. Operators forced fluid and sand into an oil-bearing formation at high pressure, creating cracks and propping them open so the oil could flow. From 1952 to 1956, this process allowed recovery of significant crude oil reservoirs in the Osage County oil fields. By 1956, many new, deep wells had been drilled out on the prairies. More steel derricks appeared, and more tilting pumps.

Most significant to large-scale oil recovery in the Osage was a technology called waterflooding that uses injected water pressure to force oil out of reservoir rock and into producing wells. Waterflooding took water from the Arkansas River, piped it in 30-inch lines to the once prolific Burbank fields, then forced the water at great pressure through a series of injection wells into the permeable rock strata of oil-bearing horizons forcing the entrapped oil to nearby wells, from which it could be pumped to the surface.

Waterflooding revived the oil industry in Osage County and brought new prosperity to towns such as Burbank, Wynona, and Pawhuska. It also

One rainy autumn afternoon ... in Pawhuska, I was struck by the swift and radical disjunctions of history. Nearby, dim and golden in a premature dusk, loomed the cut sandstone buildings of the old Osage Agency, more than one hundred years old. I shivered in the cold light, looked down from the hilltop of museums and monuments to the modest homes of the town below, and pondered the legacies of oil that lay so heavily on the peoples of this land.

⁂

carried much-needed wealth back to the Osage tribe and its headright owners. In 1940, annual individual headrights paid only $945; demand for oil during and after World War II increased prices, and by 1949 an annual headright was worth $1,560; after waterflooding began in 1950, annual payments rose to $3,355 in 1954; then they dropped again, to be revived in the 1970s by the boom triggered by the Arab oil embargo.

Jeanne Ronda, a scholar who has been researching energy developments in Osage County from their beginnings to the present, and whose work has informed this chapter, reports that Osage oil wells in 1977 produced 11,146,128 barrels. In 1978, operators drilled 602 wells. In 1979, the Osage Tribe brought in oil revenues worth $31 million; and in 1980 a headright cashed in at $26,680 a year — the highest payment ever. Then prices began to decline, bottoming out in 1986.

Oklahomans are used to this economic see-saw. They are waiting for the next peak, and maybe they are right to be hopeful, for hope is better than despair. As I write, 1,500 oil and gas employeess are still at work in Osage County. In 1994, the Osage produced more than 5 million barrels of oil, making the county the third-largest producer in the state. But Oklahomans know they cannot depend on energy for sustained economic health. They have already started to diversify their economy.

Today's Osage headright holders are much better educated and more worldly than their great-grandparents or parents. They have come to understand the ways of money and to use it wisely, but much of their old culture has been driven underground, buried with the tribe's elders. Many who stayed in Osage County have assimilated into the homogenous mix of small-town Oklahoma. And although some traditions remain, like the summer communal dances called I'n-Lon-Schka, the Osage language is mostly gone, and mixed-bloods far outnumber the few fullblood families.

Modern Osages continue to honor their warriors — heroes who fought under the American flag in World Wars I and II, the Korean War, and Vietnam. They admire members who achieved fame in modern society, such as the Oxford-educated historian and novelist John Joseph Mathews, or ballerinas Marjorie and Maria Tallchief who studied with Nijinsky and danced with the Ballet Russe de Monte Carlo and the Paris Opera Ballet, and Major General Clarence A. Tinker of the U.S. Air Force, who crashed into the Pacific Ocean in 1942 while leading a flight of LB-30 Liberator bombers over Wake Island. But there is a growing sentiment among tribal members to retrieve what they can from the ancient cultural traditions that give them a special identity.

Finally, it is only fair to mention that the oil industry that took so much wealth out of Osage County has returned some of it to communities in the form of gross production taxes, support of businesses and services, and jobs for local workers. Beyond such necessities, various companies have established philanthropic foundations, and individual oil entrepreneurs greatly benefited the cultural life of the region, the state, and the nation through charitable trusts and donations. To name a few notable examples: James A. Chapman helped endow the University of Tulsa; Robert McFarlin gave it its library;

Frank Phillips presented his Woolaroc Museum and Wildlife Preserve to the public; Waite Phillips gifted us with the Philbrook Museum of Art; E. W. Marland's fabulous Ponca City mansion and estate is now a public treasure; and Thomas Gilcrease gave Tulsa one of the world's great museums of western art.

ONE RAINY AUTUMN AFTERNOON, as I walked toward the old wooden derrick that guards the entrance to the Osage Tribal Museum in Pawhuska, I was struck by the swift and radical disjunctions of history. Nearby, dim and golden in a premature dusk, loomed the cut sandstone buildings of the old Agency, more than one hundred years old. I shivered in the cold light, looked down from the hilltop of museums and monuments to the modest homes of the town below, and pondered the legacies of oil that lay so heavily on the peoples of this land.

Later, in the damp silence after rain, I walked among rusting pumps in an abandoned oil field near Pearsonia on the Tallgrass Prairie Preserve. I noticed a few sterile, barren patches of earth that had been soaked in oil or brine. That evening, on a bluff above the horse trap, I stepped across muddy rivulets among deep tracks, watching erosion eat away soil on an old service road. Ben Johnson, Jr., had spoken of wells and streams made undrinkable from salt and brine — clear waters he drank when he was a boy. These were only a few of the industrial marks left on the Osage grasslands from a century of oil production.

Very little research exists that can accurately tally the impact oil production has had on the biological diversity of the tallgrass prairies. But at least on the preserve, studies are underway. A team including volunteers from the University of Tulsa, Conoco, Devon Energy Corporation, the BIA, and the Natural Resources Conservation Service are working with Bob Hamilton, the preserve's director of science and stewardship, to measure

A stem of sumac in autumn dew on the Prairie Preserve.
Photo by Harvey Payne

The story of Osage oil is an instructive tale that demonstrates the fragile nature of resource development and the dangers of a boom and bust economy for individuals, cultures, and the land from which wealth flows. As Aristotle pointed out long ago, every good story leads inevitably to a crisis of recognition, and beyond recognition to the working out of a resolution.

Switchgrass in a haze of prairie light.

Photo by Harvey Payne

~ ~ ~ BIG BLUESTEM ~ ~ ~

chloride in the soil, neutralize it with gypsum and other elements, and restore native vegetation.

Aside from helping to clean up environmental damage, several companies in the oil business have been generous in financial as well as in-kind contributions to the Tallgrass Prairie Preserve. Kerr-McGee, Phillips Petroleum, Chevron, Amoco, and the Williams Companies made significant cash contributions. Pipe for building bison fences and corrals has come from Helmerich & Payne, Sooner Pipe and Supply, Tektube, and other companies. Calumet Oil Company donated supplies and labor to build four scenic turnouts along the preserve's roads, as well as to grade and gravel the roads, and to install a new waterline at Headquarters. Chevron gave the Conservancy an $85,000 grant in 1991 to restore the Headquarters bunkhouse building. And in 1995 the corporation signalled its renewed interest in oil exploration throughout Osage County by donating a new "million dollar elm" to be planted on Osage Agency ground near the stump of the original famous money tree.

There is no question of stopping production on the preserve, for the Osage tribe still holds mineral rights to all land in Osage County, and they depend on what little income continues to trickle in from the oil fields. Today, according to statistics gathered by Conoco geologist Lucas Todd, there are 107 operating wells on the preserve, yielding only about 2 barrels a day per well. Over the years, production was higher, with 320 wells drilled on the Chapman-Barnard Ranch, of which 65 percent were productive. Soon, production may leap forward again, for in 1995, the Osage Tribe signed a $5 million dollar agreement with Chevron USA and Davis Brothers Oil to begin a high-tech, sophisticated exploration project in the county. Chevron will spend $4 million exploring certain areas with 3-D seismic technology, ranging into deeper horizons than anyone before could imagine. After one year, Chevron will lease the lands it finds most promising, returning the rest to open bidding by other producers. The Nature Conservancy will work with the tribe and with large and small producers so that future drilling on its land may occur in environmentally sensitive ways.

The story of Osage oil is an instructive tale that demonstrates the fragile nature of resource development and the dangers of a boom and bust economy for individuals, cultures, and the land from which wealth flows. As Aristotle pointed out long ago, every good story leads inevitably to a crisis of recognition, and beyond recognition to the working out of a resolution. This is where we find ourselves. We have realized the ephemeral nature of natural resource bonanzas, and we know that what endures is the life of the land. It seems clear to me that the final act of the Osage oil story will find its resolution on the Tallgrass Prairie Preserve as conservationists, Indians, ranchers, oilmen, and common citizens explore the renewable natural horizons of the prairie.

We have realized the ephemeral nature of natural resource bonanzas, and we know that what endures is the life of the land. It seems clear to me that the final act of the Osage oil story will find its resolution on the Tallgrass Prairie Preserve as conservationists, Indians, ranchers, oilmen, and common citizens explore the renewable natural horizons of the prairie.

White Hair's Town

"The towns that are most western have had to strike a balance between mobility and stability, and the law of sparseness has kept them from growing too big. They are the places where the stickers stuck, and perhaps were stuck; the places where adaptation has gone furthest."

WALLACE STEGNER

I HAVE SCUDDED INTO TOWN this October day on a prairie wind, and as I cruise along broad sun-wiped streets nearly empty of commerce, I wonder what it would be like to live in Pawhuska, to be one of its 3,825 remaining stalwart souls. On Main Street are two supermarkets, a liquor store, a STAX station, a Pizza Hut, a few small cafes, curio shops, and the old stone bank building that houses the Tallgrass Prairie Preserve's main office as well as some law firms. There is also the refurbished Constantine Theatre, which shows no movies these days but serves as a cultural center for the community, with home-grown theatricals and a stage for touring shows. I turn right on Kihekah Street into the colorful but depressed red-brick downtown — two blocks square, with diagonal streets centered around the Triangle Building.

Built mostly in the oil-rich early 1900s, Pawhuska was planned on the "federal" model, with the government seated on a hilltop and power filtering literally downwards. Thus, it seems older and more eastern than typical western towns which are designed in a T-shape, with perpendicular main streets emanating from a central railroad depot.

The city features 89 buildings on the National Historic Register. An octagonal house topped by a bandstand once dominated the village square, but that house was demolished long ago. The City Hall Building, which is made of cut native sandstone and began as the Osage Tribal Council House, celebrated its centennial in 1994. In the "Cathedral of the

Bluestem Restaurant window, downtown Pawhuska, Oklahoma.
Photos by Harvey Payne

Stained-glass windows from
the Immaculate Conception
Church in Pawhuska picturing
early Osage converts.

Photos by Harvey Payne

A J o u r n e y I n t o t h e T a l l g r a s s

Pawhuska in the 1880s.
Oklahoma Historical Society

Osage" housed in the Immaculate Conception Church, there are 22 stained-glass windows crafted by artisans from Italy and Germany which picture early Osage converts receiving the Word of God. And the 1920s County Courthouse, reached via a long, lamplit stairway ascending from downtown, sits in mock Grecian splendour atop Agency Hill. Framed with white columns, it looks down to the business district and further down to the dance grounds, small homes and horse pastures of the 160-acre Indian Camp.

Past the courthouse on the bluff are the modern Osage Tribal Headquarters building, welfare office, health clinic, the Osage Tribal Museum, and a couple of red-gold cut sandstone structures built in the 1880s, when the Agency settlement was new. Pawhuska (in

A pen and ink drawing of Main Street, Pawhuska in 1874.

Courtesy of the Osage Tribal Museum, Archive and Library

Osage Paw-Hiu-Skah), means "White Hair," the name of a famous chief who wore a white wig. But chiefs did not live on the bluff, for this was the home of governing whites. Oddly, the old stone dwelling that once served as the Agent's quarters now provides offices for the Environmental Protection Agency. This is about all that remains of the original Osage Agency, its Quaker agents, prison, and Indian boarding school with dormitories for boys and girls.

When I think about those old days, I am reminded of a photograph taken in 1902 of the St. Louis Boarding School for Girls in the Clear Creek area of Pawhuska, which stood surrounded by gardens. Shot on a gray-skied April day, the four-story Catholic boarding school looms solid as virtue or sin, and is topped by a wooden cross. Here, dark-eyed, black-haired children were carted by force from prairie villages to learn the ways of European civilization, which had come across oceans like the stained-glass windows in the "Cathedral of the Osage," from Rome and Germany and England. These children were taught to abandon the language and customs of their ancestors and punished severely if they did not submit. Flanked by nuns in magpie coifs and flowing black habits, the white-gowned little girls stand in graceful formations, gazing beyond new-leafed fruit trees — perhaps apple trees, or cherry, or peach — into the solemn future.

The St. Louis School for Osage Indians in Pawhuska.

Western History Collection, University of Oklahoma Library

St. Louis School Apr. 17 - 02.

Pawhuska baseball team, early 20th century.

Osage Tribal Museum, Archive and Library

At lower left, the Italian soprano Madame Amelita Galli-Curci and her husband are pictured with W. F. McGuire, Osage Chief Bacon Rind, and Rose Bacon Rind. At lower right, Percy J. Monk in Osage attire.

Photos courtesy of the Osage County Historical Museum

Anglo-Indian political relationships in Pawhuska exist side by side, but not quite together, like its monuments of marble and sandstone. "Socially," says Mayor Dave Landrum, "the Agency itself pretty much wants to be on its own. It wants to remain a sovereign nation. In other words, an Indian Camp surrounded by the city but not part of the city."

Mayor Landrum is a dentist who plys his trade in a one-story storefront on Main Street. He is tall, blue-eyed and tan-skinned, with a sweep of graying hair — a hometown boy whose father worked at the Osage Agency. And he is part Cherokee. "In Oklahoma," says Landrum, "most people have some Indian blood."

We sit in his office, decorated like many rooms in Pawhuska, with wood-paneling, a dark carpet, and framed images of wildlife — some in brilliant paint, others color photos by the region's best prairie photographer, Harvey Payne, who is also director of the Tallgrass Prairie Preserve. We talk about the economic health of the town. It's been on the decline since the oil boom of the seventies, says the mayor, "but I'm working like hell to keep it from dying. We're on the verge of a lot of things."

The Tallgrass Prairie Preserve is a focal point for the region's most recent development. "We're getting tourism thrust upon us," Landrum says. It will be good for the town, but any change can be scary.

I know from my Montana experience how difficult it can be for people who have lived well off the industries of resource extraction to adapt to the less prideful and productive jobs that the tourist business brings. Nevertheless, this small town, like so many others, is turning from an industrial economy to a tourist-driven service economy, and Landrum has worked hard to enhance tourism. The city of Pawhuska, together with the Chamber of Commerce, the Osage Tribe, and The Nature Conservancy, is building an Information and Interpretive Center that will focus on the tallgrass prairie and its many natural and historic communities — including ranching, oil, and Osage tribal history. The recently organized Pawhuska Community Foundation has purchased the Chevrolet building near the old Blacksmith's House on Main Street to house the center, with funds donated by citizens of the community and matched by the First National Bank, NBC Bank, and Osage Federal Savings and Loan.

Landrum speaks of other grand plans still on the drawing board. In the meantime, there are very few public accommodations for tourists who are already coming in greater numbers, only two modest motels (one perhaps less than modest), and a fine bed and breakfast on the outskirts of town. Nowhere enough rooms to service tour busses, which keep the tourist business going.

Most tourists will sleep the night in Bartlesville, just up the road, where Wal Mart – after a brief unhappy stay — has also gone. Still, Pawhuska is attractive because it is picturesque, out-of-the-way, and affordable. It has fine old houses built during its oil booms, and a nine-hole golf course. Perfect for retired people on fixed incomes. I ask the mayor if retirees and disillusioned city dwellers are trailing into Pawhuska the way they're swamping the Montana towns that border scenic pleasuring grounds, driving up real estate and taxes so that locals can't afford to live in their old homes any longer.

"I'm getting new patients," says Landrum. But so far, there has been no huge immigration. Just wait, I think. When ice-bound mountains and rivers lose their faddish appeal, the milder, more livable tallgrass prairies will be the new last resort for disaffected Americans seeking paradise.

The mayor looks to a more industrial future. He is encouraging manufacturers to start businesses in the abandoned carpet factory outside of town, which the county owns. The economy needs new jobs, since oil production is down and cattle prices are low. "When I came back to Pawhuska in 1956," says Landrum, "the population was 11,000. Now it's less than 4,000."

Our conversation is punctuated by a noontime siren, followed immediately by a ringing telephone. It is one of the mayor's buddies. They chat a moment about where to meet for lunch. Lunch, which is called "dinner" here, is an established country ritual and surely takes precedence over idle chatter. "Got to go," says Landrum. As we shake hands, I believe he is thinking about barbecue ribs and spicy cowboy beans. So am I.

THE BLUESTEM CAFE on Main Street is a down-home eatery with Halloween pumpkins painted on its plate glass windows. The dining area is dominated by a long central table where people come together to eat, country style. Booths line the side and back. There is an old-fashioned juke box in one corner, and the walls are hung with fading rodeo pictures, many of them signed by Ben "Son" Johnson. The place is sunny and friendly, full of local people talking and eating. I feel like the stranger I am and squirrel myself into a booth.

Most of the diners are helping themselves at a long buffet set up along the wall dividing the restaurant from the kitchen. Today's special is catfish, fried in chunks and set out in a steamer. There is a salad bar with the usual lettuce and veggies, also jello, chopped eggs, hot peppers, pickles. Side dishes include mashed potatoes, spuds au gratin, white gravy, turnips, brown beans and bacon. For dessert there will be cherry cobbler. All this for $4.75, including as much thin brown coffee as you can drink. Thoughts of barbecue fade before the fragrant catfish. I grab a tray and go for it.

The food is soft, rich, and tasty. Solace food, like macaroni and cheese or mother's milk. As I try not to gobble, a group of old men saunter through the front door wearing American Legion paraphernalia. They sit down at the long table, exchange greetings with a young couple and two elderly ladies. By eavesdropping with no shame, I learn they are World War II veterans come to town for a friend's funeral.

"Seems it's all we do these days," says one fellow, who wears a khaki Army cap studded with medals.

His balding pal says, "Someone's got to bury him."

Elizabeth Sell, waitress at the Bluestem Restaurant in Pawhuska, 1996.

Photo by Harvey Payne

Main Street, Pawhuska, 1996

Photo by Harvey Payne

The third fellow in the group is a weathered old Indian in a red satin bowling-league jacket. He remains silent, concentrated on his full platter, while in the booth next to me four ladies of the town gossip through their mashed potatoes. They are middle aged, with tightly curled permed and dyed hair. I believe they are business people because they wear the neatly pressed slacks, patterned sweaters, nylons and polished low-heeled shoes that you see worn in shops and offices all over town.

Off in a corner booth, all by herself, I notice a tiny gnome of a woman in a pale blue suit. She is humped with the osteoporosis of true old age, yet bright-eyed and sharp. This is Frances Schirmer, a retired schoolteacher, and, as she is quick to tell any visitor, the first Lady Rotarian in Pawhuska.

"I'm a descendant of Charlemagne. We go back to William the Conqueror," Frances tells me as we visit in her living room. She is a 91-year-old widow and I am amazed that such a frail creature can keep a large old house so spotless, the wood polished, every framed photograph gleaming like the windows. Her cat pounces on my shoulders, starts to lick my hair. Frances, appalled at his rudeness, attempts to lock the cat in a closet, but before we can latch the door, he leaps out, startling me, causing me to jump back, nearly knocking the old woman down. My Lord, I think. What if she fell and broke her hip because of my clumsiness?

Frances comes from strong, teacherly bloodlines. Her mother, Edith Layton, was a school superintendent in Oklahoma who lived to be 101. Her grandmother was also a teacher, as was her aunt, who taught for forty years. Frances grew up in El Reno and began teaching when she was 20 years old. Her first job was in Shidler, from 1923-28, during the height of the Osage oil boom. "I came here because the Osage paid more money — $150 a month — when they weren't paying but $70 a month in other places."

I ask Frances what it was like teaching in boom towns such as Shidler and Webb City. "It wasn't too wild," she says."It wasn't as bad as it is now. Now women aren't safe to go to the grocery store. They were killing the Indian because he had money. They were killing all the Indians," says Frances, "and I said, 'I don't want to stay here,' so I went back to school in 1929. Came back to Pawhuska in 1930."

In Pawhuska, Frances married an accountant of German ancestry ("My husband was a fullblood") and settled in for the long haul. She taught fifth grade. "Every businessman in town, I had in school," she says proudly. She retired in 1968 and was named Teacher of the Year in Osage County.

Until after the Brown vs. Board of Education decision in 1954, Oklahoma was a segregated state. "There was a colored school here, Booker T. Washington," Frances explains. "They did away with that and I had some of 'em. Black teachers came to our school, too. But they never segregated the Indian in Osage County. 'Course they were here first."

What strikes her about Pawhuska is the French visitors. "The Osage go back to France

~ ~ ~ BIG BLUESTEM ~ ~ ~

all the time, and the French come here." She is proud of notables such as Herbert Hoover, who once lived in town. After Hoover was elected President, Frances went to the White House and shook hands with him. Hoover's Secretary of War was Patrick Hurley, a mixed-blood Choctaw. "I saw him ride his white horse down the streets of Coalgate," she says.

Frances wants me to know that Patti Page is another regional celebrity, from Avant. "Her real name was Fowler. She changed it to be the name of the milk company she worked for in Sand Springs."

I am more interested in what people in town think of the preserve. "They think it's wonderful. Lots of people are going through there to see the bison." Frances likes the fact that The Nature Conservancy is preserving the natural history of the county. "You very seldom see an open prairie like that."

THINKING ABOUT HISTORY, I drive to the Osage County Historical Society and Museum, which occupies the abandoned Santa Fe Railroad Depot on the south side of Pawhuska. It is a sprawling frame building designed

Travis Barton, son of Brad Barton, in front of Bad Brad's BarBQ, famed in the region. Left, the Hat brand of the Chapman-Barnard Ranch.

Photos by Harvey Payne

to shelter wayfarers on the plains. The station past which steam engines once huffed and wheezed now sits surrounded by a spacious lawn. It is a perfect place for monuments. I would love to see a bronze bust of Chief White Hair, or the oil baron turned governor E. W. Marland, or a heroic 1930s W.P.A statue depicting an oil-field worker in the act of drilling. But there is only an old cattle car, along with a combination passenger mail-freight car, and the one-room "Liberty School, Dist. 76," which was donated by the Osage County Retired Teachers.

What I do not expect to see at the museum's entrance is a life-size bronze Boy Scout. The boy's booted feet rise above a brick planter filled with pale red geraniums. He stands at attention, his right hand raised in salute below a jaunty, snap brimmed hat. Pawhuska was where the first Boy Scout troop in America was organized. A plaque proclaims that fact, along with the organizer's name — Rev. John Mitchell — and the date, May 1909.

How marvelous. How perfectly small-town American. In *The American Scene*, Henry James remarked:

Osage County Historical Museum, in the old train station in Pawhuska, Oklahoma.

Photo by Harvey Payne

> To be at all critically, or as we have been fond of calling it, analytically, minded — over and beyond an inherent love of the general many-colored picture of things — is to be subject to the superstition that objects and places, coherently grouped, disposed for human use and addressed to it, must have a sense of their own, a mystic meaning proper to themselves to give out: to give out, that is, to the participant at once so interested and so detached as to be moved to report the matter.

To me, this Boy Scout is a perfect symbol for the county's museum of memories. He is the embodiment of virtues humble and decent, healthy, honest, and forward-looking. It is proper that he salutes forever the history of this Oklahoma town, which transplanted him from hidebound England into a brave new world of infinite outdoor possibilities and introduced him to the cultures of native America.

Inside the museum I wander among glass cases. I stop to study a beaded cradle board and a patchwork quilt made of the discarded silk shirts Osage men preferred during the lavish oil boom days. I also find ballerinas' tutus that once belonged to the Tallchief sisters, General Clarence Tinker's medals, and some fossils dug up from who knows where. The place works on my imagination like a morning dream. I could stay for hours, transfixed by the rich jumble of artifacts and photographs, treasures only partially catalogued and identified from the Osage Tribe, pioneer days, oil boom history, and relics of World Wars I and II.

The curator, Betty Smith, is a trim, attractive woman whose looks and spirit belie her actual years. Her connection to the county's history goes back before its beginning, for her parents arrived in 1905. "They had to get a permit to get into Indian Territory," she says, "before statehood was declared."

Betty has been the force behind the Historical Society since its creation in 1964, when it was housed in the Triangle Building. The society was formed by a women's club named Heeko, an Indian word meaning learning.

Made up of both whites and Indians, the organization boosted Pawhuska so successfully that they won fourth place and a $1,000 prize from the International Federation of Women's Clubs. The women added $10,000 in prizes during the next two years and donated $7,000 of that amount to start the museum. Other original donors included the Chapman and Barnard families.

From its inception, the museum was a repository for people's antiques and old photographs. But members wanted to preserve more than artifacts, they wanted a record of each family's history — a collective story about the living cultures of Osage County. The embodiment of those stories became Betty Smith's biggest and perhaps most enduring project. Over several years she and her staff, board, and volunteers compiled and edited a yearbook-style regional history, *Osage County Profiles*. Published in 1978, the bound album-sized volume is a model of its genre. In her introduction, Smith writes:

We sincerely hope the experiences related in this volume will show the character and stamina; pathos and humor; failures and accomplishments of those who helped settle and shared in the development of a new country.

Like many outspoken, active women, Betty Smith holds more than one niche in the community. She is also an advocate for ranch women, having been elected as the ninth president of the American National Cowbelles, the cowgirl counterpart of the powerful American Cattlemens Association. Her ranchwoman duties stem from a long-lasting partnership with her husband, J. B. Smith, an old-time cowboy and cattleman who was her high school sweetheart.

J. B. IS IN HIS EIGHTIES, a tall, lanky drink of water, who as a neighbor sometimes worked the Chapman-Barnard Ranch. I meet him and another longtime cattleman, Holton Payne, in Harvey Payne's law office on the fourth floor of the First National Bank Building. Holton is Harvey's father, a stout, ruddy man full of stories and good humor. He lives on a ranch near Shidler, two miles from where he was born. And he is obviously proud of his lawyer son, proud of the accomplishments that have made him a force in the rebirth of the community.

"You know, I told Harvey one time," says Holton, "I told him you don't know how lucky you are to have a poor Daddy to teach you to work."

Harvey himself sits behind his lawyer's desk, leaning back in his chair, smiling at his elders. The walls are hung with his photographs of the preserve: deer, bison, prairie chickens, grass and more grass, all tinged in the golden tones of first daylight or dusk, those "magic hours" when every living thing on the prairie seems newly-born.

Our talk runs to the old days on the Chapman-Barnard Ranch, part of which is now the Tallgrass Prairie Preserve. Chapman, he says, "was one of the wealthiest men in the U.S. — one of the nicest for someone so rich."

He remembers Barnard fondly as well. In 1958, J. B. recalls, when he was a young cowboy getting started, he wanted to lease 17,000 acres of Chapman-Barnard land to run some of his own cows. Barnard agreed to lease the land on a handshake. "You got your lease as long as we get along," he told J. B., "and you're gonna be the one getting along." The arrangement lasted 24 years, until Barnard died.

Since then, J. B. has become an owner of considerable property and cattle, but he is in declining health, having undergone open-heart surgery several years back. "They cut everything on J. B.," says Holton, "except his desire. They couldn't cut that."

J. B. likes to tell a story on himself that seems to punctuate Holton's remark. "That ranch is gonna kill you," Betty warned him one day.

"Well, if it does, I'll die happy," replied J. B. "I'm pretty well satisfied."

Which is how all three of these local men seem to feel about the Tallgrass Prairie Preserve.

Talking to Pawhuskans has taught me a little about the stamina, pathos, and humor of small-town life. That's how Betty Smith characterized the qualities of pioneers — and those qualities endure, along with a certain mistrust of strangers, especially journalists nosing around for opinions about the preserve. I, however, met with no rudeness from ranchers and lawyers, old cowboys and cowgirls, a teacher and a museum director, or the dentist-mayor. And I would be made welcome in the homes of Osage Indians, whose lives are intricately woven into this place. They would speak openly about their responses to the preserve and the changes its presence has initiated.

Romaine Shackelford lives in a tidy house in Pawhuska. He is a tall, well-built man in his seventies with a wide brow and large ears. Romaine is retired from his job as a Phillips Petroleum data processor. Like many Osage men, he is a survivor who has kicked the drinking habit. "After I retired," he tells me, "I worked up here at the Alcohol and Drug Program as a counselor." These days he is a volunteer at the Osage Tribal Museum, cataloging and identifying artifacts, "trying to make something of it."

His living room has shag carpeting and is hung with Indian art, many pictures painted with his own talented hands. A console containing a television, VCR, and Camcorder dominates one corner, for Romaine is learning to make his own videos. Shackelford's clan is the Tsi-shu-wah-sha-ta-kah, (Gentle Sky People) and though he understands the Osage language, he does not speak it. "There's only about a half dozen elders alive who know it," he says. "It's hard to revive a dead language when the people don't even think in the language anymore.

"I tried to teach my kids the traditions," he continues. "It's up to them to decide whether to use them."

His son, Harrison, is in his late thirties and a caretaker at the Agency. He is part of a group of young traditionalists who are trying to revive the old customs, and is a gifted Indian dancer.

Once, when Harrison went to New York to perform, he asked his father to let him wear the old traditional dance outfits that Romaine has carefully preserved at home. "I didn't like him taking those clothes out," says Romaine. "I hate to use the word, but they may be 'sacred.'"

Shackelford has no qualms about being part of modern society. "We get our stuff out once a year, do our dances, then put 'em away and be like everyone else. You got to conform to the world. That's all there is to it."

It is his opinion that oil money was a bad thing for the Osage people. "It killed 'em. My grandad said, 'the worst thing ever happened to the Osage was them getting all that money'." The fullbloods, he explains, "never did take to ranching or farming. They didn't like to work with their hands. If they could buy or trade something rather than make it, they did. They'd hire woodcutters. Hire house help. Take taxis to town because horses were too hard to keep." On the other hand, he continues, "A lot of the mixed bloods were living like white folks to begin with — ranching and farming. They just prospered."

~ ~ ~ BIG BLUESTEM ~ ~ ~

When I ask about the tribal response to The Nature Conservancy's Tallgrass Prairie Preserve, he tells me that at first "most Osage weren't for it. For no reason."

The tribe's suspicions go back about forty years to a time when the government wanted to individualize mineral rights in the county. Actually, their qualms go back a lot further.

History has taught American Indians to hold on to what they have, because outsiders — including government officials — have always come in to grab every asset they valued. Headright holders were especially opposed to the preserve because they believed the Conservancy was another outfit that wanted the mineral rights to revert to surface landholders such as themselves.

"Now the feelings have eased off," says Shackelford. "I go up on that preserve quite often. The Osage used to live up Buck Creek on the Kansas line, up the creek, west onto the plains."

Romaine likes to walk the ground his ancestors walked. He finds comfort in knowing that these historic lands will remain intact for his children and grandkids, too.

He smiles at me. "I'm glad they done it."

A gallery of Osage Pawhuskans from the 1920s — the work of WPA artist Todros Geller.

Osage Tribal Museum Archive and Library; photos by Harvey Payne

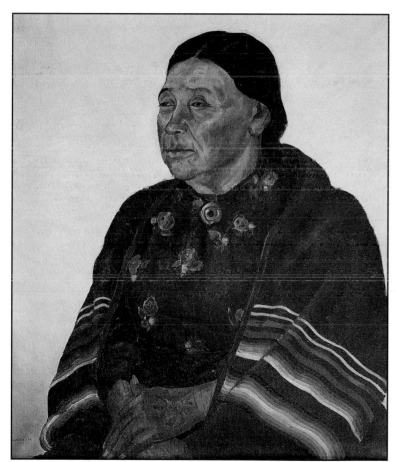

A   J o u r n e y   I n t o   t h e   T a l l g r a s s

Bill Mashunkashey, Osage.

Photo by Harvey Payne

BILL MASHUNKASHEY is not so sanguine. He claims to be the only Osage Indian developer in the county, and has written a book-length memoir to pass his story on to his grandchildren. The autobiography is called *What is Down the Road for the American Indian,* and in it, Mashunkasey says, "We developed an area for 25 Indian homes and some 25 low income homes, for others. A total of some 70 residents, which I like to believe is a contribution to the city where I live."

The Mashunkashey home is on the outskirts of town, a large, brick house built around an original old structure, with green lawns all around, a barn and outbuildings. Bill is an imposing, heavy-set, affable man of mixed blood, but definitely Osage. His wife Cleo is a pretty, Anglo woman with white hair curling around her apple-round face. They have five children, and their ample living room exhibits a colorful mix of family portraits, oil paintings of fullblood ancestors, and Osage artifacts such as a carved walnut cradle board and an otter-skin headdress.

We drink coffee and chat in the bright sun-room porch. Bill did not grow up in Osage County. He was raised in Phoenix by his white grandmother on his mother's side, and attended a military academy in Missouri. His mother had tuberculosis, and the family, which had inherited headrights, lived in high style. "We had a chauffeur . . . The chauffer's wife was my mother's maid. They lived in the servants' quarters in the garage apartment."

Bill felt little identity as an Indian, except when his parents took him on visits to Pawhuska. His great-grandfather had been the first drumkeeper of the Pawhuska Osage. A plaque at the dancing grounds in Indian Camp says that in 1884, Ben Mashunkashey, Sr., accepted the I-Lo-Skah from the Kaw Indian Tribe. But Bill learned about his Osage heritage from his fullblood paternal grandmother.

Pah-Pu-Son-Tsa, called E-ko, lived in the Indian Camp and did not speak English. She was tatooed, he writes, "from the top of her feet to her chest and from her arms to the back of her hands. The part in her hair was always colored red." One time, his father left him at E-ko's house for several weeks. The white woman who cooked for his grandmother also served as Bill's interpreter, but E-ko would not let the boy touch his food until he learned to ask for what he wanted in Osage. "Believe me," he writes, "as the hunger prevails and the food smells better, you begin to talk Osage, fluently. Tomorrow you will say bread, water, chicken, soup, cake, anything that comes to mind."

Mashunkashey enlisted in the Army in 1942, when he was 17, became an infantry sergeant, and saw action with the Marines at Iwo Jima. After he came home to Pawhuska, he tried his hand at politics, but failed to be elected. "To the best of my knowledge," he says, "I have never known an Osage Indian to be elected to an office in Osage County, Oklahoma." Later, he would work in a factory and in the oil fields, but was most successful as an insurance salesman, a job he excelled in for 14 years.

During that time, he and his family took out FHA loans to buy land and cattle. They put together a sizable ranch, part of which borders the Tallgrass Prairie Preserve. "Let me tell you," he exclaims, "we didn't have a dime, and I put this land together by any method short of murder."

As for the preserve, Bill Mashunkashey, who supported it when many Osages would not, has little to say about its aims. "Whatever their scientific findings are, I couldn't care less." Maybe he is putting me on.

I END MY TOUR OF PAWHUSKA back on Agency Hill at the Osage Tribal Museum — the first museum in the country to be owned and operated by a tribe. The museum's building was originally a dormitory for the Indian school. During the 1930s, John Joseph Mathews worked hard to establish the museum and its collection of artifacts and its archives. The building's restoration, completed in 1938, was funded as a Public Works Administration project and constructed by the CCC. John Joseph's sister, Lillian Mathews, was the museum's first curator.

Osage moccasins.

Photo by Harvey Payne

Sean Standing Bear, the young man who is the current curator, is tall and handsome, part Osage, part Sioux. We study the black spider symbol embedded in the white linoleum floor at the museum's entrance. "Spider is the traditional sign of women," says Sean. "Women were the centerpoint of Osage culture; women wove the web of community."

Sean shows me a display of blankets and explains that the colors denoted the place of a man in the hierarchical familial order of his clan: the oldest son wore a red blanket during important ceremonies; the middle son's blanket was combined red and blue; the youngest son wrapped himself in pure blue.

Left, Chief Bacon Rind. The golden eagle tail fan he is holding is considered a direct physical link between himself and his Creator.

Courtesy of the Osage Tribal Museum, Archive and Library

Hung on the walls are old photographs and drawings of traditional Mourning Dances, or War Dances, which were held to honor warriors killed in battle. In a four-day series of rituals, the tribe began the dances in expectations of retribution. Thus prepared, a war party rode off in search of the enemy. When the war party returned with enemy scalps, the dancers rejoiced, for now the spirits of their own dead warriors could rest in peace.

Because of their violent nature, these dances were forbidden under the rules of white agents.

These days the tribe celebrates each summer with dances called I'n-Lon-Schka, which take place on three weekends in June at Hominy, Grayhorse, and Pawhuska. The annual dances bring scattered clans and families together.

Originally, the far-flung festivities created alliances among old enemies. Now they create a link to the past — and with a new generation of dancers, to the future.

This 1837 Martin Van Buren peace medal was found at an Osage burial site. Above, an Osage beaded gourd rattle.

Courtesy of the Osage Tribal Museum, Archive and Library. Photos by Harvey Payne

On the previous pages, redbud trees along Sand Creek in the spring.

Photo by Harvey Payne

In glass cases along one wall sit a row of porcelain bowls painted with bright flowers and fruits. The bowls were filled with food during tribal feasts. "They represent the good meals that were shared by everyone," says Sean. "Boy, I remember some good meals!" Flowered porcelain, he remarks, "reminds us of the perpetuation of life."

The large back room of the museum is a meeting hall for the tribe. A row of WPA-funded painted portraits rings the walls — old chiefs and dignitaries in blankets and beads, scalplocks and braids, stare solemnly down at their modern kinfolk. Here, the new tribal constitution was shaped and enacted. Here, the web of communal life continues, although many threads have been broken.

The museum's artifacts, cultural materials, books, and papers help to educate contemporary Osages about their ancestral culture, which was rooted in a natural world alive with animals and plants, driven by the forces of sky, sun, moon, earth. The museum attempts to perpetuate the continuity of history in a new world of technology and materialism where many Indians feel powerless, stranded in hopeless backwaters. Places like this enable tribal peoples to find sustenance in old stories of ritual power, and to keep touch with an oral history that teaches about hunting and healing, loyalty to clan and community.

DRIVING BACK TO MY QUARTERS in the Stucco House at the Tallgrass Prairie Preserve, I think about the two museums in White Hair's town — the Historical Society with its forward looking Boy Scout, the Tribal Museum with its symbolic spider. I remember dust on windblown streets, historic brick buildings, mansions built by oil, homey restaurants, old Chevy pickups, and trailers and cabins in the Indian Camp. My day in town was a good one, but like Huck Finn I am tired of society, happy to be out of the cloistered confinements of a small town and heading for open country.

The sky over the prairies is red in the afterglow of sunset. The winding gravel road is dark. Light from my headlights rebounds into the deep blue dusk.

Then, at the edge of a barrow pit, I see glowing eyes. Not coyotes or skunks, but owls, owls, owls. I have never seen so many owls. Six fly up in the beams of my headlights. Maybe eight. I see spotlit owl faces, black-ringed eyes, distinct bars on long, hovering wings, pale heavy bodies in sudden flight. These are short-eared owls, a variety I have never seen before. They make no sound. I look up to a flurry of tawny feathers and then the owls disappear into the moonless dark.

I brake my car in the middle of the road, spewing gravel. The birds of prey are gone, but I am breathless. I feel small hairs stand up at the back of my neck. I shiver with the dread and delight of encountering owls in the night. This gathering of owls is a surpassing mystery. I begin to understand why owls hold humans in thrall. Why we think of them as spirits, omens, symbols of wisdom or death — all that and a nameless more. The owls have come to me like music from heaven, and I am blessed. I will never forget the owls that brought magic to my road.

This is what life is, I believe, why it is so important to preserve what we can of rivers and forests, mountains and prairies. For beyond the lights of anyone's town, beyond commerce and industry, culture and craft, there is a quiet darkness at the quick of things — a beating of wings that comes only from the wild.

The Politics of Preservation

"To love what was is a new thing under the sun. . . To see America as history, to conceive of destiny as a becoming, to smell a hickory tree through the still lapse of ages — all these things are possible for us, and to achieve them takes only the free sky, and the will to ply our wings."

ALDO LEOPOLD,

FROM A SAND COUNTY ALMANAC

W HEN I VISIT THE TALLGRASS PRAIRIE PRESERVE, I usually bunk in the white building named the Stucco House, or the Barnard House, or — if you ask some of the Barnard children — Jim Bob's house. This is where Bob Hamilton, the preserve's director of science and stewardship, has moved his office, and where the Conservancy houses its interns and the scientists, filmmakers, and writers who come to study the slow transformations of a prairie.

Built by H. G. Barnard's eldest son Jim Bob when he moved from Texas to Oklahoma, the Spanish-style home with its cast-iron gates, stone courtyard, and red roof seems out of place among rustling blackjacks on the edge of the grasslands, like a dream house or movie set. And when you slide back the glass doors from the patio, the incongruity accelerates.

The baronial living room has ringing floors of Mexican terra-cotta tiles and a huge fireplace, but is barren of furniture. It has become a field laboratory equipped with long tables, microscopes, computers, specimen cases, maps. You pass through carved wooden doors to a bedroom wing lined with two rows of double bunk beds. On the opposite side of the house, down a narrow passage from the blue and white Spanish tiled bathroom, is a small sitting room with a lumpy used couch, an armchair, and an old television set. It adjoins another bedroom where graduate student interns live.

Along with its forward-looking scientific accoutrements and young conservationists

A waterfall on a tributary of Sand Creek in early spring. Above, an ornate box turtle. Photos by Harvey Payne

heady with hope, the house resonates with a presence which I believe to be Jim Bob's spirit. The death of Jim Bob, it seems to me, was the beginning of the end of the Barnard family's ranch history. It marked a transition that led ultimately to the sale of the property and its purchase by The Nature Conservancy. Thus, the politics of preservation that this chapter recounts must begin with the politics of family ownership. It is a personal story with public ramifications, in which a family's loss becomes a gift to the whole wide natural world.

YOUNG JIM BARNARD, Jim Bob's son, was four when his father died. He doesn't remember him much, "only a couple of images," he says, etched in his mind like photographs. Had Jim Bob lived to control the ranch, young Jim likes to believe he would have been the next Barnard to carry on the ranching tradition. But when the old patriarch H. G. Barnard passed away, the property was joined to Chapman's estate and placed in trust with the Bank of Oklahoma to be managed by Bill Bell, a Tulsa lawyer. Income from its operation was split among the Barnard heirs and the charities that were Jim Chapman's beneficiaries.

For twenty years, from 1966 until 1986, Bill Bell managed the ranch for the trust. According to Len Eaton, who was president of the Bank of Oklahoma, where the trust was held, "Bell continued to operate that ranch much like Chapman and Barnard had. They took great care not to overgraze the pastures, and Bell continued that philosophy."

By the 1980s, great changes had occurred in the cattle industry, changing the way of life on the Chapman-Barnard Ranch as well. No longer did 20 cowboys and their families live on the place, as they had in its heyday as a working ranch. Now, "it was more like seven cowboys, who lived in town and drove their trucks out there to work each day," says Eaton. The ranch went from being a cow-calf operation to a "hotel for cattle" where steers were brought in and fattened on the tallgrass before being shipped to market. By the early 1980s, with cattle prices falling and land prices going up, Eaton recalls, members of the Barnard family began to talk of selling.

Family members mention other, more personal reasons. With Jim Bob and H.G. Barnard gone, the family began to feel less at home at the ranch. "At one point we were moved out of Mother's little house," says Mary, "into Jim Bob's house. Then, one day when we came to visit, I found the foreman's family in there. All of Jim Bob's nice furniture was piled into two of the little houses where married cowboys used to live."

There was a time when young Jim wanted to follow in his father's footsteps. He worked on the ranch summers during high school and while going to college in Tulsa, but soon found he wasn't welcomed there, either. Bill Reeds, (whom Bill Bell had hired to manage the ranch) "told me I'd be worked to death and run off," he says.

Years earlier, Jim's older cousin, Keenan (Bud's son), had also tried to become a rancher, tried to work himself up the cowboy ladder, starting as an ordinary hand. At 22, in 1969, Keenan moved into the Stucco House with his new wife. "I had idolized Uncle Jim

Tallgrass Prairie after a winter storm.

Photo by Harvey Payne

Lacy patterns in a frozen
spring along Wild Hog Creek.

Photo by Harvey Payne

Bob," he says, "I helped him build that house. It was on a rock pile . . . all sledgehammer
work."

"I was pretty green," Keenan continues, "but I ended up being a pretty good roper, a
pretty good horseshoer." After two years of bottom-of-the-barrel labor such as cleaning
piles of manure from under the scales at Blackland, Keenan knew there would be no
"career opportunity" for him at the ranch. Besides, his wife was lonely. "I realized I was a
city person," Keenan says. He cut his losses, moved to Tulsa, became a stockbroker.

Eventually, the Barnard family and their trustees decided that income from the cattle
business was not sufficient. They put the Barnard portion of the ranch up for sale. For the
Barnard family, the time for ranching had passed. Bud — H. G. and Frankie's architect
son — is a man more at home at an ambassador's party in Rome than in a bunkhouse.
Ann, the Barnards' fun-loving middle daughter, moved to California and created a new
life on the edge of the Pacific. Mary, who was the most attached to the ranch, now became
the strongest advocate for the preserve. With The Nature Conservancy in charge, she feels
the place is hers again — at least in spirit.

Ann had returned to live in Tulsa when I met her and Mary for lunch and Bloody
Marys one crisp October noon. Slowed down with emphysema, she makes her home in
the same high-rise condo that Mary and her husband share when they are not at their

house in Carefree, Arizona. Ann and Mary are best friends in their older age and I am pleased to join their easy camaraderie. Ann confesses she was never a cowgirl like her younger sister, but prized the ranch in her own way. "I loved it up there," she says. "I enjoyed every part of it. I'd take a book and go out on my horse Roany. But I didn't like the hard work." Ben Johnson, she recalls, used to tease her about that. " 'Miz Barnard,' he'd say to Mother, 'I'd give a hundred dollars for a drop of Ann's sweat.' "

Ann expresses some regrets about losing the ranch. Not so much for herself, she tells me, as for her children and their cousins — the next generation. "Dad would've loved nothing better than to have the ranch in the family, have his children and grandchildren there. But if we couldn't keep it, I can't think of any group I'd rather see own the property than The Nature Conservancy."

Helene, Mary's daughter, is a slim, elegant dark-haired woman with her own nearly grown girls. She went to the ranch often with her grandparents during school and summer vacations and keeps up her friendship with the cowboy family that befriended her there. "They would take their youngest daughter out of school when I came," she says. "I never knew it, but Grandpa told them to. He thought I should have a friend to play with."

That woman is still her best friend. Helene visits the cowboy family in their home near Wynona, but does not return to the Chapman-Barnard Ranch, which is only a few miles away. "I had my own horse," she says. "Quit going there after my horse died. Because every time I went, I would just cry."

Missy, Ann's sporty blond daughter, says she was "horse crazy" as a girl and learned to ride at the ranch. "It was like a huge playground," she tells me. "Grandmother was really a country girl at heart. I remember her wringing chicken's necks for supper, or going fishing in her red dress. But starting with the death of Grandfather, it was a great loss. I went a lot in the early 70s. Quit in the 80s."

"I felt great relief when the Conservancy got it," adds Helene. "But it still feels weird going back. I regret that my daughters haven't had access like I had. Just the land itself. You feel so small, but appropriately small. Just to roam around out there, I think it changes you."

Mary's son, Richie, was also deeply attached to the ranch. A musician and composer of what he calls "urban-rural" songs, Richie has recently moved from Los Angeles to Sacramento for the good reasons of "love and work." As the youngest cousin, for many years the ranch's baby boy, he remembers all kinds of adventures such as being saved from a striking water moccasin by Jim Bob's hired hand called "Black Clyde" to distinguish him from the foreman, Clyde Lowry.

"It was," he says, "an incredible gift to be able to spend summers up at the ranch — to be there and have free run of the place." Like his sister Helene and cousin Missy, Richie felt sad when the ranch was sold, but he believes The Nature Conservancy's management is in the land's best interests. Going back with his fiancee to celebrate the 1993 bison release was, he confides, a strange experience. "The oddest moment was seeing the remodeled Bunkhouse. There was the desk that Grandpa used to work at, and Mother's picture on the wall. It was more like being in a museum than at a working ranch."

Missy sums up the feelings of these three cousins. "That ranch was so alive," says Missy. "Supported so many families, at first. But it was already gone before it was sold. It was a great loss, but a happy ending."

Young Jim Barnard is not so happy about the ending. He is the only one of the family that still hopes to "carry on the tradition." Jim received a graduate degree in ranch management and has worked on ranches as far north as Alberta, but never got to practice his knowledge at the home place. "I really love the prairie and ranching," he says. "I'm a range man."

When I spoke with him, Jim was working in the wholesale business in Kansas City, but he still harbors the dream of owning his own spread some day. He and his sister Eugenia were the only members of the Barnard Trust to vote against selling the ranch to The Nature Conservancy. "The market had bottomed out," says Jim. "They should have advertised it more. Should have waited for prices to go up."

Jim and Eugenia believe The Nature Conservancy bought the land too cheap. If the siblings couldn't take possession of their father's share of the property, they wanted as much money as they could get from it. Although he loved the ranch, Jim never came back to it until the day of the Conservancy's bison release on October 18, 1993, an afternoon of intense and mixed emotions.

"It was odd," he says, to see "hundreds of strangers tramping around there." He took his wife to the Stucco House. "It was so changed. I was extremely sad to see the shape the house was in. My wife had never been there. She cried. She said she was crying for me, because she knew I wouldn't do it myself."

Jim has other reservations about The Nature Conservancy. "I can't argue with their desire to recreate conditions of fire and bison to restore the prairie," he says. "I just don't believe Man can duplicate the work of Mother Nature."

Young Jim Barnard is not alone in his queasiness about environmental groups taking control of range lands, or any land with resource potential. Conflicts about the fates of the few remaining swaths and patches of near virgin prairies, or old growth forests, or mineral-rich mountain ranges go a long way back and have roots in a typically western veneration for private property in which freedom to develop land is equated with individual freedoms guaranteed under the Constitution and the Bill of Rights.

Many people — especially westerners who have built their lives around work based on using the natural resources of a vast region — equate environmental groups with the regulatory arms of the federal government. They don't like government control of public lands. They oppose any person or group who might limit the private sector's capacity to make use of grass, timber, energy, water, or precious metals. They argue that because they live on the land and know it well, they are the best stewards.

Oklahoma, like Texas, has almost no federally-owned land. And that's the way many folks would like to keep it. In the 1970s, the National Park Service conducted an inventory of natural ecosystems within the United States to determine priorities for preservation. They found that the only substantial biome that had not been included in a system of national parks and preserves was that of the tallgrass prairies. Acquisition of prime tallgrass land became their highest priority. Only three sites were considered possible — all of them in the prairie ecosystem that ranges from the Flint Hills in Chase County, Kansas, to the unplowable northern grasslands of Osage County in Oklahoma.

The idea was not a new one. Beginning in the 1930s, says preserve director Harvey Payne, the National Park Service had been interested in creating a tallgrass park of some kind, probably in Kansas. When, in 1961, Interior Secretary Stewart Udall visited a proposed site in the Flint Hills (which he had been assured was available from a willing seller), he was met by armed ranchers opposed to government ownership in their county. Soon afterward a 1962 bill failed in a Senate subcommittee; and a 1971 effort by the Department of Interior, with suppport from the Kansas governor, also failed.

Rumors of the proposed federal takeover circulated for many years, Harvey explains, culminating in the 1970s, when the prairie gossip network claimed that the federal government was planning to condemn up to 350,000 acres of grasslands in Kansas and Oklahoma. Harvey has been involved in the politics of tallgrass preservation for more than a decade.

"People got stirred up," he says. "Anti-park fever took hold." Then, in 1984, Ron Klataske, a passionate advocate of prairie conservation from Manhattan, Kansas, and the National Audubon Socicty, began to take steps to make the preservationists' dream actually happen.

Northern Osage County had two large ranches that would be just right: the Chapman-Barnard Ranch, which was biologically diverse, including tallgrass meadows as well as cross-timbered sections; and the Foraker Ranch, owned by the Oklahoma Land and Cattle Company, which was almost completely tallgrass prairie in prime condition. Klataske wanted the government to buy the Barnard Ranch   or if possible, both of those places — to become its national tallgrass park or preserve.

"I was there," says Harvey Payne, when Klataske attended an August meeting of the Osage Tribal Council to present his plan to establish a prairie preserve on the Barnard Ranch. George Tallchief, the tribal council chairman, originally supported the plan, but the rest of the council members were adamantly opposed. "It was like throwing a goldfish into a tank of piranhas," Harvey remembers. The vote against Klataske was unanimous.

Harvey was a member of the original Tallgrass Prairie Preserve Association — organized by people hoping to preserve the prairie ecosystem. He was one of the few locals who participated in the long struggle for a national preserve in the Osage. Preserve is the operative term here.

"First of all, it was supposed to be a national preserve, not a park," says Harvey, "because from the start, oil drilling and production as well as cattle grazing were to be per-

Tallgrass Prairie in autumn
with tall Goldenrod (*Solidago
canadensis*).
Photo by Harvey Payne

mitted — the Tallgrass Prairie National Preserve." Federal regulatory rules for a national preserve are much more open to outside uses than the rules governing a national park.

When, in the fall of 1984, Don Nickles, a Republican senator from Ponca City, took interest in the possibility of a national tallgrass preserve in his state, the project gained momentum. Oklahoma's senior senator at that time was David Boren, now president of the University of Oklahoma. Boren, a Democrat, had supported a preserve or park from the beginning and did not need to be convinced. Responding to Nickles' concerns, Pawhuska held a town meeting, which resulted in the creation of a task force to investigate ways such a national preserve could take shape.

Six major interest groups were invited to select a representative to serve on the task force. Harvey Payne represented the Oklahoma Wildlife Federation; other local people represented the Osage County Commissioners, the Pawhuska Chamber of Commerce, the Osage County Cattlemen's Association, and the Osage Tribe. The oil interest, Oklahoma Independent Petroleum Association (OIPA), opposed the project and refused to send any representative.

As part of their research, the five task force members decided to tour several similar federal parks and preserves located near towns about the size of Pawhuska. They went to the Chickasaw National Recreation Area, whose 10,000 acres are the only National Park Service facility in Oklahoma, and found the townspeople of Sulphur very enthusiastic. "Two million visitors come there a year," says Harvey, "bringing welcome tourist dollars."

The task force also visited Jackson, Wyoming, to study the set-up in the Grand Tetons, which is one of the few national parks that allow cattle grazing within their borders. Then they visited the Badlands National Park in South Dakota.

"The consensus was, 'we need it,'" says Harvey. The task force voted unanimously to move forward with a plan.

In 1985, the group presented their recommendations to Senator Nickles and began to lobby in Washington, D.C. Their proposal received backing from the National Wildlife Federation, The Nature Conservancy, the Audubon Society, the Sierra Club, and the

Joseph H. Williams at the Tallgrass Prairie, October, 1992.

Photo by Harvey Payne

National Parks and Conservation Association. But the Osage Tribe as well as oil, ranching and private property interests were still dead set against any federal park or preserve. One of the captains of the opposition was Jack Graves, the leading independent oil producer in the Osage, whose rich Dog Creek Field dug deep into a section of the Chapman-Barnard Ranch.

On the conservationist side, one of the most influential voices was Joe Williams. In 1995, when I talked to him, Williams was in the last year of his term as chairman of the National Board of Governors of The Nature Conservancy. He had come to that position from his role as an organizer and first chairman of the Conservancy's Oklahoma chapter. But in the mid-1980s, when the debate about a tallgrass preserve was in full swing, he had been associated with the National Audubon Society as a member of its board of directors.

Joe Williams is a powerful businessman in Oklahoma, scion of a multinational pipeline and communications transmission corporation. He is also a dedicated conservationist and sportsman who, one informant tells me, has bagged as many game birds as anyone in Oklahoma. My informant is quick to add that Williams has never exceeded his bag limit, and has not shot a single game bird on the Tallgrass Prairie Preserve.

Williams was born and bred in Tulsa and was from the outset involved with efforts to create a national tallgrass preserve. "At that time," he says, "I discounted the possibility of any private organization doing anything that large. The National Park Service seemed the only answer. But we didn't realize the level of opposition."

As a way to focus debate on the proposed new Park Service preserve, Senator Dale Bumpers of Arkansas decided to hold a hearing in Washington, D.C. His committee invited four people from each side to testify. Joe Williams was one of the proponents. "It was a media event," he remembers, "the Indians in full traditional dress, the cowboys in jeans and Stetsons."

Proponents included ranchers such as Lee Holcombe and Dick Whetsell, along with Harvey Payne and Pawhuska mayor at that time, Mike Wachtman, who was also a small oil producer. Opponents included the Osage Tribe, some of the other oilmen, and some ranchers. The "cowboy concern," says Williams, was that intrusion by the federal government would "end the cowboy way of life" by taking good grazing land out of production.

The Osage Indians, Williams believes, had more credible misgivings. Since a majority of headright holders live outside the region and rely on income from their mineral rights, they fear any change that might inhibit production. And their past experience with the U.S. government's many broken treaties and promises certainly inspires no trust.

The only way to get the pro-preservation "cowboys" and the anti-preserve oilmen and "Indians" on the same side of the street was through creative compromise. All parties agree that the final legislation introduced in the Senate in 1987 by Senators Boren and Nickles from Oklahoma, as well as Dale Bumpers from Arkansas, was indeed a compromise.

The bobwhite quail, whose cheerful call is a familiar sound on the prairie.
Photo by Harvey Payne

In that bill, contrary to all precedent, Senator Boren decided that the only way to satisfy the tribe's objections would be to write the regulations governing the preserve into the legislation. Usually, such rules evolve through administrative decisions, but here it was essential that mineral rights must be guaranteed with no possibility that qualifications and procedures would later be added to make oil exploration and extraction more difficult. Regulations regarding grazing on the preserve were also included to satisfy the "cowboy"

interests. The terms of the legislation were specific. Only an act of Congress would be able to change them.

Another compromise concerned the size of the preserve and its boundaries. In its original plan, says Williams, the National Park Service proposed a preserve in which 150,000 acres would be owned by the federal government. But the compromise bill specified that only 50,000 acres would be owned in fee, with an additional 50,000 acres secured through conservation easements. With conservation easements on adjoining lands, both oil and cattle interests would be able to take advantage of government protection against unwanted intruders while continuing to reap the natural resources of the area.

The large Foraker Ranch owned by the Oklahoma Land and Cattle Company would be the heart of the preserve, with some lands included from four adjoining ranches. Its 50,000 federally owned acres would stretch along Bird Creek and Sand Creek and would include the high escarpment at the headwaters of Buck Creek. The western part of the Barnard Ranch would become part of the preserve, as well as some eastern sections of the Drummond Ranch, and an eastern piece of the Foraker Ranch.

The bill's sponsor in the House of Representatives was Congressman Mickey Edwards of Oklahoma City. Edwards, who has since retired from Congress and is on the faculty at Harvard University, had originally been opposed to the idea of a preserve, but agreed to support the bill under certain limited parameters. His conditions were: 1) Oil and gas production must continue, and would be administered by the BIA, not the Park Service, under the BIA's less stringent regulations; 2) There would be no condemnation of private lands; 3) The maximum size of any tallgrass preserve would be 50,000 acres.

The compromise legislation met all of Edwards' criteria. To ensure the bill's passage, Senator Boren convened a famous meeting to which he invited the entire Oklahoma delegation — Republicans and Democrats alike — as well as the major environmental groups that had supported creation of a national tallgrass preserve. He told them, says Williams, that although many might not like all the terms of the compromise, it was at least a beginning. And as everyone knew, in a compromise no one gets everything they want. Boren demanded that all those in attendance agree to support the bill. No backbiting. No public expression of doubts or disfavor. Surprisingly, everyone agreed.

MOTION AND THE MARKS OF MOTION

Above, mouse pawprints cross over the hoofprints of bison in snow on the preserve. Right, a whitetail doe.

Photos by Harvey Payne

"I was absolutely convinced we should do this," says Williams. Although the size and scope of the preserve was less than most environmentalists wanted, if all went well, new generations might open the doors wider. "I thought our children might be able to expand this preserve at some future time."

Congressman Edwards had made it clear to all proponents that he would accept no deviations from the compromise bill, which included his conditions of acceptance. But some out-of-state factions of the Sierra Club were not satisfied with such limits. They wanted the part of the preserve on Wild Hog Creek to be set aside as a wilderness area, where no grazing or oil production could take place. And they wanted to include more than 50,000 acres of federal land within the preserve. Then, about six weeks after Boren's meeting, a Sierra Club publication came out with an article calling the proposed preserve a sham. They argued against losing the 50,000 originally proposed acres.

The oil producers who had reluctantly acquiesced to Mickey Edwards' qualified support of the preserve were already alarmed because at that time the Sierra Club's legal arm was conducting a lawsuit against the National Park Service requiring them to enforce their oil and gas drilling regulations more stringently. That was all it took for the Osage Tribe to cement its opposition. Other borderline supporters shifted allegiances.

"It took about thirty minutes for Mickey Edwards to withdraw his support," says Williams. "Jim Inhofe, the congressman from Tulsa, also pulled out and the whole thing fell apart."

Hopes for reconciliation and rebirth of federal legislation were nulled when, in 1988, the Mormon Church purchased from the Oklahoma Land and Cattle Company a good part of the proposed preserve. The only large hunk of tallgrass prairie remaining for sale at that moment was the nearly 30,000 acre Barnard portion of the old Chapman-Barnard Ranch.

THE NATURE CONSERVANCY stepped in at that point. Herb Beattie, the first executive director of the Oklahoma chapter, had been advocating a tallgrass preserve as a federal project, but now he saw the possibilities for a private nonprofit conservation group to take up the cause. And John Flicker from the national office had already been talking to local ranchers and citizens, assuring them that the Conservancy would not alter their economy or way of life, except to make it better. Flicker, who is now president of the National Audubon Society, joined forces with Beattie, and the national office allied itself with the Oklahoma chapter in negotiations with the Barnard Trust.

"We were all so crestfallen that we lost the national preserve," Joe Williams recalls. "But it would cost 6 to 7 million to buy the Barnard Ranch, plus a whole lot of start-up and operating expenses. The Oklahoma chapter couldn't raise that much money itself, and The Nature Conservancy wasn't organized to raise money outside a state for a big project inside a state. I wondered, was there any way we could do it?"

Frederick Drummond, the Osage County rancher who is a board member of the

"It was worth it. I believe we can and must go to larger scale conservation efforts if we're going to make the difference," says Joe Williams. "In the final analysis, I think it's good that we have a private preserve rather than a federal preserve. We have more freedom."

STEWARDSHIP MADE
VISIBLE

Site of an earlier controlled burn, showing sandstone and woolly yarrow.
Photo by Harvey Payne

Oklahoma Nature Conservancy, came up with the answer. "You can't afford not to do it," he told Joe Williams. "You'll never see land go this cheap again." Williams is not a person to pass up a great deal. "So I got on the horn and started talking to people," he says.

What happened next was a lot of turmoil from within the national offices of The Nature Conservancy, and from other state chapters who also needed national fundraising for their projects. This debate occurred before the national office initiated its "Last Great Places" campaign, so the Tallgrass Prairie Preserve project was breaking new ground, a painful procedure in any long-standing organization, no matter how idealistic its goals.

When they got the go-ahead, local and national staff people, boards, and members responded with great enthusiasm. Together they raised 15 million dollars. Some Oklahoma board members and their corporate friends donated large sums of money: $750,000 from The Williams Company; $1.5 million from Kerr-McGee. The project garnered the first major gift for the Conservancy's "Last Great Places" campaign and drew support from conservationists all over the country, including the Oklahoma chapter and many members of the Sierra Club.

The successful campaign raised enough funds to buy the Barnard Ranch and to set up an endowment whose income would pay a portion of the project's yearly basic management and operational expenses. In this way the stability and longevity of the Tallgrass Prairie Preserve would be ensured.

"It was worth it. I believe we can and must go to larger scale conservation efforts if we're going to make the difference," says Joe Williams. "In the final analysis, I think it's good that we have a private preserve rather than a federal preserve. We have more freedom."

Herb Beattie, the former Oklahoma Conservancy director who started the project, agrees. Speaking as a private citizen, he says, "now we have a nature preserve that far excedes anything the National Park Service could have done."

The accomplishments of the Tallgrass Prairie Preserve have resulted in a turnaround of feelings among many local interests and citizens who initially opposed any preserve. In this, the preserve's staff deserves most of the credit, for during their first years of managing the Tallgrass Prairie Preserve, they have been good neighbors, and true to their word. They have proved to be a highly beneficial addition the Osage prairie community.

The first smart move the Conservancy made was to hire Harvey Payne to be the preserve's director. He is a local rancher's son who knows and understands the place and its people. One of the first highly visible good things that Harvey did was to buy a huge yellow fire-fighting rig — the one called "Daisy" by its devoted crew. During their first year, the preserve's crew put out twelve fires on neighboring ranches. Which goes to show there's more to being a good neighbor than good fences.

"We didn't bring in a do-gooder from outside," says Joe Williams. "The ranchers thought, 'here come a bunch of people in Brooks Brothers suits and Weejuns,' coming to herd bison, not cattle. They thought we'd destroy a whole way of life."

Hiring Bob Hamilton to be the director of science and stewardship was another good move. Hamilton is a person of the prairies — a Kansas fellow who came to Oklahoma from the Dakotas, where he had experience in raising bison. As a topper, the preserve hired Kenny Shieldnight — a true Oklahoma cowboy — to be ranch foreman. His carefully chosen cowhand crew are also Oklahomans, many of them from around Pawhuska. They ride in local rodeos, their children attend local schools, they drink in local bars. Word gets around that they are regular hands doing a good job.

"The general mood," says Joe Williams, "has, I think, become quite positive. People know we are not amateurs. They discovered we knew what we were doing. We have brought economic benefits to the town."

"When we first came in," Williams continues, "there was strong suspicion that the Conservancy would be a stalking horse for the federal government. But we're here to stay. Our goal is to protect the ecosystem that is there."

PROTECTION is what the politics that led to the preserve and will continue to influence its directions is all about. The primary protection, to be sure, is of a vital natural biome that needs preservation. But there are family and ranching heritage interests to protect, and oil interests, and Osage tribal interests, and associations with the economic interests of local communities, and protection of a more general but important cultural inheritance that defines the region's identity.

Yet, standing above all selfish interests, I sense a yearning for the common good and a shared desire that has brought these diverse groups together. The glue that holds them is love for a place — love for the life and history of that place, love that makes every positive act possible.

Jack Graves, the independent oil producer who was originally opposed to the preserve, is now a member of the board of the Oklahoma Nature Conservancy. He often leads tours through the preserve, pointing out its geological features and discussing its history of oil booms and busts. He contributes equipment and labor to grade roads, installed a new waterline, and helps do what is necessary to keep the place going.

Frederick Drummond, a third-generation cattleman and a member of the largest family ranch business in the county, is also on the board. And Geoffrey Standing Bear, the activist Osage Indian lawyer who was a leader in drafting a new tribal constitution and convincing voters to enact it, also holds a seat on the Oklahoma Conservancy's board of directors.

Many diverse interests have come together to further the goals of tallgrass prairie preservation, but the way is not always smooth. On one side, a small group of still vocal local opponents are critical of the preserve's conservation policies. On the other side are voices of some militant and idealistic environmentalists who feel the Conservancy has compromised too much. They don't like its policy of grazing large numbers of cattle on

Showy evening primrose.

Photo by Harvey Payne

the preserve. They disapprove the sale of bison for money. They flinch from the industrial landscape of oil pumps, holding tanks, roads, and telephone and electric lines. To them these compromises seem a jarring intrusion into the aesthetics and ethics of a preserve designed to protect and nurture a great natural ecosystem.

Herb Beattie is no longer with The Nature Conservancy. These days he spends his energy supporting other new projects such as the Idaho Wetlands Project, which buys wetland habitat and takes it out of production. Herb has also involved himself in an international organization called Trees for Life, and is trying to expose what he believes are "negative consequences associated with our addiction to a car-based culture."

Herb tells me that Ron Klataske, the passionate advocate of grasslands preservation in Kansas, started the chain of events that evolved into the Tallgrass Prairie Preserve in Oklahoma. According to Herb, Klataske is still preaching his gospel, still maneuvering for a national presence in the tallgrass country of Chase County, Kansas. He is talking to the feds about creating a National Tallgrass Monument there, says Herb. I, for one, hope that Klataske will win at least this small part of his battle.

As I speak to Herb Beattie on the telephone from Montana, I wonder how it feels to be out of the circle that runs the preserve. Sometimes, says Herb, "I make incognito visits to Pawhuska." There is a note of sadness in his voice.

I imagine it must feel awkward to be looking in from the outside at the Tallgrass Prairie Preserve he helped to create. But when I ask him straight out, Beattie replies with one word that seems to sum up what everyone involved feels about the end result of what has been a long and often arduous political process.

"Wonderful!" he says. "Just wonderful."

Dancing Back the Buffalo

The whole world is coming
A nation is coming, a nation is coming
The Eagle has brought the message to the tribe
The father says so, the father says so
Over the whole earth they are coming
The buffalo are coming, the buffalo are coming . .

PLAINS GHOST DANCE SONG, 1890s

NEAR THE END OF THE NINETEENTH CENTURY, when bison were gone from the Great Plains and American Indians clustered hungry, diseased, and bent with loss on sad reservations, a spiritual revival swept from Nevada to the Dakotas carrying one last surge of hope. The Messiah was Jack Wilson, known as Wovoca, a visionary Paiute from Nevada. He prophesied an imminent transformation of the earth that would sweep away white invaders and return the land to its native inhabitants. The dead would return in glory, bringing with them the plentitude of a natural world that had also died — elk and deer, grasslands swarming with buffalo. An ancient tribal order would be restored, uniting believers in perpetual youth and peace.

The ritual necessary to incite this cataclysmic renewal was the Ghost Dance. Although tribes added local variations in dress, songs, and preparations, for the most part the form of the ritual didn't change: dancers painted themselves with sacred red clay; they dressed in robes and shirts edged with feathers and adorned with symbols representing the sun, moon, morning star, as well as turtle who symbolized earth, messenger crow whose black wings connected the ghost world with the living world, and eagle — a universal symbol of the great spirit.

Men and women, old people and children joined hands in a great circle. They danced four nights in a row, and a fifth morning. From within the circle, seven priests with eagle feathers hypnotized susceptible dancers, who fell into trances, became rigid, dropped to earth in postures of death, experienced visions, then rose to sing songs reporting what they

Although some tribes danced a few years more, the fervor disintegrated, passing on to peyote visions of the Native American Church. It became clear that there would be no return to the Indians' dream of paradise. As the twentieth century progressed, more and more settlers poured into the Great Plains, and the tallgrass prairies became the agribusiness heartland of a nation devoted to cities and industrial development.

Cheyenne Arapaho Ghost Dance gathering near Fort Reno, ca. 1890.

Western History Collection, Schuck Collection #44

had seen and heard in the ancestral hemisphere. On the fifth day, everyone bathed in running waters to cleanse whatever evil might still adhere to their bodies. Every week for six weeks, devotees performed this ceremony.

In Oklahoma Territory, the Ghost Dance was a last resort for disenfranchised Comanches, Arapahos, Cheyennes, Pawnees, Kiowas and Caddos. The more wealthy, landed and less needy Osages held one dance cycle in the Big Hill country on Sycamore Creek, then skeptically gave up the practice. Meanwhile, starving and desperate Sioux in the Black Hills came to believe their Ghost Dance shirts were bullet-proof. The Sioux Uprising, which began in dancing and faith, ended in the massacre at Wounded Knee.

Although some tribes danced a few years more, the fervor disintegrated, passing on to peyote visions of the Native American Church. It became clear that there would be no return to the Indians' dream of paradise. As the twentieth century progressed, more and more settlers poured into the Great Plains, and the tallgrass prairies became the agribusiness heartland of a nation devoted to cities and industrial development. Of thirty million buffalo, only 600 survived, preserved in zoos, ranches, the Wichita Mountains Wildlife Refuge and Yellowstone National Park.

Now, we are dancing them back. One hundred years after the Ghost Dance debacle, some one hundred and fifty thousand bison are again grazing the grasses of the Great Plains. These herds did not spring from a hole in the earth or descend from the sky. We, who almost made the species extinct, have nurtured them back into the landscapes of the American West. But the story continues with new challenges, for with the return of the bison come opportunities to rekindle the vital grassland ecosystems they helped to create.

I RETURN TO THE TALLGRASS PRAIRIE PRESERVE on a frosty fall afternoon in 1995. More than six years have passed since The Nature Conservancy purchased the Barnard portion of the historic Chapman-Barnard Ranch. During those years, the preserve has grown to 34,600 acres, with an additional 2,400 acres of leased ground. It has become a profitable cattle operation, a breeding ground for bison, a scientific research center, tourist facility, and experimental grasslands laboratory. All those achievements are only means to an end, for the preserve's basic and truly important mission is to help restore the biological diversity that once existed on the tallgrass prairie's complex and interdependent ecosystem.

Bob Hamilton, the director of science and stewardship, tells me the preserve's management through the use of bison and fire is beginning to show results. He is already seeing a resurgence of biological diversity. By this he does not mean an emergence of new plants and animals — for what is there has always been there, and what has gone (elk, bear, wolves, passenger pigeons, for example) will most likely not return. When Hamilton speaks of increased diversity, he is describing changes in the patterns of distribution of existing species across the prairie's landscape.

"We inherited a very diverse landscape," says Hamilton. "It was conserved well for one hundred years, but the conservation of plant and animal life on the prairie was affected by a century of cattle grazing and management for grass to feed cattle."

Conventional range management over time on a natural ecosystem such as the tallgrass prairies results in what Hamilton calls "load-lock." Repeated management practices such as fire suppression in summer and fall tended to lock the land into set growth patterns. Grazing by cattle in place of the grazing habits of native bison encouraged species such as big bluestem while it discouraged the growth of forbs. Thus, conventional range management limited the more random historic relationships that existed among competing native species, weather, and fire and diminished ecosystem diversity.

"The whole system has been out of whack," says Hamilton. But restoring more indigenous diversity, in this case, does not mean giving up management. It means a turnaround in management philosophy and practices. Instead of managing for beef, the scientific and ranching crew is managing for diversity by carefully reintroducing seasonal fires and grazing bison.

"The preserve will always be a highly managed enterprise," Hamilton continues. "What we are doing is trying to roll back the clock and restore as much as we can of what the prairie was."

As numbers of bison increase, as areas are burned and reburned in spring, summer, or fall, as interior fences go down, fixed pasture units are becoming what Hamilton calls "patches." It is possible to literally see the changes on the preserve. Last summer, a sweep of tallgrasses that had been uniformly green the year before was transformed into a gardenlike patch of brilliant wildflowers — black-eyed susans, lemon monarda, prairie coneflower, spiderwort, and showy evening primroses.

Nature Conservancy staff at the Prairie Preserve: left to right, Bob Hamilton, Kenny Shieldnight, Mike Perrier, Perry Collins, Kevin Chouteau, Jay Taylor.

Photo by Harvey Payne

Such forbs were here before, but in much smaller numbers. Now we see the wildflowers dominant — blooming together in one large patch. That is because this patch was summer burned. Late growing season fires reduced the dominance of the primary grasses. Then, during the first growing season after the burn, the emerging grass shoots were intensively grazed by bison — who love grass but disdain forbs. With the land newly opened to sun and rain, broad-leaved plants were able to take hold. For a season or two, until the grasses return to dominance, we may enjoy the flowers' colorful display. And so can the various butterflies, bees, insects, birds, prairie chickens and other animals that depend on forbs as well as grasses for sustenance.

Eventually Bob Hamilton hopes to see the whole preserve become a patchy landscape growing helter-skelter, as it did in the long eras before the range was managed for cattle. "Diversity of disturbances leads to diversity of biology," he tells me. But given the geographical boundaries of this protected prairie island and the absence of Indian-set fires, such disturbances will be achieved only through "deliberate randomness."

Hamilton's stewardship dreams run far into the future. "We want to do something that in 500 or 1,000 years will still be thriving. We hope to maintain little lifeboats of plants and animals that will continue to function as viable ecosystems."

The information that will come from his experimental conservation efforts shall, of course, be made available to others. If the preserve's scientists can learn how this tallgrass ecosystem really functions, such knowledge, says Hamilton, could have broad applications. "It might become a tool that ranchers can use to better manage their lands."

He and Harvey and the rest of the preserve's crew are glad to be part of a grand experiment. "It's never been done before," says Hamilton. "I hope it'll still be going in 200 years."

THE CORE STAFF AND CREW who run the preserve's multi-faceted enterprise are a capable bunch — stalwart, flexible, and humorous. Perry Collins, the assistant foreman, lives with his wife Danna and their several children in the white frame house adjoining the preserve's Headquarters. This was Frankie Barnard's Little House, and the home of foreman Ben Johnson, Sr. It has been expanded and remodeled for a modern family. There is a swing-set in the yard, Halloween pumpkins at the doorway, and a stuffed scarecrow. To my surprise, I also see about 25 bison clustered along Perry's reinforced fence as if waiting to be fed.

"What is this — a zoo?" I ask Perry, who has driven up in one of the white Conservancy rigs recently donated by General Motors.

"Just moved them into the new bison pasture," says Perry, a stocky, affable man wear-

He and Harvey and the rest of the preserve's crew are glad to be part of a grand experiment. "It's never been done before," says Hamilton. "I hope it'll still be going in 200 years."

RELEASING THE BISON

The bison release on October 18, 1993 was broadcast round the world by CNN, NBC, CBS, and ABC.

Photo by Harvey Payne

~ ~ ~ BIG BLUESTEM ~ ~ ~

ing Carhartt coveralls and a cap. "Guess they're curious."

These free-ranging bison are wonderfully sleek and healthy, their ruddy winter coats shining as if just groomed. They have flourished since being released onto the prairie in October of 1993. I notice many youngsters poking alongside their mothers.

"They did real good, this year," Perry says. "There's 120 summer calves. Lots more than we expected."

In 1994, only 39 new calves were born on the preserve, not counting the 10 born during the winter of 1993-94, shortly after the original 300 head had been set free in the tallgrass. Damn good, I think. A threefold increase in two years.

"We're going to round 'em all up next week. Cull about 60 bull calves and yearling bulls. Keep the heifers." Perry grins wide. "It's a new experience every day."

I wish I could be there to witness the roundup. It will take place in the new bison trap and the strong pipe corrals and pens that the crew has been building all year. When you see that setup looming huge on the plains, you realize the difference

Bison graze on a patch of prairie that was the site of an earlier prescribed burn. Bison are strongly attracted to the new growth following a burn.
Photo by Harvey Payne

A J o u r n e y I n t o t h e T a l l g r a s s

between herding cows and herding bison. The holding pens are equipped with thick metal shields, scratched and gouged by the bisons' deadly horns. The head-high pipe fences and gates look more like a fortified prison than any corral you have ever seen.

Perry and his men, working under foreman Kenny Shieldnight, will mount their four-wheel all-terrain vehicles and pickups (horseback bison-herding being a rarely practiced, dangerous, and lost art) and push the 450 wild beasts into the enclosure. Sometimes, Perry explains, you have to stand up in your ATV to see over the quick-footed, huge humped animals. It can be more thrilling than anyone hopes because even on wheels, a man is no match for an enraged bull.

"Rounding up bison with a four-wheeler," adds Kenny, "you have to keep them front to you or back to you." By this I gather you don't want to be sideways to those horns.

"Bison are easier to drive than cows. Bison will go into the first hole. You don't herd 'em like cattle, you haze 'em. Give them 50 to 75 yards, don't ride them close up, like cattle."

Since the preserve has no wolves or prairie grizzlies — historic natural predators that kept bison herds genetically strong — preserve managers cull the herd. They round up and sell the weak, the sick, the very young and old animals. They also sell some young bulls. Their purpose is to mimic predator selection patterns. Proceeds from such sales help support the preserve.

Once safely in the corrals, the bison to be sold are separated from the rest and tested for brucellosis and tuberculosis. The others don't need to be tested because the original 300 head herd was tested and certified disease-free before being shipped to the preserve, and again one year later all animals obtained since then were also tested before being allowed into the herd. It is best for both crew and bison to keep contact to a minimum.

In nature, heifers are culled along with bulls, but the preserve's policy is to save heifer calves in order to accelerate the growth of the herd. The heifer calves are vaccinated against brucellosis to ensure the health of their eventual offspring. They are also equipped with electronic chips called transponders embedded under their skin. The transponders hold identifying numbered codes that are read by waving an electronic scanning paddle over them. The scanned transponder number is then automatically fed into a personal computer where the animal's individual file is retrieved.

Coded information includes age, sex, weight, calving success, where the animals came from, when and to whom they were sold. It's all part of the research. A conjunction perfect for the millenium: prehistoric beasts transmitting electronic data.

KENNY SHIELDNIGHT is a blue-eyed Oklahoman in blue denim, his round face weathered in smile-lines and crinkles — a cowboy conservationist. He and his wife, Royce, and their young daughter Billie Jean live in a rambling ranch house near the entrance to the preserve. A day room lined with saddles and tack leads in from the driveway and barns. There is a long formica kitchen

Since the preserve has no wolves or prairie grizzlies — historic natural predators that kept bison herds genetically strong — preserve managers cull the herd. They round up and sell the weak, the sick, the very young and old animals. They also sell some young bulls. Their purpose is to mimic predator selection patterns. Proceeds from such sales help support the preserve.

counter, and beyond it an open living room carpeted in shag and furnished with plaid-covered easy chairs.

Royce joins me for a smoke. She is lean and narrow-hipped, with shoulder-length gray-streaked hair. Raised on New Mexico ranches by a cowboying family, she rests easy on the Oklahoma prairies. Royce does the cleaning chores at the preserve's Headquarters and the Stucco House. She cooks hearty lunches for the ranch crew and helps out with the horses and cattle that she and Kenny raise on their place. Royce exhales a small cloud. "I love the space and the freedom out here."

Kenny goes to the kitchen to fetch a cold, end-of-the-day beer. He tells me the work on the preserve is not that different from work he's done on other big ranches: building fence, running cattle, building more fence, running bison. "It's still a ranch," he says, "and I'm the working end of it."

But it is not really the same. "Cattle business, you've got a lot of burnout in it. Cattle day after day after day." Here, Kenny is not bored. He is learning new things. For example, he has learned that to control brush, fall burning is more effective than the common practice of spring burning. "In fall, there's up to a 90 percent kill. Spring burning, it'd take three to four years straight to kill off the same brush."

"When I was cowboying," he continues, "there was grass, and there was weeds. Now I know all the names of the grasses, and the weeds have become wildflowers."

At first, Kenny and his crew were often hassled by other ranchers and cowboy neighbors, mostly because the preserve didn't run any cattle for a couple of years. "Some guy'd come along and ask what I was doing." Kenny laughs. "I'd look him in the eye and say, 'I'm countin' butterflies today.'"

These days folks are much more friendly. "That's because we're good neighbors," says Kenny. "I'll go out of my way to help them. Word gets around. If you're a good neighbor, you'll have good neighbors.

"I'm not retired out here," he says, grabbing up his daughter. "I'm going to die out here. Only problem is me and my girl don't have enough time to go fishing, do we?" The child shakes her head, blonde curls flying. "The truth is, I believe in what we're doing."

BOB HAMILTON also believes. He better believe, for he is largely responsible for the prairie's management. We sit in the preserve's Pawhuska office. Bob is tired, having just delivered 44 calves from the Wichita Mountains Wildlife Refuge to increase the genetic diversity of the Tallgrass Prairie Preserve's herd. He is late for dinner, but Bob's enthusiasm is unbounded as he catches me up on progress.

"We've been building fences and bison corrals, restoring buildings, buying fire equipment. It takes a lot to run this place," says Hamilton.

He feels good about the accomplishments of the last two years. "I feel a lot more comfortable about summer burning and free-ranging bison, things I had never done before."

Summer burning is the most destabilizing activity you can do, he says, because "you push succession backwards.

"The bison," he adds, "are using the land as they see fit. They're using some patches more than other patches — even patches of patches." But the bison are thriving in the tallgrass. Hamilton is delighted at the high rate of calving this year. He is ahead of his goal, which he describes as "bisonization of the preserve over time."

The preserve released its original 300 head in 1993. In eight to ten years they expect to have about 2,000 bison ranging free on the core ranch. Starting with 5,000 acres in bison pasture, they have added some 800 acres this year. By winter they will have added 1,400 acres, and plan to increase forage by 2,000 to 3,000 acres each succeeding year until the whole range (except for several thousand acres dedicated to cattle and control use) is populated with bison.

Wild turkeys (*Meleagris gallopavo*) are still found on the Preserve. Below, a wild turkey feather.

Photos by Harvey Payne

"We've figured out the carrying capacity in AUM's (Animal Unit Months)," says Hamilton. "A bison AUM assumes that an adult will consume 2.5 to 3 percent of its body weight each day for one month. For a 1,000 pound bison, that adds up to 30 pounds of air-dried forage each day, or 900 pounds per month, or 10,800 pounds a year. USDA soil survey maps for the entire preserve have been computer digitized, allowing for forage production estimates of all pastures. Determining when and how much acreage needs to be added to the bison unit consists of calculating herd forage needs, and dividing by land productivity to achieve a target forage removal rate."

The preserve leased pasture for intensive summer grazing for 10,000 yearling cattle in 1995, and plans to lower the number to 9,200 in 1996. They will also overwinter a bunch this year to see how winter grazing will affect grass production. That's a lot of cattle, but as the bison increase, says Hamilton, the cattle will decrease until they occupy fewer than 1,000 acres.

About 1,400 acres have been set aside as a control unit — no fires, no grazing by cattle or bison. With this control, they will be able to compare traditional set-aside conservation practices, which Hamilton calls the "reductionist approach," with a more risky "experimental/dynamic holistic management approach." As part of this research, his scientific staff is gathering information about the effects of bison/fire management on invertebrate, bird, and plant communities. The results will be part of a larger project that gathers information from three Conservancy Great Plains preserves that manage with fire and

bison — the Tallgrass Prairie Preserve, the Niobrara Valley Preserve in northern Nebraska, and the Cross Ranch in North Dakota. Their data will be compared with data from the Konza Prairie Research Natural Area in Kansas, which studies plots of land under fixed management conditions.

The preserve is also part of a satellite research project being conducted by Augustana College and the Earth Remote Observation Survey (EROS) Data Center (a U. S. Geologic Survey Facility), both in Sioux Falls, South Dakota. These researchers will track the productivity and forage qualities of the preserve's grasslands using satellite images from which they compile data. I would love to see those space pictures — the great sweep of big bluestem, the peninsulas of blackjacks colored scarlet or chartreuse — infrared imagery charting by color the nitrogen content of the earth. I could talk research with Bob all evening, but he is hungry and so am I.

The historic building that was once Chapman-Barnard Ranch Headquarters now houses special events, provides an office for Conservancy staff, and welcomes visitors. Some 30,000 visitors a year come to see and learn about the Tallgrass Prairie Preserve.

Photo by Harvey Payne

LIFE AND DEATH

Sunset on the tallgrass prairie. Even the husk of a prairie tree is useful, providing insects for woodpecker feasts, and offering nesting and roosting possibilities for various birds. Below, right, cumulus-like clouds flower from the flames that will scorch and renew the earth.

Photos by Harvey Payne

BY SEVEN O' CLOCK, a bunch of us tallgrass enthusiasts are sitting at a long picnic table in Pawhuska's proudest eating establishment, Bad Brad's Barbecue. Mary Barnard Lawrence is there, and my editors Paulette Millichap and Sally Dennison, and Scott Edward Anderson, director of development with the Nature Conservancy of Alaska, and the Oklahoma chapter's new director, Brita Haugland Cantrell, and preserve director Harvey Payne.

We puzzle over the menu. Shall we have pork ribs or beef ribs, chicken, sausages, or brisket? For side dishes, will we dare order the spicy cowboy beans or stick with brown beans, coleslaw, fries, salad? And, will we have room for blackberry cobbler, or peach cobbler, or cherry? And do we want ice cream on top? It's a tough life, but someone's got to live it.

An elderly couple passes our table and stops to chat with Harvey. These are two of the preserve's core of 80 volunteer docents. On Wednesdays and Fridays, weekends and holidays from mid-March through mid-November, the docents greet tourists and local visitors at the Headquarters office. They direct hikers to nature walks, tell them where to find bison, explain the history of the Bunkhouse and ranch, describe the preserve's goals, sell hats, tee-shirts, books.

It's an important job, for visitation has increased at least 10 percent each year. In 1995, says Harvey Payne, more than 12,500 people signed the guest register. Since probably half the visitors don't bother to sign in, he estimates from 25,000 to 30,000 guests passed through that year. And although most are from Oklahoma and surrounding states, a great many are foreign tourists — with 28 countries represented in 1995.

"The attraction," says Harvey, "is to see tallgrass prairies being recreated." Another attraction is the ranching heritage. "Tourists love visiting an authentic ranch from the golden age," he continues. "You'd have to go to Texas, to the King Ranch, to see another ranch that has this tradition."

During the six years the preserve has been in existence, Harvey has observed a big change in local attitudes. "More and more community people are becoming involved. Support, like the bison numbers, grows exponentially."

Harvey finishes his brisket and digs into his beans. "Wide-eyed, shrill-voiced conservation does not work here," he explains. "The Conservancy's businesslike, science-based approach is much more effective."

There have, of course, been problems, like a few oil and salt water spills from some of the hundred producing wells on the preserve's land. But Harvey sat down with the oil pro-

ducers and they developed plans to treat the affected areas. Energy exploration is ongoing. Chevron has concluded a deal with the Osage tribe to purchase a 20-year lease for exploration in the county. Although much of the preserve is leased, some new ground will be affected. Harvey and Brita have already met with the Chevron people. "They have the best technologies," says Harvey. "We will work with them to keep disturbances to the land at a minimum. It just goes to show that we can have a world-class preserve and have ongoing economic activities such as oil and gas production. The two do not have to be mutually exclusive."

The Oklahoma Nature Conservancy has also been working with Conoco and Devon Energy to restore land that was damaged long ago. The University of Tulsa is involved. "We're a great field lab for them," says Harvey.

Oil, bison, grasshoppers, forbs, fire — the research opportunities are only beginning. There are innumerable grasslands studies to be done, and a burn study conducted with Oklahoma State University, and ongoing bird counts — even studies on butterflies.

"Public education is an equally important goal," adds Brita Haugland Cantrell. Brita is an attractive, open-faced Nordic woman, straight-talking and friendly. She is a lawyer by training, having come to the Conservancy from the Oklahoma Attorney General's office, but is particularly interested in expanding educational activities associated with the preserve. To facilitate an educational program, the Oklahoma field office has recently hired

Tiger swallowtail butterfly on butterfly milkweed.

Photo by Harvey Payne

an education and outreach coordinator. Projects in place include an Oklahoma teacher-training program in the field of Conservation Science. And Tic-Tac-Toe Bison — a game that teaches principles regarding the science of prairie species.

Brita and her staff are encouraging schools to bring students to the preserve on field trips. She says, "the tallgrass is a living laboratory for students." Brita loves the prairie, but admits there are constant challenges. "We're learning as we go. Eventually it will even up. Our mission is biological growth through sound science as this tremendous habitat unfolds."

By now, all of us are sated with barbecue, but I cannot pass up fresh blackberry cobbler — with a tiny scoop of ice cream. Brita agrees to share bites. She tells me about her first visit to the preserve to meet the staff. "Harvey said, 'wear boots'. By the time we'd finished hiking, my pants were yellow with goldenrod dust. One eye was swollen shut. I was sneezing. Harvey gave me a roll of toilet paper." She laughs. "That's how I met all those people.

"I have been amazed about how almost apolitical this organization is," Brita continues. "Our work draws people irrespective of whether they're liberals or conservatives. A tallgrass visit is healing."

Mary Barnard Lawrence is listening. My editor, Paulette, touches Mary's arm. She smiles. "Mary is the heart of the place," says Paulette.

The collared lizard is at home on the sandstone boulders and rocks of the preserve.

Photo by Harvey Payne

A J o u r n e y I n t o t h e T a l l g r a s s

Aerial view of the Tallgrass
Prairie Preserve.

Photo by Harvey Payne

NEXT MORNING at the Headquarters bunkhouse, Mary is up at first light. She pads into the airy, whitewashed kitchen wearing a robe, slippers and a woolly sheepskin vest. Harvey pours her a freshly brewed cup of coffee and Mary warms her hands around the steaming mug. "It's chilly," she says.

Much colder than her house in Carefree, Arizona. But Mary does not mind the chill. She is anxious to get out on her morning walk in the tallgrass.

Several years ago, on October 18, 1993, Mary was a key person in the bison release ceremony — a media event that introduced the Tallgrass Prairie Preserve to the American public. That morning, too, was cool, and it was foggy. General Norman Schwarzkopf took center stage in his role as a new board member of The Nature Conservancy. Secret Service men mixed with crews from three networks and CNN. The crowd at the bison pens included ranchers, oilmen, environmentalists, school children, patrons of the Con-servancy, an Osage tribal delegation that would soon give the General his Osage Indian name. It also included Mary's children, siblings, nieces and nephews.

There were, of course, speeches. The most eloquent was by then-Senator David L. Boren, who had championed a national tallgrass preserve in Congress and continued his support when The Nature Conservancy made the dream real. Boren referred to Alexis de Tocqueville's observation that America was a place where ordinary people cared for the common good and volunteered to achieve communal goals. He praised Oklahoma's foresight in preserving bison when they were endangered. And he honored the spirit of stewardship that had conserved this prime tallgrass prairie. It was, he said, a heritage of care that began with Native Americans such as the Osage, was continued by responsible ranchers such as Chapman and Barnard, and will thrive under the hands of The Nature Conservancy.

"It is impossible . . . to fully understand America without seeing the prairie."

Grass is where I began my journey, and in grass I will end it. I have come a long way into the stories of tallgrass, and I have learned that bison, humans, even grass and oaks mingle in a tenuous earthly balance. Fire is different. Today the grass glows red as fire. Red light seems to be emerging from the earth. The universe is made of fire.

"It is impossible," said Boren, "to fully understand America without seeing the prairie. To walk through the tallgrass under a boundless sky is to understand in a new way the spiritual integrity of Native American culture. . . . To experience the prairie is to experience that sense of possibility, of a chance for a fresh start and a new beginning, and of the hope carried west by every pioneer."

In the ceremony's culminating moment, 300 bison were released from their pens. The bison never hesitated: they swept in a broad curve past grandstands loaded with spectators, and trailed into the tallgrass. This was no thundering herd, but still, the ground shook. Involuntary tears rose in many eyes.

Remembering that day, Keenan Barnard said, "Grandpa would take a lot of pride in the fact that this ranch is giving so many other people joy."

"I drove up with my brother and mother," recalls Mary's daughter, Helene. "Mother was practicing her speech. It made me and Richie cry so hard I had to stop driving."

Mary's speech was direct and personal. "I remember trying to visualize buffalo on the land rather than the herds of whiteface Herefords I had grown up with — and finally laughing at my poor efforts," said Mary. But now that the buffalo were actually there and running, it was no longer a laughing matter.

"All of us here today are surely a part of history in the making," she concluded. "This is sacred land; it is time for the bison to come home. With the coming home of the bison, I can't help but feel that some part of me is coming home too."

ALTHOUGH I AM STILL a stranger in these parts, I have that same powerful sense of coming home as I hike up into the rounded blackjack hills from the Stucco House on a cere November evening. The woods open when I reach the ridge and I look over the prairie in a soft rain. I see the deep sienna color of oak leaves and the orange-tipped bluestem grasses. Thunder booms in the distance and lightning is a flash of blue on the horizon.

Below me in the valley, I see yellow lights in Perry's house and in the cowboy shacks behind it. I see the dark shapes of dappled and roan horses grazing calmly in the horse pasture. Coyotes sing to each other in the falling dark, and I hear the cry of a great horned owl, who rests stone-still in the gnarled arms of a lone post oak. A deer crosses my path and disappears into the undergrowth. Although there is barely a breeze in the rain-still air, when I walk between twin oaks that arch over my head like a tunnel, their leaves rattle, hiss and whisper as though inhabited by ghosts. I shiver and turn back toward the solitary comforts of a shot of whiskey and a clean, warm bed.

Next morning is Sunday, overcast and drizzling. I head for the crossroads in the bison unit, where I know part of the herd is grazing last summer's burn. Pickups pass by me on the gravel road, drivers waving in the habit of the country. A white Buick full of white-haired oldsters on a Sunday drive cruises slowly by. The cars pull to a stop near a patch of blackened ground where about 60 bison quietly graze the bright green new shoots of grass that have emerged in fire's wake.

I join the motley visitors who stand almost reverently before the bison. Some approach nearer the free-ranging animals with cameras. Some stay back, content to see the humps, horns, dainty hooves, wide-set round eyes close up through the lenses of binoculars. A few hunters in camo gear and scarlet vests pile out of a pickup. The prairie chicken hunting is bad, they say. Fewer birds every year. Everyone whispers, as though in church. Parents with small children hold them close.

From distant ridges I hear the chuck-chuck-chuck of oil pumps beating like the Osage drums of another century. We will never know what the prairie was before we stepped into it. Some of its elements are irretrievable. It is hopeless to try to replicate the past. This is the prairie of now — a living, pulsing organism — a compromise that seems to be working. City people are here, and local country folk, foreign tourists, and hunters who have come to see the native beast on its native land, never mind roads and pumps and telephone wires.

Later, near the abandoned foundations of the ghost oil-boom town of Pearsonia, I take my own camera out, for I have happened on the perfect symbolic image. But I have been profligate in my picture-taking and discover I am out of film. I decide to chase the image anyway, imprint it on memory, where it belongs.

The time is near sunset. I walk down a draw through big bluestem stalks seven feet high. The tallgrass drips from this afternoon's rain, and my jeans are soaked. But on the western horizon, black rain clouds are rising up the sky, dispersing.

Across a wetland creek bottom stands a bull bison, his thick brown winter coat fringed in the tones of a lion's mane, back-lit by the setting sun of America's West. He will be my foreground. Behind him is an abandoned oil field with rusting pumps arrested in mid-motion like huge pecking crows. Still further back, in middle perspective, is the wide and rolling prairie, speckled with grazing cattle from some modern cowboy ranch.

But it is the far distance that astonishes. Here is an apricot sky running with silver-edged clouds, washed with patches of bird's-egg blue, like a Venetian painting. The heavens are opening. Under wings of light, grasslands of big bluestem spread in the four sacred directions — a luminous circle of grass.

Grass is where I began my journey, and in grass I will end it. I have come a long way into the stories of tallgrass, and I have learned that bison, humans, even grass and oaks mingle in a tenuous earthly balance. Fire is different. Today the grass glows red as fire. Red light seems to be emerging from the earth. The universe is made of fire.

I stand in the tallgrass after rain, feeling insignificant as a grasshopper or a spider under the red sun. Soon I will be heading sunward. I will drive across the Great Plains toward my Montana mountains and this prairie will ride with me in memory and imagination, and my way will be made better.

GENERAL WORKS ON THE GREAT PLAINS

Walter Prescott Webb, *The Great Plains* (1931). The pioneer work; now outdated in many ways but still worth reading. Available as a University of Nebraska Press paperback.

Carl F. Kraenzel, *The Great Plains in Transition* (1955). A foundation work published by the University of Oklahoma Press. Not currently available in paperback.

James C. Malin, *History and Ecology: Studies of the Grassland* (1984). Currently available as a University of Nebraska paperback. Malin was the greatest of all the grassland historians. The chapter in this book entitled "An Introduction to the History of the Bluestem — Pasture Region of Kansas: A Study of Adaptation to Geographical Environment" is the single most important essay ever written on the bluestem region.

Brian W. Blouet and Frederick C. Luebke, eds., *The Great Plains Environment and Culture* (1979). An important collection of essays published by the University of Nebraska Press.

United States Department of Agriculture, *Grass: The Yearbook of Agriculture for 1948*. Considered by many to be the classic volume dealing with grasslands. A beautiful book and essential for understanding the Great Plains.

William Least Heat-Moon, *PrairyErth (a deep map)*. (1991) Currently available in paperback. Certainly the model for what should be done in the Osage. This is a superb book, one based on careful archival research and the willingness to become deeply invested in the life of Chase County.

Pasture and Range Plants. Fort Hays State University, 1989. Deservedly well-known as a wonderful introduction to the subject.

OSAGE TRIBAL HISTORY

The very best general introduction to Osage tribal history is the work of Terry Wilson. Wilson has written two outstanding books: *The Osage* (Chelsea House, 1988) and *The Underground Reservation: Osage Oil* (University of Nebraska Press, 1985). Readers might well begin with Wilson's 1988 book and then move on to the 1985 scholarly monograph.

John Joseph Mathews, *Talking to the Moon: Wildlife Adventures on the Plains and Prairies of Osage Country*. (1945) — the result of ten years of observing nature and wildlife from a stone house among blackjack oaks; *Wah 'Kon-Tah, The Osage and the White Man's Road*, an account of reservation life under Quaker agent Major Laban J. Miles 1878 through 1931; and an autobiographical novel, *Sundown*, about a mixed-blood Osage born into the twentieth century. All available from the University of Oklahoma Press. Relevant for anyone studying the Tallgrass Prairie Preserve is *The Osages, Children of the Middle Waters*. Based on interviews with Osage elders, it tells the story of the tribe from mythological beginnings through assimilation. Available in paperback from the University of Oklahoma Press.

Dennis McAuliffe, Jr., *The Deaths of Sybil Bolton*. (1994) A recent book on the Osage Reign of Terror.

Bureau of Indian Affairs. *The Osage People and Their Trust Property*. (1953) Very important for understanding the tribe and the mineral estate.

In 1957 and again in 1972 the Osage Tribe issued interesting booklets commemorating important milestones in tribal history. *The Osage Indians Semi-Centennial Celebration (1907-1957)* and *The Osage Indian Tribe Centennial Celebration (1872-1972)* may be found in the Pawhuska Public Library.

Linda Hogan, *Mean Spirit*. (1990) A novel about the Osage Reign of Terror.

Osage Indian Customs and Myths, by Louis F. Burns is also useful. Published by Ciga Press, Fallbrook, California.

RANCHING IN THE OSAGE

Robert M. Burrrill, *Grassland Empires: The Geography of Ranching in Osage County, Oklahoma, 1872-1965*. Ph.D. diss., University of Kansas, 1970. Currently available on request from UMI Dissertation Services. This is the fundamental work on ranching in Osage County. Burrill did massive archival research and also worked with Dick Whetsell at the Adams Ranch. Nothing else can take the place of a careful reading of Burrill.

Terry Hammons, *Ranching from the Front Seat of a Buick: The Life of Oklahoma's A.A. "Jack"Drummond*. (1982) The Drummond family remains one of the most important ranching families in the Osage. Toward the end of his life, Jack realized that his wheeler-dealer image and constant court battles had caused his larger family more than a little consternation. This book was his way of explaining his actions and answering his many critics. Despite its obvious biases, it offers a fascinating account of the times, and a rare glimpse into a fast-changing industry. Read this account for what it is: a revealing self-portrait of a feisty entrepreneur whose competitiveness and acquisitiveness were sharpened by life in the Osage.

The late John Roy Drummond wrote a general family history that was privately published some years ago. It is available in the Pawhuska and Hominy Public Libraries.

Ellen Jayne Maris Wheeler, ed., *Cherokee Outlet Cowboy: Recollections of Laban S. Records.* University of Oklahoma Press, 1995. Chapter 3 contains Records's account of the 1870s in the Osage county. A valuable early account.

We have found two books by Harold L. Oppenheimer helpful in understanding the business of ranching: *Cowboy Arithmetic* (1961) and *Cowboy Economics* (1971).

OIL IN THE OSAGE

Kenny A. Franks, *The Osage Oil Boom* (1989). Usually cited as the standard work on the subject.

Robert Gregory, *Oil in Oklahoma* (1976). A brief introduction.

Mary Elizabeth Wood, *Historical Review: Bird Creek Basin from 1800.* Originally prepared for the U.S. Army Corps of Engineers and reprinted in 1979 by the Skiatook Historical Society. Hard to find but contains some valuable information.

Carl N. Tyson, James H. Thomas, and Odie B. Faulk, *The McMan: The Lives of Robert M. McFarlin and James A. Chapman.* (1977) An authorized biography that must be used with great caution; has some valuable information on the history of the Chapman-Barnard Ranch. Published by University of Oklahoma Press.

Osage County Profiles, published by the Osage County Historical Society in 1978, is a treasure trove of information not readily available elsewhere. It is a real testimony to the dedication of Mrs. Smith and her volunteer staff.

Arthur H. Lamb, *Tragedies of the Osage Hills* (undated but probably published sometime in the 1930s). Many readers come upon this little book and misunderstand its nature. It is a compilation of newspaper accounts of Osage county violence. It must be used with great caution.

The Deaths of Sybil Bolton by Dennis McAuliffe, Jr. is the story of a journalist tracing the mysterious death of his Osage grandmother back to the oil-greed murders of the Reign of Terror in the 1920s. Published by Random House in 1994. Linda Hogan's novel *Mean Spirit* is a fictional rendering of the story.

GRASSLANDS

John Madson's, *Where the Sky Began, Land of the Tallgrass Prairie,* Sierra Club Books, is the best book for learning basic prairie ecology. Also by Madson, with photos by Frank Oberle, is The Nature Conservancy's picture-book, *Tallgrass Prairie.* Published by Falcon Press, it lists tallgrass prairie sites from North Dakota to Texas and Mississippi.

Richard Manning's *Grassland: The History, Biology, Politics, and Promise of the American Prairie,* from Penguin Books, USA, offers a recent, environmentally-focused study of the plains.

Grasslands, by Lauren Brown, an Audubon Society Nature Guide to birds, wildflowers, trees, grasses, and insects, is a necessary component of any grasslands hike. Published by Alfred A. Knopf.

Pasture and Range Plants, published by Fort Hays State University in Kansas, is a beautifully illustrated botanical compendium of tallgrasses, forbs, and legumes.

Grass: The Yearbook of Agriculture for 1948, a classic and beautiful grasslands resource published by the United States Department of Agriculture.

Louise Erdrich's "Big Grass," in The Nature Conservancy's collection *Heart of the Land,* available in a Vintage paperback. Finally, of course, is the poetry lovers' masterpiece — Walt Whitman's *Leaves of Grass.*

EXPLORERS AND NATURALISTS

Journal of an Indian Trader, Anthony Glass and the Texas Trading Frontier, 1790-1810 is one of the earliest personal accounts about the southern plains region. Edited by Dan L. Flores, it is available from Texas A & M University Press.

Also edited by Dan L. Flores, *Jefferson & Southwestern Exploration, The Freeman & Custis Accounts of the Red River Expedition of 1806*, records the second major expedition into Louisiana Purchase territory – the first being Lewis and Clark's more famous northwestern expedition. It is available from the University of Oklahoma Press.

Thomas Nuttall's *A Tour of Travels into Arkansas Territory during the Year 1819* is a classic by one of the nineteenth century's great naturalists. Edited by Savoie Lottinville, this book, too, is available from the University of Oklahoma Press.

Washington Irving's *A Tour of the Prairies* recounts his adventures in Arkansas and Oklahoma Indian territories in 1832. Possibly the most widely-read historical account of the region, it is available in paperback, edited by John Francis McDermott, from the University of Oklahoma Press.

On the Western Tour with Washington Irving, The Journal and Letters of Count de Pourtales, edited by George F. Spaulding, is a charming account by a young Frenchman who traveled with Irving. Published by the University of Oklahoma Press.

George Catlin's *Letters and Notes on the Manners, Customs, and Conditions of North American Indians* reports on the artist's eight years of travel in Indian country, from 1832-1839. The whole work is a visual and literary delight, but Letters No. 37 through No. 45 are most relevant.

Tixier's *Travels on the Osage Prairies*, edited by John Frances McDermott, recounts a French explorer's experiences among the Osages in 1839-40. Published by the University of Oklahoma Press in 1940.

A Naturalist in Indian Territory, The Journals of S.W. Woodhouse, 1849-50, edited by John S. Tomer and Michael J. Brodhead, depicts the camp life and observations of a naturalist on a Creek boundary expedition in northern Oklahoma. It was recently published by the University of Oklahoma Press.

Thomas Jefferson's "Letter to Senator John Breckinridge" (1803), and his "Letter to Elbridge Gerry" (1799) may be found in *The Portable Thomas Jefferson*, edited by Merrill D. Peterson, a Viking Press book, available in paperback from Penguin Books.

PIONEERS AND SETTLERS

Joanna L. Stratton's *Pioneer Women, Voices from the Kansas Frontier* offers compelling voices from prairie women. It was published by Simon & Schuster in a paperback Touchstone Edition.

Other good sources on pioneer women include Julie Roy Jeffrey's *Frontier Women: The Trans-Mississippi West, 1840-1890;* Sandra Myres's *Westering Women and the Frontier Experience, 1800-1915;* Glenda Riley's *The Female Frontier: A Comparative View of Women on the Prairie and Plains;* and Susan Armitage and Elizabeth Jamison's compilation, *The Women's West.*

More specific to the Oklahoma and Kansas plains experience are *Oklahoma Memories*, edited by Anne Hodges Morgan and Rennard Strickland — a University of Oklahoma Press paperback.

Osage County Profiles, published in 1978 and edited by Betty Smith, is a yearbook-style collection of reminiscences by residents of Osage County. Including memoirs of settlers, ranchers, oil people, and Indians, and illustrated with portraits and historical photographs, it is available from the Osage County Historical Society in Pawhuska.

Angie Debo's *Prairie City* is a case history of the evolution of town life on the Oklahoma plains starting with the land rush of 1889. It is available from Council Oak Books in Tulsa.

In *Plains Folk: A Commonplace of the Great Plains*, and *Plains Folk II: The Romance of the Landscape*, Jim Hoy and Tom Isern have collected oral histories and folklore as told by the diverse peoples who make their homes on the American prairies. Published by the University of Oklahoma Press.

In *The Glory of the Hills: The Flint Hills Editorials of R. A. Clymer*, edited by William Galvini, we hear the voice of an old Flint Hills newspaperman in love with the grasslands. Including black-and-white photographs, the pamphlet is available from the Butler County Historical Society, El Dorado, Kansas.

INDIAN TERRITORY – GENERAL HISTORY

For a readable overview of Oklahoma's history, I recommend *Oklahoma, A History,* by H. Wayne Morgan and Anne Hodges Morgan, published by W. W. Norton as part of their series, *The States and the Nation.* It includes a Historical Guide prepared by the editors of the American Association for Local History.

W. David Baird & Danney Goble, *The Story of Oklahoma,* is a useful textbook which focuses on the diversity of Oklahoma's land and peoples. Published by the University of Oklahoma Press in 1994.

Grant Foreman's *Indian Removal,* available from the University of Oklahoma Press, recounts the sad history of the Trail of Tears and the forced emigration of the Five Civilized Tribes to Indian Territory.

Angie Debo depicts the aftermath of that story in her classic study, *And Still the Waters Run, The Betrayal of the Five Civilized Tribes.* First published in 1940, it has been reissued in paperback by Oklahoma University Press.

Ben Yagoda's fine book, *Will Rogers, A Biography* presents the life, times, and words of Oklahoma's Cherokee Kid – a mixed-blood cowboy turned humorist and, finally, American sage. From Harper-Collins West.

References to the Ghost Dance phenomenon are from James Mooney, *The Ghost Dance Religion and the Sioux Outbreak of 1890,* originally published in the Fourteenth Annual Report of the Bureau of Ethnology, reprinted by the University of Chicago Press. Chief Plenty Coup's vision is reported in Frank Bird Linderman's *Plenty Coups, Chief of the Crow,* Bison Books. University of Nebraska Press.

BISON AND FIRE

Larry Barsness's *The Bison in Art, A Graphic Chronicle of the American Bison,* published by Northland Press for the Amon Carter Museum of Western Art in 1977, offers a rich mixture of history and art depicting the story of the North American Bison.

Wayne Gard's *The Great Buffalo Hunt* is a lively account of the destruction of the huge bison herds, with quotes and anecdotes from original sources. First published in 1959, it is available as a University of Nebraska Press Bison Book in paperback.

The Time of the Buffalo by Tom McHugh is a more recent telling of the bison's story. Another University of Nebraska Press book.

For some of the many firsthand accounts, see Alexander Ross's *The Fur Hunters of the Far West,* University of Oklahoma Press; and Alexander Majors, *Seventy Years on the Frontier,* as well as Granville Stuart's memoir *Forty Years on the Frontier.*

Bison populations and movements were directly affected by prairie fires. Discussions of such inter-relationships, as well as data regarding fire and grasslands ecology may be found in *Fire in North American Tallgrass Prairies,* edited by Scott L. Collins and Linda L. Wallace, a 1990 publication of the University of Oklahoma Press.

Fire Ecology, United States and Southern Canada, published in 1982 by John Wiley & Sons is the premier scientific reference on the subject. For a theoretical and historical overview, see Stephen Pyne's *Fire in America: A Cultural History of Wildland and Rural Fire,* Princeton University Press.

ANNICK SMITH AND JAMES P. RONDA

ACKNOWLEDGMENTS

Pages 19-20 Reprinted by permission of Simon & Schuster from *Pioneer Women* by Joanna Stratton. Copyright ©1981 by Joanna Stratton, pp. 43-46.

Pages 20-23 Reprinted by permission of University of Oklahoma Press from *A Tour on the Prairies* by Washington Irving. New edition copyright ©1956 by University of Oklahoma Press, p. 90, pp. 175-76.

Pages 38-41 Reprinted by permission of the Butler County Historical Society, El Dorado, Kansas from *The Glory of the Hills: The Flint Hills Editorials of R. A. Clymer,* edited by William Galvini, 1989, p. 1.

Page 41 Reprinted by permission of Simon & Schuster from *Pioneer Women* by Joanna Stratton. Copyright ©1981 by Joanna Stratton, pp. 43-46.

Page 41 Reprinted by permission of Random House, Inc. (or any of its subsidiaries) with The Nature Conservancy from *Heart of the Land,* "Big Grass," by Louise Erdrich. Copyright ©1994, p. 149.

Page 45 Reprinted by permission of University of Oklahoma Press from *A Tour on the Prairies* by Washington Irving. New edition copyright ©1956 by University of Oklahoma Press, p. 90, pp. 175-176.

Pages 50-55 Reprinted by permission of University of Oklahoma Press from *The Osages: Children of the Middle Waters* by John Joseph Mathews. Copyright ©1961 by University of Oklahoma Press, pp. vii-xiii, 10, 45, 80-84, 210, 383, 424, 450, 572, 649, 719-720.

Page 53 Reprinted by permission of University of Oklahoma Press from *Talking to the Moon: Wildlife Adventures on the Plains and Prairies of Osage Country* by John Joseph Mathews. Copyright ©1945;1981 by University of Oklahoma Press, p. 142.

Page 55-60 Reprinted by permission of University of Oklahoma Press from *Jefferson & Southwestern Exploration: The Freeman & Custis Accounts of the Red River Expedition of 1806* edited by Dan L. Flores. Copyright ©1984 by University of Oklahoma Press, pp. 234, 271.

Page 61-62 Reprinted by permission of University of Oklahoma Press from *Thomas Nuttall: A Journal of Travels into the Arkansas Territory During the Year 1819* edited by Savoie Lottinville. Copyright ©1980 by University of Oklahoma Press, pp. 162, 178, 205.

Pages 62-64, 68 Reprinted by permission of University of Oklahoma Press from *A Naturalist in Indian Territory: The Journals of S. W. Woodhouse, 1849-50* edited and annotated by John S. Tomer and Michael J. Brodhead. Copyright ©1992 by University of Oklahoma Press, pp. 96, 109, 110.

Pages 89-90 Reprinted by permission of Springer-Verlag: New York from *Fire in the Tropical Biota, Ecosystem Processes and Global Challenges,* by J. G. Goldammer, ed.: W. Schule, "Landscapes and Climate in Prehistory: Interactions of Wildlife, Man, and Fire," chapter 13, 1991, pp. 274-315.

Pages 97-98 Reprinted by permission of University of Oklahoma Press from *Jefferson & Southwestern Exploration: The Freeman & Custis Accounts of the Red River Expedition of 1806* edited by Dan L. Flores. Copyright ©984 by University of Oklahoma Press, pp. 234, 271.

Page 98 Reprinted by permission of Simon & Schuster from *Pioneer Women* by Joanna Stratton. Copyright ©1981 by Joanna Stratton, pp. 43-46.

Pages 98-99 Reprinted by permission of the author from *Where the Sky Began* by John Madson. Copyright ©1985 by John Madson, pp. 188-189.

Page 102 Reprinted by permission of University of Oklahoma Press from *Alexander Ross: The Fur Hunters of the Far West* edited by Kenneth A. Spaulding. Copyright ©1956 by University of Oklahoma Press, p. 283.

Page 104 From a publication of Reprint Services Corp., *Seventy Years on the Frontier* by Alexander Majors, 1893, pp. 194-200.

Page 104 Reprinted by permission of Amon Carter Museum from *The Bison in Art, A Graphic Chronicle of the American Bison* by Larry Barsness. Copyright ©1977 by Larry Barsness, pp. 13, 22.

Pages 106-108 Reprinted by permission of University of Oklahoma Press from *Tixier's Travels on the Osage Prairies* edited by John Francis McDermott, translated by Albert J. Salvan. Copyright ©1940 by University of Oklahoma Press, p. 197.

Pages 109-110 Reprinted by permission of Alfred A. Knopf from *The Great Buffalo Hunt* by Wayne Gard. Copyright ©1959 by Wayne Gard, p. 266.

Pages 112-114 Reprinted by permission of University of Oklahoma Press from *On the Western Tour with Washington Irving: The Journals and Letters of Count de Pourtales* edited by George F. Spaulding, translated by Seymour Feiler. Copyright ©1968 by George F. Spaulding, pp. 69-70.

Pages 114-115 Reprinted by permission of University of Oklahoma Press from *The Osages: Children of the Middle Waters* by John Joseph Mathews. Copyright ©1961 by University of Oklahoma Press, pp. vii-xiii, 10, 45, 80-84, 210, 383, 424, 450, 572, 649, 719-720.

Page 116 Reprinted by permission of Amon Carter Museum from *The Bison in Art, A Graphic Chronicle of the American Bison* by Larry Barsness. Copyright ©1977 by Larry Barsness, pp. 13, 22.

Pages 116-117 Reprinted by permission of Alfred A. Knopf from *The Great Buffalo Hunt* by Wayne Gard. Copyright ©1959 by Wayne Gard, p. 266.

Pages 120-121 Reprinted by permission of Harper & Collins from *Plenty Coups, Chief of the Crow* by Frank Bird Linderman. Copyright ©1962 by F. P. Linderman, pp. 227-237.

Pages 127-128 From *The Portable Thomas Jefferson* edited by Merrll D. Peterson, Penguin Books, pp. 494, 477.

Pages 128-130 Reprinted by permission of University of Oklahoma Press from *The Osages: Children of the Middle Waters* by John Joseph Mathews. Copyright ©1961 University of Oklahoma Press, pp. vii-xiii, 10, 45, 80-84, 210, 383, 424, 450, 572, 649, 719-720.

Page 132 Reprinted by permission of University of Oklahoma Press from *Indian Removal: The Emigration of the Five Civilized Tribes* by Grant Forman. Copyright ©1932, 1953 (new edition), and 1972 by University of Oklahoma Press, preface.

Page 134 Reprinted by permission of University of Oklahoma Press from *The Osages: Children of the Middle Waters* by John Joseph Mathews. Copyright ©1961 by University of Oklahoma Press, pp. vii-xiii, 10, 45, 80-84, 210, 383, 424, 450, 572, 649, 719-720.

Page 137 Reprinted by permission of W. W. Norton from *Oklahoma, A History* by H. Wayne Morgan and Anne Hodges Morgan. ©1984 by H. Wayne Morgan and Anne Hodges Morgan.

Page 137 Reprinted by permission of University of Oklahoma Press from *The Osages: Children of the Middle Waters* by John Joseph Mathews. Copyright ©1961 by University of Oklahoma Press, pages vii-xiii, 10, 45, 80-84, 210, 383, 424, 450, 572, 649, 719-720.

Pages 137-138 Reprinted by permission of University of Oklahoma Press from *Wah 'Kon-Tah: The Osage and the White Man's Road* by John Joseph Mathews. Copyright ©1932 by University of Oklahoma Press.

Page 142 Reprinted by permission of W. W. Norton from *Oklahoma, A History* by H. Wayne Morgan and Anne Hodges Morgan. ©1984 by H. Wayne Morgan and Anne Hodges Morgan.

Page 145 Reprinted by permission of Chelsea House Publishers from *Indians of North America: The Osage* by Terry P. Wilson, Frank W. Porter III, gen. ed. Copyright ©1988 by Terry Wilson, p.56.

Page 145 From Senate Report 59th Congress, 2nd sess., no. 5013.

Pages 152-153 Reprinted by permission of University of Minnesota Press from *The Day of the Cattlemen* by Ernest Staples Osgood. Copyright ©1929 (1970) by Ernest Staples Osgood, pp. 26-27.

Page 155 Reprinted by permission of Alfred A. Knopf from *The Great Buffalo Hunt* by Wayne Gard. Copyright ©1959 by Wayne Gard, p. 266.

Page 158, 160 Reprinted by permission of W. W. Norton, from *Oklahoma, A History* by H. Wayne Morgan and Anne Hodges Morgan. ©1984 by H. Wayne Morgan and Anne Hodges Morgan.

Pages 187, 191, 194-198 Reprinted by permission of the Oklahoma Heritage Association from *The Osage Oil Boom* by Kenny A. Franks. Copyright ©1989 by Kenny A. Franks, pp. 67, 74-75, 77, 79-95, 111, 127.

Pages 198-199 Reprinted by permission of Western History Collections, University of Oklahoma from *W.P.A. Writers Project on Oil in Oklahoma.*

Pages 199, 201 Reprinted by permission of Osage County Historical Society from *Osage County Profiles,* edited by Betty Smith. Copyright ©1978 by Osage County Historical Society, pp. 435-436.

Page 202 Reprinted by permission of University of Oklahoma Press from *Ghost Towns of Oklahoma* by John W. Morris, copyright ©1977 by University of Oklahoma Press, p. 64.

Pages 202-205 Reprinted by permission of the Oklahoma Heritage Association from *The Osage Oil Boom* by Kenny A. Franks. Copyright ©1989 by Kenny A. Franks, pp. 67, 74-75, 77, 79-95, 111, 127.

Page 213 From a publication of University of Michigan Press, Ann Arbor from *The American West as Living Space* by Wallace Stegner. Copyright ©1987 by University of Michigan Press, Ann Arbor.

Pages 224-225 Reprinted by permission of Penguin Books from *The American Scene* by Henry James. Copyright ©1994 by Penguin Books.

Pages 225-226 Reprinted by permission of the Oklahoma Heritage Association from *The Osage Oil Boom* by Kenny A. Franks. Copyright ©1989 by Kenny A. Franks, pp. 67, 74-75, 77, 79-95, 111, 127.

Page 230 Reprinted by permission of the author from *What is Down the Road for the American Indian* by Bill Mashunkashey. Copyright ©1990 by Bill Mashunkashey.

INDEX

Annick Smith is author of the critically acclaimed book *Homestead* and coproducer with Robert Redford of the movie *A River Runs Through It*. Smith was also executive producer of the feature film *Heartland*. With William Kittredge, she coedited *The Last Best Place: A Montana Anthology*. Her essays and stories have appeared in many magazines and anthologies. A native of Chicago, she has lived most of her adult life on a ranch outside Missoula, Montana.

ABOUT THE PHOTOGRAPHER

Photographer Harvey Payne grew up on a ranch eighteen miles west of the Tallgrass Prairie Preserve; he took up photography as a hobby after finishing his education and opening a law practice in Pawhuska, Oklahoma. His wildlife and nature photography has appeared in numerous magazines. Today he continues to practice law in Pawhuska and serves as director of the Nature Conservancy's Tallgrass Prairie Preserve.